My Turn

William Hall, who assisted Norman Wisdom in the writing of his life story, is a biographer, broadcaster and critic. He is the author of more than a dozen biographies, including Michael Caine, James Dean, Frankie Howerd, Larry Adler and Dick Emery.

MY TURN

Memoirs by
NORMAN WISDOM
with
WILLIAM HALL

CENTURY

Published by Century in 2002

7 9 10 8

First published in the United Kingdom in 1992 by Century
The Random House Group Limited
20 Vauxhall Bridge Road, London SW1V 2SA

Random House Australia (Pty) Limited
20 Alfred Street, Milsons Point, Sydney,
New South Wales 2061, Australia

Random House New Zealand Limited
18 Poland Road, Glenfield
Auckland 10, New Zealand

Random House South Africa (Pty) Limited
Endulini, 5a Jubilee Road, Parktown 2193, South Africa

The Random House Group Limited Reg. No. 954009

www.randomhouse.co.uk

A CIP catalogue record for this book is available
from the British Library

Papers used by Random House are
natural, recyclable products made from wood grown in
sustainable forests. The manufacturing processes conform to
the environmental regulations of the country of origin

ISBN 0 7126 23930
Typeset by MATS, Southend-on-Sea, Essex
Printed and bound in Great Britain by
Clays Ltd, St. Ives plc, Bungay, Suffolk

This is for my lovely Mum,
for my dear brother Fred,
and for my kids, Nick and Jackie.

I would like to thank Richard Dacre for the invaluable information contained in his book *Trouble in Store*, which helped me with the accuracy of this autobiography.
I'd also like to thank my dear old army chum, Patrick Dickinson, for helping me with so many happy memories.

FOREWORD

I first saw Norman Wisdom at the Hippodrome, Brighton, after an urgent phone call from Billy Marsh, one of my associates for many years, sent me hurrying down on the train to catch the evening show. That was in March 1948.

Within minutes of seeing this extraordinary young comedian I knew I had to have him on my books. It marked the start of a long and fruitful association which has lasted to this day.

We are also great friends. Which is why I am particularly delighted that he has at last written his long awaited autobiography. With Norman, there is no generation gap. People of all ages warm to his unique appeal, and wonder at a talent that has taken him from the old variety days to ice-skating spectaculars, lavish musicals and on to world-wide stardom in films that still bring laughter to millions.

He has reached the heights of comedy, and been compared to Chaplin. But for me, and I suspect for his fans all over the world, there can only be one Norman Wisdom.

I'm proud of him.

– BERNARD DELFONT

INTRODUCTION

Wednesday, 6 February 2002, 12.30pm. The Lancaster Room of the Savoy Hotel, London.

Six hundred of the great and the good, the creative artists, culture vultures and intellectuals, gather for the annual awards luncheon of the South Bank Show, that bastion of British culture which, this year, is a very special occasion indeed. It marks twenty-five seasons of the TV series that has written its own place into our national heritage as a reflection of the arts and culture of the country. A clutch of opera singers, conductors, painters, pianists, actors and ballet dancers mingle with TV's top brass.

So what is Norman Wisdom doing among the celebrated names filling the chandelier-hung banqueting room?

Answer: getting a standing ovation, that's what.

He threads his way through the tables on the way to the stage to shake hands with Melvyn Bragg, chairman of the judges, at the rostrum. Knight of Laughter meets Lord of the Arts.

It is turning out to be quite a week for Wisdom ('Don't call me Sir . . . Norman's just fine!') Two days earlier he had packed his bags at his home on the Isle of Man to celebrate his 87th birthday with his family, flying in to be with them for an informal get-together. Nothing special, just a curry from the local Indian take-away round the corner from his flat in Epsom, Surrey.

Now here he is, presenting the trophy for best comedy to Ricky Gervaise for the popular BBC2 show *The Office* – and finding himself the only star to get people rising out of their seats to cheer him all the way to the stage.

At the star-studded champagne reception beforehand, celebrities such as Jane Asher, Honor Blackman, painter Frank Auerbach, Elvis Costello, Angus Deayton, opera legend Kiri Te Kanawa, Wayne Sleep, Ben Kingsley, Lynda La Plante, Johnny Vegas and Ken Russell smile across at him, wave or come over to shake his hand. Photographers crowd round.

Mel B. passes by, stunning in a bright red dress. 'Will you pose with Mel B?' a photographer requests.

'Sure,' says Norman affably. 'Where is he?' Mel B. tosses her dark locks and stalks off.

Just kidding. The Spice Girls adore Norman, or so they said when they all appeared together on a Des O'Connor Show, and he admits he rather fancies them. Which one? 'All of them! Pity they had to split up.'

On the stage he pretends to trip, which has been expected of him ever since he did just that in front of the Queen when Her Majesty knighted him in Buckingham Palace the previous year. He gets the laugh. And he offers to sing *Don't Laugh at Me* but, alas, explains Melvyn Bragg, the event is being televised and the clock says there isn't time for unrehearsed songs, though a spot of ad-lib patter goes down well.

Shame, really. Our Norm is timeless, ageless, and the clock has yet to be invented that will curb his boundless enthusiasm.

Back at table 11, with more cheers and laughter following like an obedient bloodhound, he winks at me.

'Did I do all right, then?'

Yes, Norman. You did.

Do you really need to ask?

William Hall, London 2002.

CHAPTER ONE

I was born in very sorry circumstances. Both my parents were very sorry! That's an old music hall gag, but in fact it wasn't very far from the truth.

When I talk about my childhood, friends inevitably compare me to Oliver Twist. And that wasn't so far from the truth, either.

I was actually born in Marylebone, London, on 4 February 1915. I've usually kept that date quiet. But now I'm getting on a bit, why not chance it and be honest! I weighed 7 lbs 2 oz at birth and as I grew up I was always small for my age.

My father Frederick was a chauffeur, and my mother Maude was a dressmaker at Nabob's in Curzon Street. She was pretty and petite, with warm brown eyes and a great sense of fun. She once made a dress for Queen Mary, and she was mighty proud of that. I would sit at her feet for hours in fascination just watching her sew and weave.

It was a small flat, just one bedroom on the ground floor of a run-down old house in West London, with a parlour, a small kitchen and a toilet – but no bathroom. We had to wash in the kitchen sink and take our baths in a tin tub in the parlour at the rear. The actual address was No.91 Fernhead Road, Paddington. We all slept in that one bedroom, my parents in a double bed, while I shared a single bed with my brother Fred, who was two years older.

Outside in the street the gleaming Daimler my Dad drove

would be parked, but inside we were close to the poverty line. My father would repair my one pair of shoes by cutting up old tyres and glueing them to the soles. At least I was walking an inch taller. And that was before the bad times came.

It sounds unbelievable, but my first memory is of sitting on the stone steps outside the house looking up at the sky – this was during World War One – when suddenly an enormous German Zeppelin drifted silently into sight. It hovered there like a giant grey cigar, and my mouth must have been as wide open as my eyes as I gazed up at it in fascination.

Then my Mum came rushing out, scooped me up in her arms and ran back inside. I must have been about two years old.

In those early days our family life seemed quite normal, though I was aware that my parents seemed to quarrel a lot. What I didn't realise until later was that my father drank – and when he had a few he became a changed man. He was of average height, slim, but very strong, and when he came home in that condition my brother Fred and I took to our bed. He never hit Mum, but there were the most awful shouting matches that would leave her in tears. Father would storm out again to the Chippenham pub round the corner, and when the door slammed behind him, Fred and I would scramble out of bed and run to comfort Mum. The three of us would just hug each other. I must say my father didn't beat us, not then – but there are worse ways of destroying a family and abusing your children, as we would find out.

At the age of four I went to St Luke's Infant School up the road. I was in a striped jersey, short trousers and a coat with huge lapels. Mum dressed me the same as Fred, and there was no doubt we were brothers as we walked hand in hand up the road with her for my first day at school – even down to the floppy hats we both wore. The only difference was that I was crying all the way. I didn't want to go to school.

It was a forbidding place, a large grimy Victorian institution with a playground surrounded by high iron railings. That first day was a raw January morning. There was no central heating, but my classroom had a small fire in a huge chimney place at the back of the room.

My teacher was a kindly middle-aged woman with her hair in a bun at the back. She took a small stool, led me over to the fireplace and sat me down behind the big brass fireguard in the hearth. There she allowed me to stay for the whole day – and the next. You could say I found myself warming to school life.

I tended to mix with boys older than myself, Fred's pals, and of course I was the smallest in the gang. They didn't call me Tich as you might expect – I was always Wizzie, a nickname that would stick with me right through my Army days. When they closed the gates on us after school the streets became our playground, with energetic games of football and cricket up against the wall of a builder's yard. Often our ball was just a lump of scrunched-up paper tied with string.

I was nine when the blow fell. Fred and I came home from school to find the flat oddly quiet. Father was sitting in the gloom in the parlour with the curtains drawn. His face was bleak – and he was stone cold sober. 'Your mother's gone,' he said simply, without any preamble.

We couldn't take it in at first. I didn't burst into tears, because I didn't understand it. Our Mum gone? Where? Why?

The 'why' was self-evident. In the next few months my father became more and more brutal towards us. The 'where' turned out to be in Willesden, where she had turned for solace to another man whom she would later marry and happily settle down with for the rest of her life – but it meant she didn't get custody of us when my father divorced her.

Now came a period in our young lives that really could have come straight from the pages of a Dickens novel. Father started going away for long periods, leaving us totally alone and uncared for to fend for ourselves. Ostensibly his job as a chauffeur took him all over the country. At one point he got a job in Oban in Scotland with a family firm called Jasper Sinclair. But another time a letter from him dropped on to the mat out of the blue, together with a photograph – from Ceylon! Why he went there I never did find out, but I had a harsh reminder of his home-coming.

Up the road was a dairy called Welford's. When the sun shone they would pull down an awning to shield the milk and cream in the window. They were very tolerant of us kids, and didn't seem to mind that one of our games was to swing upside down on the steel bars at either end of the awning. A few days after the letter from Ceylon dropped through the letter box, I was larking about with my mates, hanging by my legs from the bar, swinging gently and laughing with them, when I saw a familiar figure striding up the street – familiar even though I was seeing him upside down.

'Hullo, Dad!' I called in surprise as he loomed nearer.

His slurred words gave no hint of what was to come: 'Why don't you learn to behave yourself?'

And as he walked past he clenched his fist – and *wham!* He slammed it into my stomach. I fell head first on to the pavement, half-stunned . . . and watched dazed as his figure receded up the road. He didn't look round or say another word.

By now Fred and I were going to school barefoot. That was nothing unusual in those days and in that area of extreme poverty and deprivation. It was only a quarter of a mile up the road, and your feet soon become hardened to the pavements.

We didn't tell any of the teachers when our father went away, because we were both too scared of what he would do to us when he came home. His behaviour became more aggressive as the months wore on. He never took a strap to us, but a clout round the earhole was a regular event. One day when he was in a foul mood, I said something that upset him. He picked me up bodily and threw me from one side of the parlour to the other. My head actually hit the ceiling before I came crashing down on to the sideboard. As I said, Dad was strong – and I was small. At least I was learning to fall.

Fred and I became street urchins, and the streets became not only our playground but our battleground for survival. Our mates were Wally and Arthur Noble and Johnny Taylor and his three brothers. Sometimes their parents would invite us home for tea, so we would get something to eat, ravenously gulping down bread and jam or cakes until we were stuffed.

But often it was either steal or starve. Our target became the street market in Harrow Road, where the traders sold everything from second-hand carpets to fruit and sweets. Greengrocers would display all their wares out on the pavement, which made them particularly easy pickings.

If I was Oliver Twist, then Fred was the Artful Dodger! We would stand close to the stalls with one of us holding out a newspaper to hide the hands of the other snatching the goodies. Best of all with the street traders, we would pretend to listen in admiration to their patter as we swiped the apples or oranges under their noses.

I became a specialist in eggs. You had to be particularly nimble and gentle in order not to leave a sticky yellow trail as you made off, and I never broke a single egg. Nor, astonishingly, were we ever caught.

Another pastime which took up many happy hours was searching for fag ends in the gutters. I was smoking at the age of nine, but in the teeming working-class streets of the twenties, nobody took any notice or cared. The gang would collect fag ends from all along the streets. Then we would meet up by the builder's yard that also served as our cricket pitch (the lamp-post being the wicket), climb up over the eight-foot wall using each other's backs as stepping stones, and hand the filthy bits of tobacco around. We would then sit solemnly smoking them till we were blue in the face.

An unpleasant memento of that builder's yard has left its mark on me to this day. There were six-inch nails embedded into the top of the wooden gate and along the length of the wall to discourage kids like us getting over. One day our paper parcel football sailed over – and as usual I was delegated to retrieve it. I was just scrambling back with it when a policeman appeared at the end of the road. 'Oi, you kids!' he shouted.

The others scarpered for their lives. I was trapped. In desperation I hoisted myself over and jumped for it – only to feel a searing pain in my left hand and find that I was impaled on one of the nails. I actually hung there with my feet a yard above the ground as the policeman came pounding up. When he saw the blood flowing down my hand and staining the wall he grabbed me round the waist, and eased me up so that I was able to slide my hand free.

'Off with you, sonny,' he said. 'And get that hand seen to.'

I ran home to bathe it in hot water, lucky that it never became infected. I was even luckier my father was away.

In those times the police were extraordinarily tolerant of the noisy kids who ran riot in the streets. They had the sense to herd us into nearby Queen's Park where we could get rid of our energy without the risk of being run over.

In fact, we often evaded them and enjoyed the street life, making nuisances of ourselves with our games of 'Chicken' – like running across the road in front of a car, or hanging on to the back of a bus and jumping off when the conductor came at you. Once I jumped off facing the wrong way, and nearly knocked myself out as I bashed my head on the tarmac and rolled into the gutter – more useful practice for the future!

One game that nearly went dreadfully wrong was when Fred balanced on a window ledge at least twenty feet above the ground while the other boys dared him to jump. I can still hear the others chanting: 'Windy, you haven't got the guts!'

But he had. Fred didn't answer, but I knew he would do it. He jumped – and hit the ground with a frightful thud. When he got up his eyes were staring, and he was bent double like a little old man as he limped away trying to disguise his pain. Oddly enough, I felt in some way it damaged his eyes – because after that they seemed to bulge out in a strange way. I suppose he was lucky he didn't break his back – but sadly it led to a glandular problem later on in life.

It was a tough area, and as well as being street-smart we had to be prepared to stand up for ourselves.

One day after school Fred got into a brawl with a boy who was much bigger than he was. It started out as a quarrel over some sweets, then two more lads joined in and started hitting Fred really hard. A ring of shouting youngsters formed round them – until without thinking I burst through, laying into the bullies with fists and feet for all I was worth.

When I came round I was on my brother's back being carted off home – but I was the hero of the hour. I found out that the biggest bloke had thumped me once and knocked me clean out, which scared all the others into stopping the fight.

It taught me one important lesson, even at that young age: I always believe that if you're being bullied – hit out once, smack him on the nose, get one in. He may half kill

7

you, but he won't pick on you again. Sometimes you've got to take a chance, risk getting hurt. Up to then a lot of the lads had picked on me from time to time because I was the little fellow. But after that day word spread round the school, and from then on both Fred and I were left in peace. I reckon it was worth the headache!

We never had any toys, not even a teddy bear. The first and only one that came my way was when I reached the age of ten. Mum had been seeing us secretly, perhaps half a dozen times in a year, suddenly appearing at the school gates just to take my hand and reassure me she was there, and thinking of us even if she couldn't get nearer than a kiss outside the playground.

She would say: 'Don't tell your Dad, whatever you do.' But once she brought me a small pedal cycle, a present for my tenth birthday, and the first thing I had ever owned in my life. I took it home in triumph, pedalling away like mad along the pavement. My father saw it that evening when he came in from work – via the pub.

'Where did you get that?'

I forgot my mother's advice. 'Mum gave it to me. For my birthday.' Before I had finished my father grabbed it in one hand – and smashed it against the wall. Then he threw it on the carpet and stamped on it till it was bent and mangled. My tears of protest meant nothing.

I made my second mistake when I picked up the battered bike and tried to mend it. My fingers became caught in the chain, and started bleeding. In the end I gave up and went indoors to the sink to wash off the blood.

Father said: 'How did you do that?'

'I'm trying to repair my bike,' I told him – and *wallop!* His hand exploded against my jaw. Dad believed in rough, instant justice . . . The sad thing is, looking back, I can honestly say that I never got any love from my father, ever.

I stayed at St Luke's School until I was ten and a half, and although I did not exactly excel in the academic area I was able to hold my corner. My headmaster was Mr Hill – do we ever know our teachers' Christian names? Mr Hill cut an impressive figure, rather like Arthur Lowe in Dad's Army – haughty, small of stature, always impeccable in a long jacket, grey trousers and a top hat.

One day another boy gave me a great big sweet, a real gob-stopper. I put it in my mouth, and was happily sucking away when Mr Hill suddenly took it on himself to inquire: 'Wisdom, are you eating, boy?'

All I could answer was: 'Mmmpph

'Open your mouth!' he ordered.

He actually put his fingers into my mouth, pulled out the offending sweet, and flung it on the fire. At four o'clock when the bell rang for the end of lessons I waited for the classroom to empty before quietly going over to the fire to rake among the cinders and rescue my half-chewed gob-stopper. I washed it under the tap, then thoroughly enjoyed it.

St Luke's was a mixed school. When I was feeling hungry I would raid the girls' cookery class on the first floor and scrounge the remnants of their culinary endeavours. Sometimes it tasted awful – but when your stomach's rumbling you don't stop to ask too many questions. At least it was something to eat.

As soon as I was old enough to realise the value of money I started running errands. We kids would roam over a wide area, from Kilburn all the way down to Hyde Park. We also soon found our way into Paddington Station, where we would carry passengers' bags for a few pennies.

On Saturday mornings we would walk across half London to the British Museum. We could get in for nothing, and spent hours wandering around staring at objects that made my young mind boggle. It was on one of these outings that I stumbled on a novel idea for making money. I was dashing across Bayswater Road when I ran straight into a bicycle being sedately ridden by a well-dressed lady in a wide-brimmed hat. I was knocked flying – and somehow my ear got caught in the spokes of the spinning front wheel as I lay in the road!

My pathetic yells of pain filled the air, and the lady was crying too, obviously concerned for me. 'I'm so sorry,' she said, and fished in her handbag to produce a sixpenny coin. 'Please take this. I hope you'll be all right.'

Sixpence in those days could buy a lot of sweets. I treated my mates to bullseyes and ice-cream, and became extremely popular. For the next few weeks I spent Saturday mornings running across Bayswater Road whenever a cyclist appeared, trying to get knocked down. Finally a policeman appeared and grabbed me by the collar.

'I've been watching you,' he said. 'Just what do you think you're trying to do?'

Meekly I told him the truth. 'I'm trying to earn some money.' He gave me a quiet kick up the backside and told me to get moving and not show my face there again.

This guttersnipe life went on for almost two years. Finally my father came to his senses and realised his sons were turning into vagrants. He placed us into the care of guardians who had a farm in Roe Green, in what is now the green belt of Hertfordshire. The family's name was Denmark, and a whole new vista of country life opened out for us, totally removed from the squalor of the city streets.

Fred and I helped milk the cows and feed the goats. The farm was a noisy, squawking mass of cattle, goats, chickens and ducks. One odd memory I retain is of putting my small hand inside a cow's mouth and feeling its rough tongue sucking on it!

Our local school at Hatfield was three miles away, which meant an early start each morning. I loved it, gulping down my breakfast so that I could set off across the fields with Fred – in fact we would always run rather than walk, for the sheer joy of it, in a daily race to the school gates.

Fred invariably won. Two years makes a lot of difference at that age. School broke up at four o'clock, and I would start before him across the fields, and look over my shoulder to find Fred panting along behind me, determined to catch up. If he thought I was going to win he would, in fun of course, grab me by my jersey collar and trip me and send me sprawling before racing on with a loud horse laugh.

There was one master at that school who took an intense dislike to me, and took a sadistic delight in making me squirm. He was a big man with thick black eyebrows and a nasty expression that seemed to blend into his face. He used a heavy old-fashioned round ruler to keep us in check, and he would stalk up and down the classroom and tap a boy sharply on the head if he thought the lad was not paying attention. One morning I was silly enough to answer him back, and, when he beckoned me up to the front of the class, I knew I was in for it.

'Hold out your hand,' he commanded. When I obeyed he lashed out with the ruler. The pain was almost unbearable, but I didn't utter a sound or shed a tear. Almost immediately the hand began to swell, and became puffy and red. He had broken my finger – and the bone on my right forefinger has been weak ever since.

I managed to stammer: 'Can I go to the lavatory please, sir?'

When I got there I caved in and cried. Nobody else ever knew. The only good thing was that the teacher realised he had gone too far, and never hit me again.

In truth, Fred and I were a couple of little devils. We would go scrumping for apples in local orchards. But unlike in the Harrow Road street markets, we would get caught time and again by the enraged owners, who would grab us by the ear or collar and march us back to our guardians. After six months the Denmarks couldn't stand our bad behaviour any more. They sent a message to our Dad, who had to come and take us away and find new guardians for us.

Another reason for our short-lived stay turned out to be that Father had fallen behind with the weekly fee of five shillings apiece for our board and keep. So with a lot of heartache my brother and I turned our backs on the delights of the countryside and headed for Deal in Kent.

We were starting to feel like gypsies. Father found us fresh guardians, a coal-mining family in a pleasant little house in Isleworth Walk, a quaint alley-way off the main street. They soon found that the pair of us were too much to handle, but at least they were more tolerant than our previous custodians. They kept my brother – and slung me out!

By good fortune I ended up in the care of a Mr and Mrs Blanche who lived nearby in a small house in Downs Road, Walmer.

By now I was learning better manners. There were no social workers in those days, and if we were a nuisance, our temporary keepers simply threw us out. The Blanches stood no nonsense, and I would get a swift clip round the head if I was cheeky. They were firm but fair. So fair that when eventually my father failed to come up with the payments they still allowed me to stay on, for free.

That picturesque old Cinque port would become a focal point of my life, with its bracing sea air, colourful timbered streets and a sense of permanance I had never really felt till then.

There was also a busy little railway station where I found I could earn a bob or two carrying passengers' luggage. Everyone had been in too much of a hurry at Paddington Station to make the job worthwhile, but in the sedate atmosphere of Deal it seemed much more promising. And so it turned out to be: on my first morning I went down to the station and carried four bags, calling it a day when the last passenger gave me the unheard-of tip of a shilling. I was getting rich! But other times I carried two cases fully half a mile for fourpence; so it evened up in the end. My method was simple:

I hung around the station until a train came in, then darted up the platform searching out the pale, weaker looking passengers I could approach with a cheery: 'Carry your bag, sir (or ma'am)?'

Canada Road School, where the Blanches sent me, was a much happier place than either St Luke's or Hatfield. I found I was becoming skilled at painting and sketching, and even won a prize for a water-colour of a landscape.

Even better from my point of view was that the school was mad on sports. Several of my pals were the sons of Royal Marines stationed at the local depot, and they were able to use the barracks gymnasium for nothing. I became crazy about sport in no time at all. I was never a great academic – but I was the keenest sportsman in the school.

I was actually starting to enjoy school. In fact, I had never been happier in all my childhood. I joined the Sea Scouts, and along with the other lads I built up my arm and shoulder muscles rowing the long-boat around Deal sea front.

One day I was walking home in my Sea Scouts uniform after a meeting, and on the quayside I came across a group of people milling around a camera on a tripod, with lights and steel boxes. It was a film unit, and the place was awash with actors and extras. They were filming a scene around the Walmer Lifeboat, and nobody seemed to mind when I hung around, fascinated at the bustle and confusion of my first glimpse of show-business.

I ran home to tell Mrs Blanche. 'Could I stay out and watch them tonight?' I pleaded.

'Certainly not,' she said briskly. 'It's bed for you at the usual time.'

I climbed into my pyjamas, and got into bed. Mrs Blanche saw me safely tucked in – and I waited a whole hour before I slipped out of bed and quietly got dressed again. My room was on the first floor. I clambered out of the window and hung from the sill by my finger-tips before letting go and plummeting into a flower bed.

On the quayside they were night shooting a storm scene, with a rain machine sending squalls of water into the faces of the men in the lifeboat as it rocked up and down in the sea. The film crew were so friendly they even offered me tea and sandwiches in their break. I stayed there all night, and it remains one of the great nights of my life, as vivid now as it was then.

Somewhere around 7.30 in the morning I crawled home – and to my horror found Mr and Mrs Blanche up and about in the kitchen. With typical schoolboyish enthusiasm, I hadn't actually given any thought as to how I was going to get back into my room.

I tapped timidly at the back door, and the pair of them gazed down at me incredulously. 'Where on earth have you been?' boomed Mr Blanche.

'Down at the harbour,' I owned up. 'Watching them film –'

Mr and Mrs Blanche almost elbowed each other out of the way to see who could get to me first. Mrs Blanche won. 'You disobedient little devil!' she yelled. And – *Whack!* My ear stung. But it was worth it.

I expanded the scope of my odd jobs. A newspaper round brought in one shilling and sixpence a week, but lasted less than a month after I stayed away with a chill. On Saturdays I ran errands for a butcher, rarely finishing before eight o'clock at night, but earning half a crown for my time.

When I left school at fourteen I became a full-time delivery boy for a local china shop, with a barrow load of cups, saucers, plates and ornaments I would take from the warehouse to the shop. I walked v-e-r-y carefully, and never dropped or broke a single plate. For this I was paid a handsome ten shillings a week – and handed over 9/6d to the Blanches. It seemed fair. After all, they had looked after me for so long – for nothing. In retrospect, I suppose this can be seen as acclimatizing me to the rigours of the tax man in later years. In those days it just meant that I stayed poor.

By now I couldn't wait to get a better job. A month later a vacancy came up a few doors down the High Street at Lipton's the Grocers on the corner of Park Street, and I was round within minutes of hearing about it. To my delight a bicycle went with the job. A plate under the crossbar displayed the famous name, and in front of the handlebars was a basket for the deliveries.

The manager, an angular man with a pencil moustache, took one look at me, and didn't seem to like what he saw. 'A little small, aren't you?' he said, looking from me to the bicycle and back. He was right. When he stood back to supervise my riding test I found to my horror that I couldn't reach the pedals. Thinking quickly I shifted from the saddle to the crossbar, and just managed to get a foothold. The manager looked dubious, but he agreed to give me a try.

The streets of Deal became a race-track, with every delivery a personal challenge to see how fast I could get there and back. Soon I achieved the reputation of being the fastest errand boy in town, bar none.

In the next six weeks my fame spread. One day I was riding up the High Street when the manager of the Home and Colonial, the great rival to Lipton's, stepped out from the pavement and signalled me to stop. 'How would you like to come and work for me?' he asked.

I said: 'How much will you pay me?'

He said: 'How much are you earning now?'

I said: 'Ten shillings a week, sir.'

He said: 'I'll give you twelve shillings.'

I hurried in to the manager at Lipton's and blurted out: 'I've been offered twelve shillings a week by the manager of the Home and Colonial.'

He looked up. I noticed that his moustache was quivering. He said: 'All right, I'll give you twelve.'

I rushed to the far end of the High Street and burst in on the manager of the Home and Colonial. 'Sorry, sir,' I said. 'The manager at Lipton's is offering me twelve shillings.'

He said: 'All right, I'll make it fourteen.'

By now I was getting to realise the value of competitive negotiation, so I belted back to Lipton's.

'The manager of the Home and Colonial says he'll pay me fourteen shillings a week.' Breathless and confident, I waited for the next offer.

The manager of Lipton's looked at me, and said: 'All right, shove off!' And that was the end of that.

On my new Home and Colonial bicycle I pedalled the country roads around Deal, whistling cheerily as I took deliveries to farms and villages within a five-mile radius of the town. The crunch came six weeks later when Home and Colonial bought a brand new delivery van – and I was out of work.

So much for a fourteen-year-old entrepreneur trying to better himself.

CHAPTER TWO

It was time for a change. I called in at the Deal Labour Exchange.

After a lot of riffling through papers, an official said: 'Like to try your hand at being a commie-waiter? Nice place called the Artillery Mansions Hotel.'

He then broke the news that it was in London.

I took the train to London on a ticket bought by the Labour Exchange. All my belongings were crammed into one very small case, but my step was light as I made my way to Victoria Street, and I was looking forward to a new start and a new challenge.

I was taken on as an apprentice at twelve shillings a week, and was given a small room of my own about the size of a boot-box with a bed, a chair and a wash-basin. They also decked me out in a waiter's uniform. As I adjusted my bow tie in the mirror, I couldn't help thinking I'd come up in the world from a barefoot urchin scrounging in the gutter for fag ends, and I determined that I would look as well-groomed as possible.

I was living in, eating well for free, sleeping in a comfortable bed, and had more money than I knew what to do with. Twelve bob seemed to go a long way, and at the end of my first week I thought I would show off a bit. I bought myself a second hand navy blue suit with a double-breasted waistcoat, a pair of pointed black shoes (new) and topped it off with a silver grey trilby. Make way for a man about town, growing up fast!

I marched down the stairs and out to the taxi rank across the street. Hailing a cab, I got in and ordered the cabbie: 'Drive round the block, will you please!'

The driver took one look at my diminutive frame, all four-foot-ten of me dressed up like a dog's dinner, and shrugged as only London cabbies can. 'Right you are, guv'nor,' he said, keeping his face straight. He took me in a swift circle and three minutes later we were back at the steps of the hotel. The fare was two shillings – a colossal cheek, I thought. After that I went everywhere by bus.

The head waiter liked me, and I got on well with the two other waitresses. They taught me the art of carrying a tray on one shoulder – 'Keep your back upright and look straight ahead' – and to start with I served the manager and other members of the staff with their meals, progressing to coffee in the lounge for the residents.

After three weeks of training I was judged capable enough to be sent round the rooms in the morning collecting the breakfast trays. Some would be on the floor outside the door, others meant a discreet knock and a polite: 'May I take your tray, sir?' The hotel had five floors, and it would normally take me the best part of an hour.

My job came to an abrupt end after one month of this. I had cleared four floors, and was on the fifth with a tray loaded with the leftovers of two breakfasts on my shoulder – porridge, eggs and bacon rinds, bits of toast, butter, marmalade. I reached the end of the corridor and pressed the bell for the lift.

Nothing happened. I slid the iron-trellis gates open – in those days the safety regulations were nowhere near as strict as they are today and leaned over, shouting down to the page boy: 'Lift, please! Send up' – That was when it happened. The tray slid off my shoulder and hurtled five floors down the lift shaft with a horrendous clatter, smearing the walls with an unsightly mess of porridge and egg and marmalade and smashing the cups and plates to smithereens at the bottom.

I was tempted to follow the tray. Instead I trudged reluctantly down the stairs to face the music. The head waiter was already there, standing at the bottom with his arms folded. He eyed me more in sorrow than in anger. It was the nicest way I've ever had the sack. 'Norman, if I get you another job, will you leave?'

True to his word, he found me a job as a page-boy at the Ladies' Forum Club near Hyde Park Corner, another living-in post complete with a royal blue button-and-braid uniform and pill-box hat. My pay had dropped to eight shillings a week, but the work reflected the money: there were six of us simply running messages, and I spent most of my time sitting around on a quilted bench waiting for the hall porter to snap his fingers at me.

There is a great camaraderie in hotel life, a club without a name where everyone gets to know everyone else. So I was mingling with waiters and page-boys from other hotels, and joined them on regular outings to a dance school in Chelsea. After half an hour of instruction, the lads and girls would get together for a general knees-up – and it was then that I realised what my size, or lack of it, meant.

The girls looked down on me, often literally, from my Brylcreemed black hair to my patent leather shoes – and would politely decline my invitation, or say they had reserved the dance for someone else. Sometimes they were rude enough to laugh out loud in my face – and that hurt most.

My eye fell on a pretty waitress named Sally, who had a perky manner and a bright smile to match it. I was still only just fourteen, but I plucked up my courage, walked into the dining-room as the luncheon plates were being cleared away, and put on my most confident manner. 'Would you like to come out with me some time?' I ventured.

She smiled, then burst out laughing, and I wanted the carpet to open up and swallow me. Finally she said: 'But you can't afford it.'

So that was it! Not my size, just money. 'If I saved up enough, will you come out?' She nodded, and I almost danced out of the room.

Two weeks later I had eight shillings in my pocket – enough to paint the town pink, if not quite red. Sally was the first girl I had ever taken out, and I was determined to do my best. When I approached her and told her I had the money, she seemed pleased and agreed on the spot.

I really wanted to impress her. I donned my posh outfit, and we met an hour later. We walked from the Forum Club to the Metropole Cinema opposite Victoria Station, queued for forty-five minutes and finished up two rows from the back in the one-and-nines. I forget the title of the film, but I was too excited to take in much of it anyway.

When we came out I asked her if she was hungry. She smiled and said: 'Yes, Norman, dinner would be nice.'

I figured that with less than five shillings left, I had to use my loaf – if you see what I mean – so I ushered her into the nearest cafe. It was hot and crowded, and we couldn't find a seat, so I pushed through to a ledge by the window where we could stand. Then I went back to the counter and ordered egg and chips for two. I wouldn't say Sally's face was happy, but with money running out the choice was limited.

We finished our meal – well, I did – and then I followed her out as she left the cafe in what seemed rather a hurry. Sally lived in Vauxhall, a bus ride away. I tried to hold her hand, but she was almost running towards the nearest bus stop. The bus came – but as she jumped on and the bus moved off I suddenly realised I hadn't given her any money for the fare. I chased the double-decker down the middle of the road, waving a sixpenny coin and shouting at the top of my voice: 'Sally, here's your fare. Sally! Hey, *Sally*!'

I caught a glimpse of her contemptuous expression before she turned away and ran up the stairs to the upper deck. Then I made my dejected way back to the Forum Club, alone.

Next day when Sally arrived for work, I hurried up to her with my best smile – but she turned her back and walked off. She never spoke to me again.

Put six bored page-boys together, and you're asking for trouble. We were all in one big room, a dormitory on the top floor under the roof. We were a mischievous bunch, and our favourite sport was to indulge in keyhole capers – peering through keyholes in the bathrooms on each floor where the 160 ladies would perform their ablutions.

We were never caught, and my only worry was that I might find another eye peering back at me.

After a few weeks the job began to bore me. I told one of the other page boys how I felt, and to my surprise he said he felt just the same. His name was Joe, he was fifteen – just a year older than me – with a strong Welsh accent.

He said: 'I tell you what, why don't we go and work down the mines? You can live with me and my family at Glandwr – it's near Cardiff.'

I didn't hesitate. 'You're on,' I said. 'But we're skint. How do we get there?'

'We'll walk,' he said. 'And we'll nick some food from the kitchen.' That was good enough for me. I handed in my notice on the spot – but Joe didn't. He said he needed more time to think about it. That was no use to me, because it meant that I would be out in the cold with nowhere to sleep and no money coming in.

On the day my notice expired I spent a forlorn day

wandering around the streets before finding myself back at the Forum Club – looking in from the outside. Joe spotted me from the foyer and came out. I must have touched his conscience, because he brought with him one of the cooks, a motherly woman who took pity on me. 'You can come home with me dear, while Joe makes up his mind,' she said – and she was as good as her word.

Her husband was a policeman, a burly London bobby who made no complaint at finding a young stranger sharing his home. I stayed with them for three days. On the third day the doorbell rang – and Joe was standing there with a shoebox full of food tucked under one arm and a grin spread across his face.

'Right,' he said. 'I haven't bothered about giving notice. Let's go.' It took us two weeks to cover the 183 miles, and we really did walk the whole way. We slept rough in dry ditches and haystacks – and as the days wore on the whole thing took on the air of a madcap adventure. We actually started to enjoy it. The weather was fine. It was high summer, the sun shone, and insects hummed in the hedgerows.

We rationed out the food, drank water from streams, and even if the sandwiches became hard and curly at the corners they tasted fine.

It's a funny thing about sleeping rough. When you've only had the briefest taste of the good life, and don't know any better, a haystack makes a marvellous bed, thick and soft and all-enveloping! You don't think about fleas or rats, and normally we were so dog-tired after a day on the road that we just sank into an exhausted sleep.

When we finally limped in to Cardiff, I couldn't wait for Joe to take me to his parents where I could have a hot bath and rest my aching feet. It would be lovely to have somewhere to stay, with regular food – and a job. But something was wrong. Joe wouldn't look me in the eye as he started stuttering something I couldn't quite grasp. Finally I got it out of him: he had not even mentioned my coming to his parents, and worse, I got the impression he didn't want me around any more.

We had a fierce argument on the pavement in the city centre. I accused him of letting me down. I shouted: 'You mean I've walked for two weeks just to hear *this?*' Joe only hung his head – and then suddenly turned and ran off down a side street and ducked out of sight round the corner. I was too tired and too dispirited to chase him. After all, what good would it do? I was alone in a strange town with no money, no friends and nowhere to sleep.

I looked round, and found I was standing outside the Hippodrome Theatre, where there was a variety bill that week. Without really thinking I pushed the door open and found my way to the stage manager's office. I knocked on the door.

From his desk the manager saw a tousled head appear round the door, and a dirt-smeared face blink appealingly at him. 'Excuse me, sir,' I said.

'What is it?'

'Er – I'd like to get into show-business.'

Now it was his turn to blink. 'What can you do?'

I did a little soft-shoe shuffle on the faded carpet in front of him, and piped up: 'I'm forever blowing bubbles . . . pretty bubbles in –'

The manager laughed. 'On your way, son. You've got to do better than that.'

Years later I would play the Hippodrome as the star of my own show. Sad to relate, it wasn't the same manager. If only – but that would have been too much to ask.

I trudged off with no idea where to go. A salty tang was in the air – and suddenly it occurred to me: hey, this is a port. I might get a job at sea. Where are the docks? I heard the sound of ships' sirens, saw the cranes and derricks silhouetted against the sky, and followed my nose until I was standing by the huge gates leading on to the wharves.

Groups of dock labourers were sitting around a burning brazier tucking into their lunchtime sandwiches and drinking mugs of hot tea. Nobody challenged me as I slipped through the gates and stood watching them longingly. Pangs of hunger ran through me in spasms.

Then from the watchman's hut by the gates came a shout: 'Oi, you kid there. Get out!'

A guard was gesticulating through the window. I turned my grubby urchin's face towards him, as he waved an angry fist at me. *'Get out!'*

But as I turned to flee, the foreman called out from the group:

'Just a minute, son. Where have you come from?' He was a big, friendly giant with a weatherbeaten face.

'London,' I replied. 'I'm trying to find a job.'

'How did you get here?'

'I walked.'

A ripple of ribald laughter ran through the group. The big man looked down at me quizzically. 'Show me the soles of your shoes.'

I raised them one after the other – to reveal holes that went through to my feet. Even my socks were worn. He nodded slowly. 'So you did, son. C'mon over here' . . . And ignoring the gateman he beckoned me to join the others round the brazier, handing me a sandwich from a newspaper and offering me a mug of tea. 'How would you like to be a cabin boy?'

I plucked up my courage and replied: 'Oh yes, sir. Anything, sir.' 'This way,' said my new-found friend, and led me off along the wharf past huge baulks of timber to another section of the docks where the freighters were moored. He stopped by one ship, and I stared up at the towering hull, gleaming with new grey paint, to read the name on her:

Maindy Court. 'I know the skipper,' he said, leading the way up the gang plank.

The Captain looked at me suspiciously as his friend insisted: 'This kid's got guts. He's just walked all the way from London. Take a look at his shoes.' Once again I held my footwear up for inspection.

'Um,' said the Captain, a man of few words. He paused. Then:

'As a matter of fact we do need a cabin boy for this trip. We sail tomorrow.'

'Where to, sir?' I asked, hardly able to believe my luck.

'Argentina,' said the Captain briefly. 'Get yourself ready. You can sleep aboard tonight.'

I was ready. All I had in the world was one brown paper carrier bag, and I took it down below to the cabin I would share with the steward, and stowed the contents away in a drawer under the lower bunk where I would sleep for several months. Then I gratefully shook hands with the big dock worker, and promised to look him up when I got back – whenever that would be.

We sailed on a brilliant sunny morning with the sky a blue canopy overhead. Outside the galley I peeled the first of innumerable buckets of potatoes, and watched as the Welsh hills faded into the distance and the coastline of North Devon slid past and disappeared. Then it was time to get down to the serious business of my duties as a cabin boy – the lowest of the low. But who cared? I was bound for new horizons, new adventures, and for a fourteen-year-old kid it was like a page out of *Boy's Own Paper*.

The *Maindy Court* was a big ship, I would say around 8,000 tons, taking out coal and bringing back grain and meat. I learned we would be away for almost five months, and my pay would be ten shillings a week.

Until we weighed anchor and headed for the Atlantic I never knew what hard work was. My day started at 6.00 a.m.

with a trip to the bridge carrying a mug of tea for the first officer. Then I had to go round the cabins waking the Captain, the chief steward and the first mate with tea, and on to the galley to help the second steward – my cabin mate – prepare their breakfast.

After breakfast I washed up, and made the beds for the Captain and the officers. I swept the galley. Then it was time for the chore I grew to hate most: peeling potatoes. It meant collecting bucketfuls from the hold at the stern, lugging them to the galley, and getting down to it. That took me to lunchtime.

In the afternoon I went round polishing the ship's brass – and I never realised how much brass even a freighter carries. Then I had to clean the officers' cabins, collect up the papers, and make sure the rooms were neat and tidy. Then there were three meals a day, which meant carrying the food from the galley to the Officers' Mess for the steward to serve up. I never finished before 11.30 at night, when I would tumble into my bunk and go out like a light.

At first I suffered from seasickness, hardly helped by having to endure cooking smells from the galley. My legs felt weak, I had dreadful nausea. But still I kept smiling because I felt so free and happy – even as I was heaving to in the Bay of Biscay. Then suddenly, after two days, the nausea disappeared and I never felt sick again.

The other problem was tiredness. I was kept working so hard that I finally overslept one morning – and paid for it dearly. I was roused from my dreams by a hoarse voice bellowing: 'You lazy little swine! Get out of it!' I opened one eye, just in time to glimpse the massive figure of the first mate, biceps bulging as if they would split his shirt sleeves, with one huge fist poised above me. Then – *wham!* He hit me full in the face, and I felt the salty taste of blood in my mouth.

'Get up and get to work! Do you hear?'

I heard. My head was spinning, but one thing was sure: I wouldn't stay in bed a moment beyond my allotted time in future.

I didn't mind the hard work. Life aboard ship was never dull. When I had a spare moment I would wedge myself by the rail at the stern of the ship and throw lumps of bread in the air for the albatrosses that would come screeching out of the sky to grab them. Other times I would look out for dolphins, and marvel at their sleek grey shapes and graceful movements as they kept easy pace with us one minute, then raced off with a blinding turn of speed the next. And they always seemed to be grinning!

I was the smallest and by far the youngest aboard ship, and the crew virtually adopted me as a mascot. They pulled my leg a lot, but they were never cruel. Like most sailors they were handy with their fists, and as the freighter ploughed steadily on its sou'-westerly course across the great ocean, they would relax with boxing sessions on deck under the hot sun.

I watched from the sidelines. Eventually one of them said: 'Want to have a go, son?'

I looked at their beefy bodies, bearded jaws, and saw fists the size of hams. 'No thanks,' I said, hastily.

'C'mon, it's all right,' another one joined in. 'We won't hurt you.'

'Promise?'

'Promise! In fact we'll teach you –, 'Oh, all right then,' I said.

They found me a set of gloves that fitted, and set about showing me the rudiments of the sport. Lead, bonk, shuffle ... To my surprise, I found I had a natural ability for it. Soon I was mixing with the best of them, and getting cheers from the watching crew when I landed a good one. It was great exercise, and on the eight-week voyage I became fitter than ever. Even the Captain came to watch, leaning above us on the rail with a pipe between his teeth, occasionally giving a nod of approval.

I was addressed variously as Wizzie, Son, Hey you, and Oi! By the time the *Maindy Court* docked in Buenos Aires I was one of the shipmates, and felt part of this special, if temporary, family.

Once the cargo was unloaded, we were free to explore the city. On deck as we prepared to disembark, I spotted a group of my mates huddled together, occasionally glancing over at me. Finally they approached me like a delegation.

'We've got an idea to make a few quid, Wizzie,' said the leader, a burly northerner named Reed.

'Have you?' I said. 'What is it?'

'Well,' said the seaman. 'You've become pretty useful with your fists, though to be honest you don't look it. We know a boxing booth where they put on a bit of a show, and you can challenge the local champ. And surprise him. You can make us – er, and yourself, of course – a bit of dough. Are you game?'

'Not really,' I said. 'But I'll go along with you and have a look.'

The booth was part of a fairground in a large field on the edge of the city. We made our way through streets with surprisingly tall buildings, quite different from the shanty town I had imagined the place to be. The boxing ring was set up in a marquee in the centre of the field. Inside were wooden chairs filled with expectant customers – and the occasional dope who would take on the resident pugilist.

I didn't like the look of him – a stubble-jawed Argentinian, bigger than me of course, with an ugly scowl more suited to a mugger in a dark alley. Reed and his pals pointed to a board. 'If you can stand up for one round, you get a pound, see? Two rounds, they double it. If you're still conscious and standing after three rounds, you get a fiver. Just don't let Pedro clobber you. C'mon – you can do it, Wizzie.'

'Yeah,' chimed in another sailor. 'You're bloody good now. Remember, we taught you to box – so don't let us down!'

What could I say after that? 'All right,' I agreed reluctantly. With a whoop they dragged me off to the ring owner, who took me to a side room where I could change into shorts and singlet. I put on a lumpy pair of brown gloves that had obviously been used by the previous contenders to push themselves off the floor, and with my heart pumping I marched back into the marquee.

I was a lamb to the slaughter, all five stone of me. There was no referee, just a time-keeper with a loud bell. Pedro stood menacingly in the middle of the ring as I clambered through the ropes. He must have been a good nine stone, and I started wondering if this was such a brilliant idea after all. My mates were in a group to one side, and there were at least two hundred people there to witness the sacrifice.

We touched gloves – and went at it. The marquee was filled with cheers and jeers, it was hard to distinguish which. The crew were egging me on, and I heard cries of 'Box him! Box him! Don't go mad.'

I didn't go mad – I went down. Pedro caught me with a cracking right hook that practically lifted me off my feet. 'Stay down, wait till nine!' came the despairing cry from the side. I was up at the time-keeper's shout of nine – and then the round was over and I was a quid richer.

I stayed in for the second, and was down again. I managed to climb to my feet, using the ropes to get me off the canvas, and spent the rest of the round scampering gamely around the ring trying to avoid another howitzer punch. Two pounds in my pocket! But I was starting to hurt, and my right eye was closing.

In the third round I found blood trickling into both my eyes from a cut on the forehead, and running down my chest. Pedro snarled and growled – and came in on my blind side, landing another haymaker on my jaw. Down I went again. I don't remember getting up, but the old saying came through the mists of pain: the best form of defence is attack.

The blokes told me afterwards how I suddenly became a tiny tiger, getting stuck in, and every now and then landing one for Britain that made him grunt. When the final bell went after what seemed an eternity the cheers could have been heard back at the ship.

I was covered in blood, exhausted – but conscious. And still on my feet, just about. My mates half carried me from the ring, slapping me on the back, and the rest of the audience backed them up with loud applause. Pedro gave me a wave and bared his yellow teeth in what passed for a sporting grin.

In that moment I felt so proud that I forgot the pain. My ribs were bruised black and blue, my right eye was closed, my forehead was swelling up, and there was blood everywhere. My teeth had a bit of a rattle, but nothing was broken. I had taken a pounding – but I knew I had won their respect.

'See you outside, Wizzie –' They left me to get cleaned up.

Ten minutes later when I emerged – they'd gone! My mates had collected my money and disappeared to spend it, I found later, in the nearest bar.

I made my lonely way back to the ship, suddenly aching all over. At least the evening couldn't get worse.

Wrong again.

I walked straight into a street riot. Not having seen a paper or heard a radio, I was totally unaware that Buenos Aires was in a serious state of unrest at that time, and that mobs were on the streets looking for trouble.

I dodged into doorways and ran up side streets to avoid the crowds. Somehow I made it back to the docks – only to duck as stones and lumps of coal began whistling past my head. A band of youths had spotted me, and I forgot my aches and pains and sprinted for the dock gates.

The crew was still ashore drinking and carousing away my money, but one sailor had been left to guard the ship. He was a fat Greek engineer named Dimitri, and during the trip over I had noticed him occasionally staring at me with a fixed look that he would soften into a wet-looking smile when I caught his gaze.

'Hullo, Norman,' he said in a thick accent, his swarthy features appearing suddenly out of the shadows as I stepped off the gangway on to the deck.

Norman, eh? No-one else had ever called me that.

He reached out for me with both hands. 'Come here, Norman . . . His sweaty face leered into my battered features like a stranger offering sweets to a young child. 'You been in trouble? Maybe I can help –' I blinked at him. His fat lips glistened in a smile as he clasped me in a bear hug that I thought was a genuine sympathetic welcome. But his affectionate embrace grew tighter, and it dawned on me that this time I was in trouble of an entirely different kind.

There was a pause. Then he said: 'I think you're nice. I want you, Norman!'

My yell cut through the night as I struggled free and bolted for it, hollering fit to bust. "Elp! Somebody stop 'im! 'Elp! Anyone there . . . ?'

Dimitri literally chased me all over the ship, scuttling up and down gangways, in and out of doors, through passages, around the deck. Every now and then I would hear his panting gasp: 'Norman – don't be silly!' which spurred me on to greater speed.

Blimey, what a night! I'd been laid out flat in a boxing ring, stoned by a mob, and now I was being chased around a ship by a poofy sailor.

The chase ended as suddenly as it began. Unknown to me, a second crew member had been left aboard. The chief steward had stayed on to prepare the officers' grub. The first I knew of him was when I scurried round a corner on the upper deck, to encounter a large figure in a white apron clutching a heavy shovel in both hands. I ducked underneath – and as Dimitri came round – *Clang!* The steward swung the shovel right into the Greek's eager-looking face. The impact laid el Greco out on the spot.

'You're all right now, son,' the chief steward said. 'Come on to the galley, and we'll get some steak for that eye.' He strode off without a backward glance at the recumbent figure on the deck. I followed him to the galley, and was treated to the best steak of my life, courtesy of Argentina.

Dimitri left me alone after that. He had a black eye and a puffed face for a week, but I seldom saw him on deck and none of us ever spoke of it again. I just felt lucky I was fit and nippy. My own bruises healed quickly. Next morning I was a hero. All my shipmates came up and ruffled my hair and said 'Well done' – but no-one offered me a share of the prize money. To be truthful, I didn't care. In those past hours I felt I had become a man.

Buenos Aires is on the southern estuary of the River Plate, or Rio de la Plata in local lingo, that divides Argentina from Uruguay. With our coal unloaded and a large supply of meat in the hold, we bade our farewells to the city and cast off the ropes – but instead of setting sail for home we turned west and headed inland to pick up a load of grain from a village on the River Plate. Through the shallow waters – maximum only ten fathoms deep – that in 1939 would become the graveyard of the German pocket battleship *Graf Spee*, scuttled off Montevideo – we slid quietly up-river for a full hundred miles to the verdant web of the great rain forest.

I had never seen so many colourful birds nor heard so much noise. The screech and caterwauling kept me awake at night, and I would lie in my bunk with my hands behind my head listening to the sounds of another world, and weaving fantasies of my own around them.

We stopped off at two or three shanty villages on the way, with names like Diamante and San Nicolas, berthing at rickety old wooden jetties under the uninterested eyes of the locals. It was in Villa Constitution that some of my shipmates decided it was time the cabin boy really grew up. Reed again. The big Geordie had noticed that I was starting to take more than a passing interest in the pin-ups adorning the various locker doors of my shipmates, and he sat me down in the Mess Room and looked me straight in the eye.

'Beginning to fancy them, are you Wizzie?'

'I wouldn't know what to do,' I answered defensively.

'Now listen,' he said. 'First off, you've got to find someone who likes you – 'How would I know if she does?' 'Loads of ways,' he said. 'For instance, if a lady gives you a present, it means there's something about you she likes, and she fancies you. And if she takes you indoors – rest assured, it's a dead cert.'

'Cor,' I said eagerly. 'Right, I'll remember that.'

The *Maindy Court* docked at the jetty around noon, and we had the rest of the day to ourselves. I watched the rest of the crew heading en masse for the nearest waterfront bar, before I decided to go off and explore the back streets. The place was quiet, and seemed to be mainly inhabited by dogs and small children who ran around barefoot.

A small store with baskets of fruit displayed at the front caught my eye. I was idly looking at the colourful display when the owner appeared in the doorway. She was a large, motherly woman with jet-black hair and broad hips, aged around forty, with a friendly smile. She wore a simple black peasant's dress, and addressed me in Spanish. 'Ingles?'

I shrugged, and smiled apologetically. 'Sorry, no comprende.' I must have had that hungry look as she smiled at me.

'Ah,' she said with a knowing wink. 'Ingles!' And she took an apple out of a box and pressed it into my hand.

I looked down at it, and suddenly thought: Hullo, a present! I couldn't believe what happened next.

The woman moved back to the doorway, beckoned me over and then took my hand, leading me into the cool gloom out of the midday heat. It was a small room with only a table, a couple of chairs and a settee. She indicated the settee, and I sat down.

She put the kettle on and came towards me carrying a plate of cakes. It was obviously tea-time.

Right, I thought. This is it! And in the first subtle eagerness of youth I put my hand right up her skirt!

Her reaction took me by surprise. With a shriek that might have raised the dead she walloped me right across the ear, sending my head reverberating like the clocktower of Notre Dame. I rolled off the settee, picked myself up and fled from that place as if the local demons were after me. I even left the apple behind, so you could say I abandoned the fruit twice in one day. And I never did let on to my mates.

Finally we sailed for home. Initially we made for Rotterdam to unload our grain. I was seeing the world, but peeling those potatoes bored me stiff, and I decided to do something about it.

The *Maindy Court* had a complement of twenty-eight officers and crew. Twice a day I had to fill two buckets with potatoes from the hold, and carry them to the galley to peel them.

The potato locker was located at the rear of the ship, almost on the water line, away from everybody. The plan I had devised back in Buenos Aires was simple: I would fill two buckets – then sling them Out through the port-hole. Then I would fill the buckets again and take them up to the galley. For every two I took up, two went overboard. The same thing happened in the afternoon.

Half way across the Atlantic, strangely enough we ran out

of potatoes. The steward got the blame, and he was more baffled than anyone.

The end of the voyage was in sight – but first we ran into heavy weather in the notorious Bay of Biscay. My route from the galley to serve the officers in the Mess with their meals took me along the deck for about thirty feet, a perilous journey in rough seas for which the only protection was a life line stretched four feet above the deck. We would hang our arms over it and cling on in case any heavy seas came over to whip us overboard.

On our return trip the weather was so foul that we were blown ninety miles off course, and found ourselves ploughing doggedly through great green waves the size of a house that made the freighter pitch alarmingly. Being brave or ignorant I never bothered with the life line, preferring to keep an eye out for any monster waves and take quick evasive action.

Even in that heaving sea I was never sick. And the officers were hungry. On this particular day I came staggering up from the galley with a huge tureen full of pea soup, enough for the six officers who were waiting for it. I was half-way along the scheduled route when the ship dipped sharply – and a whacking great wave came over the rails and took my feet from under me, washing me into the scuppers, still hanging on to the now empty tureen. The ship came level again, and back I went, soaked to the skin, for a refill. This time I did use the life line – so that when another great green wave came over I clung grimly on, and watched the sea splash liberally into the tureen.

I made it to the Mess, to find my cabin mate the steward impatiently waiting to dole out the portions. He handed a bowl of green pea soup round to each of them, and I stood there sweating, wondering if they'd notice anything, because I knew what was in it. At last the silence was broken by the first officer. 'Gentlemen,' he said. 'If I were you, I

35

wouldn't put any salt in it until you've tasted it.' I quietly edged back to the galley.

After unloading the grain at Rotterdam, we sailed on to Barry to get rid of the meat. It was the week before Christmas when I signed off with a mixture of regret and anticipation, collected all my wages for my five months at sea, and said goodbye to the crew who had been my shipmates on my voyage of discovery. The *Maindy Court* was not due to sail again for several months, or I would probably have stayed with her.

The future beckoned. I had a few quid in my pocket, I had been half-way round the globe, and the world was wide open.

How could I know I was about to experience the worst day of my life?

I packed my things in their paper bag and made my way to the Labour Exchange in Cardiff. They questioned me about my background, and agreed to try to fix me up with a job in London on the lines of the work I had been doing before. I was not yet fifteen, but I was self-sufficient, ready to face the world, and willing to work.

Meantime they sent me to a youth hostel which took in sixteen boys and housed us in four dormitories. For the week before Christmas I did find a part-time job with a bakery selling fresh rolls door to door in the back streets, but that was all there was going.

The hostel farmed out all their kids on Christmas Day to different families who took them under their wing as a charitable gesture for this special day of the year, and gave them a wonderful time. If the *Maindy Court* had made it back earlier and not been delayed by the weather I would have been one of them. As it was, I was too late and 'missed the boat', as it were, by two days.

On Christmas morning 1929 I woke up to the sound of laughter and excitement in the dormitory. The other boys put on clean shirts and smartened themselves up to look their best. I remember one brushing his hair in front of the bathroom mirror until it shone. One by one they left as the doorbell rang and someone came to collect them. The building grew emptier and my footsteps sounded hollow on the bare wood floor as I wandered through the deserted rooms, the only boy left in the house.

Lunch time came. Christmas lunch, and I sat alone in the canteen at one end of a long trestle table eating sausage and mash. I stared around the empty hall, and for once I did not try to hide my tears.

Cook, a matronly figure in a white apron, had pushed the plate through the hatch from the kitchen with a brief: 'Merry Christmas' – and gone off for her own family celebration.

It wasn't that I hadn't received a Christmas present. Or that I was worried about nobody caring for me – I had grown used to that. But after the camaraderie of shipboard life I was suddenly back to that unutterable loneliness that I felt when Joe had abandoned me months before.

Alone in that deserted hostel I realised I had nobody to love me. I was never so empty in my whole life.

CHAPTER THREE

New Year's Day, 1930, and the Labour Exchange found a
job for me – and gave me the train fare into the bargain. A
pub in Henley-on-Thames needed a barman. I pocketed the
money for the train and headed out to the Great West Road
with my carrier bag, thumb raised hopefully in the air. And
this time I got lucky. Two lifts, and I was walking over the
bridge on the Thames to the pub on the corner to report for
duty.

The owner, a red-faced man in tweeds, answered my
knock. When I told him I was the new barman he simply
looked down at me and said: 'Son, I need someone who can
hump barrels of beer up from the cellar. Don't be daft!' And
he slammed the door in my face.

I walked back to London. It took me two days, but I was
fit and eager when I reported to a domestic servants agency
in the West End. They had a vacancy for a scullery boy in a
posh house in Earl's Court. A butler answered the door,
summoned me inside, and showed me to my room. 'The
kitchen is downstairs,' he said loftily. 'I will see you later.'

The kitchen was empty, and I was hungry. I stood by the
big oak table for a few minutes waiting for someone to
come, then started nosing around. I opened the pantry door
– and there, joy of joys, was a whole cooked chicken, sitting
temptingly on a plate. It seemed to be just waiting for me.

I reckoned that, now I was part of the staff, I could help

myself. I grabbed it with both hands and tucked in ravenously, and was just polishing off the last blissful wing when the sound of someone clearing his throat came from inches behind me. It was the butler.

'Just what do you think you are doing?' His face was a curious shade of purple.

'Er – I was hungry,' I said lamely. Looking at the carcass on the table it was a pretty obvious remark.

'*Out!*' was all he said. And I followed his pointing finger out of the front door and into the street, pausing only to grab my carrier bag on the way. I hadn't even had time to unpack. I suppose it's quite rare to be sacked before you've even started, but at least I got a free meal out of it.

With nowhere to sleep, I called in on my grandparents – on my father's side – at their terraced house at No.21, Shirland Road, Kilburn, and asked them if I could stay. In one voice they gave me their answer: *no*. 'Why don't you go to your father – he's responsible for you,' advised grandma, a trim, grey-haired lady in her late sixties.

She gave me Dad's address. He had married again, and was living in Earl's Court. It had been a long time, and I knew I had to see him, if only to clear my mind of the dark memories of the past.

I knocked on the front door of a large house in a leafy square in Earl's Court. A lady answered it. 'Yes?' She was a pleasant woman with a kindly air about her.

I plucked up my courage. 'Can I see Mr Wisdom please?'

'What do you want?' she asked.

I took a deep breath. 'I – I'm his son, Norman.'

The silence seemed to go on for ever as she stared at me. Finally she opened the door wider. 'I'm Mrs Wisdom,' she said. 'You had better come in. He's still at work, but he'll be back shortly.'

My new stepmother ushered me in to the front room, and left me. I sat down on the settee, and waited. Like so many 'front rooms' of the day, it was functional, cold, impersonal, scarcely lived in except to entertain visitors. My hands were moist, and my heart was pounding. I had no idea what I would say to my father, I hadn't seen him for nearly four years, but somehow I thought: It's going to be all right. We'll get together again. All those bad memories belong to the past.

After half an hour of listening to the clock ticking on the mantelpiece I heard the front door open. Hurried footsteps ran over linoleum to meet him. A muffled conversation took place in the hall – then the door opened, and there stood my father, dark and burly in his smart grey chauffeur's uniform, brows knitted, but his face utterly devoid of expression.

Apprehensively I rose to greet him. I felt unexpected tears welling in my eyes. I stretched out my hands, wanting to say the right thing. 'Dad – ?'

But my father stood back, and uttered just two words to the son he had not seen in four long years.

'Get out!' he said.

That was all. He held the door open, his face like stone, and watched without another word as I walked slowly out of the room and down the front steps to the street.

There I turned, in time to see my father closing the front door. In a choked voice I called up to him: 'I'll never see you again.' And I never did.

It was back to the hard pavements. I had a few bob in my pocket, not a lot, but I wasn't going to spend it on digs. I found a bus shelter near Victoria Station, where I could wrap myself in newspapers – the old tramps' trick of keeping warm – and settle down for the night underneath the seat.

I varied my sleeping quarters, as much for personal safety as anything else. After my experience with the Greek sailor I knew there were blokes who would be after me like a trout up a stream, and I had to watch out for myself. I was small and skinny – but I was also muscular, and I didn't have an ounce of fat on me. I reckoned I could out-run, if not out-fight, anyone who came after me. I relied on my wits and my speed.

If you are really tired you can kip anywhere. I would find my way to the warm air vents around the Savoy Hotel and lie down there with the tramps on the pavement. Passers-by would just step around us. After a time I recognised a few familiar faces swaddled in old clothes and mufflers, but we weren't an army in those days, and there was no such thing as Cardboard City. Today I read about the beggars and the vagrants and the kids who leave home to live rough, and I feel sorry for them. Me, I didn't have a home to leave .

Finally I found a place I could call my own: a favourite spot behind the Marshal Foch statue that stands in a small garden opposite Victoria Station. I would sleep on the stone steps, hidden from sight, and I was never disturbed.

An all-night coffee stall nearby was my salvation. It was run by an ebullient bald-headed man with a Mexican moustache and a spotless white jacket that always looked as if it had just come out of the wash. Around three o'clock in the morning, when it was usually very quiet, I would creep out from my hideaway, and up to the stall where I could just get my face above the counter to peer up at him appealingly. The owner would peer back at me, shake his head, and without a word hand me a hot pie and a mug of Bovril. I would mutter my thanks, and slink back to my hiding place.

I survived like this for a month. How, I don't know. In the afternoons I would take refuge in a local cinema, usually the Metropole. I would wait unobtrusively by the Exit doors until someone came out, and then slip through to make my way to a seat in the darkness and warmth and stay there for the rest of the day, seeing the same film round and round. At the end of the week, when the film changed, I reckon I could have recited the dialogue backwards. Just before the lights went up I'd head for the toilet, and dive back after the interval. No-one ever challenged me, and it was a great way to stay warm.

Often I would fall asleep, and it was always the National Anthem that woke me up, like a subconscious signal that it was time to go. I would head back to the statue, give the Marshal an ironic salute, and settle down to snatch some more sleep. Somehow I always managed to look clean. I would wash in the public lavatories on the Embankment or in the station, and I made sure I never looked like a tramp.

Perhaps this made an impression. Because finally my coffee stall friend had a few words to say. He leaned down over the counter, handed me a pie and Bovril, then said: 'You know, this sort of life will do you no good. If you've got nowhere to go, why don't you join the Army?'

'I'm too young, Mister,' I replied. 'And I'm too small.'

'But they take lads of fourteen in the Army band,' he said. 'How old are you?'

I munched the pie. 'Fourteen,' I said. 'But I don't know anything about music.'

He winked. 'Don't let that worry you,' he said. 'Bullshit them. Tell 'em you do. Then you might get a chance to learn.'

I had nothing to lose. Next evening I reported to the Army recruiting office, which was based at Scotland Yard opposite Big Ben. Two large soldiers at the gate informed me that the recruiting section was closed for the day and that I had better come back next morning.

'Oh,' I said. I put on the little-boy-lost look, which wasn't far from the truth. 'That's terrible. I've got nowhere to sleep.'

They exchanged a quick glance. 'All right, sonny. If you're signing up you may as well come in,' said one, gesturing me to the guard room. They gave me a meal and a blanket, and let me kip down for the night on a bunk. It beat Marshall Foch out of sight, and gave me my first good impression of the Army.

Next day I underwent a medical examination. And passed it with flying colours, despite my size. I managed to get a glimpse of the papers: Height: 4 feet 10½ inches. Weight: 5 stone 9 lbs. Then I was summoned to the Bandmaster's office.

He was big and bristling. But I had a feeling he was human too. He finished reading my report, looked up from his desk, and barked:

'You know all about music, do you?'

'Yes, sir,' I replied brightly.

'What's a sharp?' he demanded suddenly.

'Pardon, sir?'

'I said *what's a sharp?*'

I had to confess. 'I don't know that one, sir.'

'What's a flat?'

'I don't know that one either, sir.' We could have been playing riddles.

'You don't know anything about music then, do you?' He glared at me.

'I'm sorry, sir. No – but I'd like the chance to learn. I was hoping I could bluff my way in, but now I see I can't. I apologise for taking up your time.'

'You should have said that in the first place,' he said, but his tone had softened. 'I'm putting you on the waiting list. You'll hear from us in due course. I need your address.'

This flummoxed me, because I had no home and no address. Suddenly I remembered my grandparents. No. 21, Shirland Road went into my file. I got up, stammering my thanks. He waved an airy dismissal – but I detected the hint of a smile behind it.

I tried the Job Centre once again, and this time they found me a job that suited me down to the ground. The Marble Arch Pavilion (later the Odeon) became my new employers: I was taken on as a page boy at £1 per week. On the strength of my having a regular job my granny agreed to take me in – particularly after she heard how my father had treated me. I said my farewells to Marshal Foch and moved in to Shirland Road. Grandma took fifteen shillings out of my weekly pound, which didn't leave me too much to throw around.

At the Pavilion my main job was to take VIP guests up in the lift, in one of those Waygood-Otis elevators where you turn a handle and the cage responds to your bidding. One evening I was on duty when Joan Crawford arrived as guest of honour at a premiere of her film *Untamed*. The love goddess not only smiled down at me, but ruffled my hair and suddenly kissed me on the forehead. All I could do was gulp. Thirty years later I would sit next to her at a Hollywood luncheon and she would put her hand on my knee under the table. But as a fourteen-year-old page-boy, I settled for the hair.

Reginald Foort was the resident organist, a splendid old professional who practised every day in front of a vista of empty stalls. He would go over the music again and again, and I used to lean on the rail entranced by the great sounds swelling up from the heart of the mighty Wurlitzer.

One day he turned and gave me a friendly grin. 'Do you like it?'

'Oh yes – but why do you keeping playing the same piece all morning?' I couldn't help asking. 'Why don't you try something else?'

'You have to keep going until you get it absolutely right,' he replied, and it was something I took to heart and never forgot. It was a code I have lived by to this day.

Soon after, a buff envelope dropped through the letter box of No. 21 Shirland Road. I had been accepted as a drummer boy for the King's own Royal Regiment at Lichfield in the Midlands.

I said ta-ta to my grandmother, and off I went – to one of

the happiest surprises I could imagine. Army life was everything I had dreamed of, and as a very junior drummer boy I spent most of the week learning the basics of music, with very little square bashing.

After three months I was given a generous fortnight's leave on full pay, and decided to spend the time in London. I moved back with Grandma. One morning I answered a knock at the front door, and was astonished to find the postman standing there with a parcel – addressed to me. More important, on the back was the address of the sender ('If not delivered, please return to . . .') and inside was a birthday present of a hairbrush . . . from my mother!

My heart leaped. I could hardly remember the last time I had seen her. How many years was it? At least four – no, five. The address was near the Old Kent Road, and an hour later I was in a bus bound for Peckham. It was my mother's sister, Auntie May, who answered the door. (I had met her a couple of times when I was still at school.) Her mouth dropped open when she saw me – and she grabbed my hand and raced round to the post office to send a telegram to my mother.

Mum was there the same evening, rushing in to gather me in her arms and give me a long, long cuddle that chased the years away. She looked absolutely wonderful, in a fur coat and jewellery, and seemed quite prosperous. More than that, she looked happy.

'I am,' she said. 'And you too, Norman? My, it's lovely to see you.' She was living with her second husband Sydney Poulton in a flat in Russell Square, a very high class part of London near the British Museum, and she had become a successful dress designer. We sat down over a cup of tea to catch up on five lost years. The two sisters shook their heads in wonder at my adventures, though I didn't dwell on sleeping rough in the streets or mention the name of Dimitri. 'We must never lose touch again, Norman,' Mum said, firmly. 'What are you doing with yourself now?'

45

When I proudly told her I was in the King's Own Regiment, Fourth of Foot, I was amazed to see tears well up in her eyes. 'That's no career for anyone with ambition,' she said. 'I'll get you the right job. You've got to make something of yourself.'

I couldn't see it. In the three short months I had been with them, the Army had done more for me than anyone else ever had. I was enjoying myself. Why chuck it all in? But perhaps Mum was right. Maybe I could be with her, and have a career that meant something as well. In the days that followed I moved into the Russell Square flat, and every day Mum and Sydney kept on at me. In the end I gave in.

'All right,' I said. 'But what – ?'

'You told us you used to be good at drawing,' she said. 'You can be an architect.'

When my leave ended Mum took the train with me up to Lichfield, and paid over £35 on the spot to buy me out of the Army. It was as easy as that, and we were back home the same day.

Through her dress-making, my mother hobnobbed with the wives of some quite influential businessmen, and a week later she was able to get me a job with the Trust Concrete Steel Company whose impressive offices looked out on to the Thames. I was to be a trainee draughtsman. She insisted on taking me into the West End and buying me a smart suit, new shoes and a couple of shirts.

I certainly looked the part when I reported for duty at 9.0 a.m. prompt on the Monday morning, even if I didn't feel like it. The chief draughtsman was thin, precise and wore pebble glasses. He led me into a drawing office with long picture windows with a marvellously distracting view of the river traffic passing below, and allocated me a high stool beside a big sloping desk. As I perched on it he asked: 'What do you know about trigonometry?'

I came clean from the start. 'Nothing, sir.' I wasn't even

sure what it meant. 'But I can draw.'

'Oh well,' he said without enthusiasm. 'I suppose that's a start. I'll find someone to show you the ropes.'

While I waited I looked around. There were a dozen other similar high desks and stools with young men in shirt sleeves bowed intently over huge sheets of graph paper, measuring lines with set-squares, compasses and slide rules. The silence was so profound that the only sound was the scratching of pencils on paper. It reminded me of a school examination. Or a scene from Dickens – all that was missing were the quill pens. I turned back to watching the tugs and barges on the river four floors below.

Two fellows appeared at my elbow. They spread out a large plan in front of me. It was some kind of building, filled with lines and scrawled figures. 'Hullo, you're the new architect, right?' said one. I nodded. 'Good. Well, this is extremely urgent. Take a look at this office block. It's going up Thursday, along the river near Blackheath. Get it ready, check the figures to make sure the ratios are right. Watch out for the pillars on the sixth floor, and mind where the pipes go. The best method is Pythagoras, using the hypotenuse *there!*' He prodded a spot half-way up the building. Then they turned on their heel and walked out of the room.

What on earth had they been talking about? I sat there, numb, staring at the outline in front of me, willing it to go away. It was a bewildering jigsaw puzzle that meant nothing. I picked up a pencil, and put it down again. I was so overcome with dread that I could have turned to stone. Finally I asked for directions to the lavatory.

But I didn't go to the loo. I picked up my coat and walked out of the building and into the fresh air. I had lasted less than two hours. The thought came to me: What a pity my mother hadn't realised my education was far below the requirements for this type of job.

Outside, I rested my elbows on the Embankment wall and stared out at the river. What was I going to tell Mum? Where would I go now? It was much later that I realised that it had been a practical joke, and that the prize pair were a couple of other trainees pulling my leg. By then it was too late.

I stayed by the river for a whole hour. Finally I took a deep breath – and headed for Scotland Yard and the Army recruiting office.

CHAPTER FOUR

In the fearsome heat of an Indian summer I marched proudly through the white-washed walls of the barracks and into the square at Lucknow. Like the rest of the troops, I was in khaki, with riding breeches and puttees, and wore a topee with the brass badge of the 10th Hussars emblazoned on it, gleaming in the sun. The badge was a plume of ostrich feathers over a coronet and a ribbon: *Ich Dien* – 'I Serve' – which is, in fact, the motto of the Prince of Wales, taken originally from the blind King John of Bohemia.

That was 1335. This was Lucknow, 1930! I could hardly believe I was here. It was a name I had heard only in geography at school. Thank heaven the interview back in London had gone well. Same office, different bandmaster. I wondered what the first one would have said if he had been sitting there when I marched in to sign on all over again? Something like: 'Try and stay with us a little longer this time, will you?' Actually I hadn't told them I'd been in before – I was afraid it might cause problems.

But this new bandmaster had merely sat back and inquired:

'What's a note?'

I replied instantly: 'A note is a sign used to represent the relative pitch of a sound – sir!'

'Ummm . . .' he said. Then: 'What's a key?'

I responded: 'The height or depth of a sound, sir.'

49

'What's harmony?'

'Two or more notes in combination, sir.'

I had learned all this invaluable information from a music book in the few weeks at Lichfield, and now I was putting it to good use. I could tell he was impressed, but I also felt that his next question was intended to catch me out – and I was right. He smiled . . .

Then he gave me the big one – and he thought he'd got me. 'What is enharmonic?'

Who had ever heard of enharmonic? Well – I had. I answered smartly: 'In the case of the voice or various instruments, enharmonic is applied to an interval smaller than a chromatic semi-tone, sir.'

He looked at me for a long moment. Then he said slowly: 'My God! Alright – you're in!'

He bent to study my file, then looked up. 'India suit you?' he asked.

'Cor,' I said. 'Not arf – sir!'

The bandmaster explained that the Hussars would be in India, and since I vaguely equated hussars with horses it meant I might get to ride as well. For a fifteen-year-old ex-street urchin, it was an incredible chance to see the world, be educated – and be paid for it. First I had to kick my heels for two and a half weeks at Aldershot, as a bandboy learning the rudiments of music attached to the 8th Hussars. Suddenly the call came through. The first I knew of it was when I was marched off to the medical room and pumped full of shots for all sorts of nameless diseases, including the main scourge: malaria. Next day I found myself aboard the troop ship SS *Southampton,* bound for Calcutta and the 10th Hussars via the Suez Canal.

Six weeks later we were marching through the teeming streets to the railway station, and put on a train for the 600-mile journey through the burning red scrub and desert to Lucknow. The first sights and sounds of India, as anyone who has ever been there will tell you, is something you never forget. My senses were assailed by the crowds, the clothes, the sheer mass of humanity pressed around us – as curious about the khaki figures in their midst as we rookie soldiers were about them.

Lucknow was the capital of the province of Oudh, set on the placid waters of the River Gunti, to the north-west of Calcutta and only 200 miles from Katmandu and the foothills of the mighty Himalayas. As I stepped from the railway station my eyes took in a bewildering maze of tumbledown shacks, narrow streets full of stalls, beggars crouched in doorways with their hands pathetically out-stretched, and simply masses of people. The first thing that struck me was that despite the distressing squalor, they all seemed so extraordinarily cheerful. The second was the incredible range of colours, as if a rainbow had settled on every corner I came to as we marched in double file from the station to the barracks. The stalls were hung with muslins and shawls exquisitely embroidered with gold and silver, while others sold all kinds of glassware and pottery.

Two hundred of us had arrived from the ship to swell that particular garrison. We were there to keep up the 'British presence', and we would train to be ready for anything. On that first, unforgettable arrival through the old town we passed the ruins of the original fort which had been so gallantly defended against the mutineers in the legendary uprising of 1857.

As we passed through the big iron gates, with two white-helmeted sentries snapping to salute at the guard-house, my eyes were watering – but not from the searing mid-day sun. They were tears of pride running unashamedly down my cheeks, and in that moment I was probably happier than at any time in my young life.

I was marching with my comrades, part of a special regiment in one of the most exciting and glamorous countries on earth. To some people I may still have looked like a boy. But suddenly, in my pith helmet, uniform, puttees and polished boots, I was a man. I swung my arms with renewed vigour and passed under the arched gate and into my new life.

Our quarters were in a low red-brick barracks with a sloping roof of shiny black slates. After settling in we were given a pep talk by the CO, Lieutenant-Colonel B. O. Hutchinson, who despite his somewhat unfortunate initials was a suitably commanding figure from the Old School.

He reminded us that we were in a strange country with totally different customs, that we must remember at all times that we were representing King and Country, and gave us a dire warning of what would happen to us if we stepped out of line. Straight back home on the first ship! But we were also privileged to be part of an elite regiment, and we could find enormous enjoyment in the life if we put our hearts into it.

I needed no second bidding. The Army would clothe me, feed me, keep me fit and educate me. As bandsmen, among four squadrons numbering eight hundred men, we were even known as 'the Gentlemen of the Regiment'! What a turn-up for a one-time Oliver Twist. Right then, I couldn't ask for more!

Just look at the alternative. The blokes would sit around the Mess or in their bunks before turning in, and often the talk would turn to what was going on back home. It was a grim picture they painted.

Britain was sinking towards the depths of the Great Depression of 1933, with three million people unemployed, an average weekly wage of £2 10s, and dole queues stretching around the block. This was the time of the Jarrow Marchers, when hundreds of shipbuilders closed in on London after William Palmer's yard shut down in the north.

If I had stayed, I wouldn't have had a chance.

My Turn

I set out to make the most of where I was. I started with my fellow soldiers – which ones I should pal up with in the months ahead? Looking around the dormitory on that first night, I discovered to my surprise and delight that I wasn't the smallest in the regiment: that privilege belonged to the Smith brothers, Jim and George. Another bond we shared was that they had come from an orphanage in Dover, and were relishing their new life as much as I was.

Next day the bandmaster called us into the Music Room at the end of one of the buildings. Mr M. Roberts was tall and amiable, with a splendid moustache of which he was inordinately proud, judging by the way he would give it a frequent surreptitious twirl. Behind his back we called him Robbo. To his face, he was always 'Sir'.

We lined up in front of him as he consulted the list of new arrivals. 'Ah, Wisdom. Let's have a look at you.' He stepped up close, and examined my lips with his fingertips to judge the embouchure – the shape of my mouth and tongue – for the tautness with which I could grip a reed cap. 'Purse them. . . now smile. . . open wide. . .' I felt like Muffin the Mule.

Cor blimey, I thought. He's not a dentist as well, is he? The thought occurred to me that he might hold out a trumpet and say:

'Spit in this!'

Finally Mr Roberts stepped back. 'I'm putting you on clarinet, Wisdom.' Then he turned to the others, and an hour later we all knew our instrument: trumpet, trombone, oboe, bassoon, euphonium ... It was a proper military band, with all mod-cons. It was only when he came to Simpson, who had somehow got through despite the drawback of a hair lip, that Bandmaster Roberts paused momentarily. Then he said crisply: 'Simpson – drums!'

'Yeffir!' said Simpson, happily.

The first weeks passed swiftly, with seldom a minute to ourselves. The Army saw to that. For hours on end I sat on a bench in the Music Room learning how to blow into the clarinet properly, eventually graduating to scales and keys until I felt ready to try a tune. Once I set out to master something, I never wanted to give up. It would take at least a year to master that instrument – but meantime there was something else. The trumpet.

This was an entirely difference kettle of fish. We were going to learn to sound the Regimental Posts like Reveille, Cookhouse, On Parade, Officers' Mess, and, of course, the Last Post before lights out at night. Not forgetting the Regimental Call – if you can imagine *We are the Tenth, the shiny, shiny Tenth!* put to trumpet blasts.

With the trumpet, you have no valves to worry about, but an awful lot of puff is needed. There were twelve of us bandboys. In common with the other new arrivals, I was issued with a lovely brass trumpet which I would hang on a lanyard on my personal hook by the lockers in the Music Room. Over the next weeks I was introduced to the mysteries of 'tongueing' and 'double tongueing' – you've heard the *Pip-p-p-p-pip!* of a military trumpet call, but it needs breath control to get it right and avoid the embarrassment of running out of air in the middle. Cardinal sin and a firing squad for that!

It isn't as simple as a lot of people think – or anything like that legendary movie line from from Lauren Bacall to Humphrey Bogart: 'You just put your lips together and blow.'

That's whistling. Trumpet playing is an art in itself.

Two months had gone by when the band was summoned to go with part of the regiment on a tour into hill country. Four trumpeters had to stay behind to sound duty calls, and as a newcomer I was one of them. It was called 'Trumpet Guard', a twenty-four-hour-round-the-clock duty. When your turn came it meant kipping down on a bunk and staying in the guard room for the twenty-four hour period by the gate until 5.30 a.m., trumpet at the ready, to sound the change of guard an hour later at dawn.

Your duties were laid out precisely, and never varied. Reveille at 6.30 a.m. I would cycle across the parade ground, my trumpet on its halyard round my neck, through the eerie dawn with the first flush of pink staining the sky and the cockerels starting to crow. Then I would sound my wakey-wakey call from all four corners of the square, and hear the stirrings and growled oaths from men rudely jolted out of sleep as I cycled past the mosquito-meshed windows. Regular cries of 'Piss orf!' would pursue me back to the guard house.

We were more popular sounding 'Cook House' for breakfast, lunch and dinner, plus 'Parade' when the troops were called to muster, 'Guard' when the guard changed, and of course the haunting Last Post for lights out, which meant kip time.

One terrible incident occurred during my second year in Lucknow that cast a shadow over my entire time with the Tenth. I was on 'Trumpet Duty' in the guard house with three other soldiers, and as usual we would take turns to sleep on the bunk in one corner of the room. It was just a concrete hut, very basic, with a table, four chairs and a bed.

We would spend the hours till dawn playing cards, reading or grabbing a nap when we felt tired. On this particular night we were seated round the table getting the cards ready for a game of poker. Trooper Johnny Chisholm was on my left reading a newspaper while I sifted through the pack to check all the cards were there.

Another trooper named Mike was cleaning his rifle on the seat next to me, peering down the sights and pulling a cord through the barrel with the flannel cleaner. He thumbed in a couple of rounds, and suddenly – *crack!* The rifle went off and shot poor Mike right through the head. He went crashing back on to the floor, and died on the spot.

I was stunned. We all were. The echoes of that shot seemed to reverberate for ever in the confined space. I was just a kid of fifteen, even though I had seen more of the world than most boys my age. Up to that moment I had been under the impression that all weapons we used were loaded with blanks. Now I knew better. It was real ammunition.

That night was the first time I ever saw anybody die, and I felt sick for days afterwards. Especially as the band was away and I needed company.

Sometimes the band was away on engagements for two or three months. I used to wish I could go with them, but it would be close on a year before I was skilled enough to join them. Meantime I had to nose around to see if I could find an instrument that no-one else played. One hot afternoon I was rummaging around the large store room when I came across a dusty old xylophone hidden behind some boxes. I pinged it with my fingers, and found the notes actually worked. I rooted around until I found a couple of appropriate sticks with the knobbly ends, then sorted out some music and started picking out a tune, parrot fashion. After that I practised every day – and by the time the band came back from the hills I had two numbers up my sleeve, 'Snowflakes' and 'Two Imps'. You have to learn a xylophone by ear – you can't play and read sheet music at the same time.

Bandmaster Roberts greeted us cordially, as the musicians left to hold the fort. He was sorry to hear about the drama in the guard house and invited me to join the next day's practice. It was great to be among a crowd of my mates again, twenty-four good men with all their musical talent, and I joined in with gusto on my clarinet. Normal practice time was from 9.00 a.m. to 12 noon, but invariably they ran out of music by 11.30 a.m. when the bandmaster would say: 'Does anyone fancy anything in particular?'

This time I piped up: 'Can we have 'Snowflakes' please, sir?'

He bent a stern gaze on me. 'Has Christmas come early this year, Wisdom? 'Snowflakes' is a xylophone solo.'

Above the general laughter I pressed on. 'I know, sir.'

The bandmaster raised an eyebrow. 'Don't tell me –'. He stopped. 'All right. Where is it?'

I wheeled the instrument out from the store room, and after a few tentative thumps with the sticks went hell-for-leather into 'Snowflakes', my hands blurring over the keyboard. At the end there was a stunned silence. Someone broke it to say: 'Cor, how about that?' Then they all broke into applause. At the very next Troop Concert I sat in the front row of the band with my clarinet, and, at the right moment, I moved forward to perform my xylophone solo. My first chance, and I took it with both hands, literally! That was the first time in my life I had ever been applauded, and it was nice. I can almost compare my excitement to my first appearance at the London Palladium.

During these concerts the band used to sing sea shanties, and one day I went to the bandmaster and said, 'Excuse me sir, but why is it that nobody ever sings the solos?' He said, 'Because Wisdom, we haven't got anybody who can sing well enough.' I said, 'I'm sorry sir, but I think you have.' With an expression of disbelief, he gazed skywards, and then muttered, 'All right Wisdom, sing me a song, so I did. I sang an Old Jack Buchanan number called 'You Must Say Yes to Mr Brown'. Once again he looked surprised and walked away almost shouting, 'All right, that'll do me. Start learning your solos for the next concert.'

Sure enough I did and there I was, once again, on the stage in the front line of the band with my clarinet. It was 'Snowflakes' followed by sea shanties and more applause – oh yes! I was beginning to get the bug.

The bandmaster was impressed. 'Well done. We'll put

that into the programme.' From then on I had my solo spot when we gave concerts for the garrison – and I was always in the front row.

What else did India do for an impressionable youth who wanted a chance to be as good as the next man? A taste for curry, for a start. Sunday lunch was always curry, Gandhi's Revenge we called it, and I have relished a curry ever since – hot, but not volcanic.

The Army also taught me to be tidy, fastidiously so. It is almost an obsession, and I am happy to admit that I still cannot bear to see anything out of place or left dirty.

To this day if someone moves an armchair in my house, I'll shift it back so that the legs are in the same spot in the carpet! It is all due to the weekly kit inspections we had to endure. All our clothing would be laid out in neat piles on our bed, and Sergeant Cox would go striding down the centre aisle between the beds with his baton under his arm, ripe for trouble. Woe betide the man whose shirts were untidy or boots unpolished. The incentive was that the best kit was excused next week's inspection – and I reckon I won six out of ten.

The Army also gave me my education. Along with the other lads of similar backgrounds I attended classes three times a week, and finally obtained a First Class Certificate of Education.

But just because we were called the Gentlemen of the Regiment did not mean we escaped the drill or training. I was taught to fire a rifle – I became a marksman – plus map-reading and survival in rough terrain. The bonus was a beautiful chestnut mare standing all of twelve hands high, and I was introduced to her in my first week, the day after being issued with my riding gear: breeches, boots, spurs, puttees. The spurs still hang above the desk in my study, and what memories they evoke.

'All right Wisdom, you take Number 16.' The riding

instructor was a big man in jodphurs with a face that reflected years in the open air under a tropical sun.

I had already done a recce of the stables, and found most of the horses to be fearsome-looking brutes that rolled their eyes at you as if sizing you up for breakfast. I had never been on a horse in my life. Number 16 was big for me – they all were – and I had to lead her out to a nearby wall before I could even take a jump into the stirrups! I immediately dubbed her 'Sixie', and what a lovely horse she was. We first learned in a classroom how to handle the reins and the bit, and the theory of jogging with every other bounce when trotting was explained to us. It was when I got into the saddle that my nervousness evaporated. The ground was a long way away, but somehow it didn't worry me in the slightest.

We went through the motions like any other riding school: start with walking your mount, then a trot. Grip with your knees, turn your toes up – if they're down, you can't grip. Now a canter . . . then dig your spurs in, and suddenly I'm away at a full gallop across the parched red scrub and stones of the plain. And we're all shouting *'Bloody marvellous!'* at the tops of our voices in a headlong gallop that leaves us breathless and the instructor shaking his head. 'Lads, lads – keep 'em in control. I'm telling you.' The instructor's name was Jaye, and his rank was sergeant-major.

As we got to know him better we found he had a devil-may-care disposition – and a sense of humour to match. He had a reputation in the camp for 'rough-riding', and finally we found out what that meant. One morning he lined us up in the stables, and said crisply:

'Right! You've all passed riding school?'

'Yes, sir!' Somehow we had.

'Then mount up – and follow me!'

We scrambled into our saddles – and suddenly I was in the middle of the Charge of the Light Brigade, Lucknow version. 'Tally ho! Follow me – and keep in my tracks,' bellowed the sergeant-major – and off he went at full pelt into the scrub, choosing the trails that he knew and we didn't. I have never seen so many bodies bite the dust at one time. It was like Beecher's Brook on a bad day in the Grand National. The diminutive Smith brothers were flung headlong into the bushes at one and the same time, an amazing coincidence I thought as I galloped by, clinging to the mane of Sixie and desperately trying to stay in the saddle.

Finally the galloping sergeant-major reined in, and surveyed the carnage. 'That's the way you're going to have to ride if ever it comes to the chase,' he announced. 'No prisoners, understand? You'll be out on your own, and you're going to learn to stay in the saddle.'

He never did explain who would be chasing whom, and to be truthful it had never entered our heads. We were all too exhausted to ask questions. The Smith brothers limped back to base with their mounts. I had stayed on Sixie, and took extra trouble over her grooming that night. She had done me proud.

She did me less than proud a month later. By now I was already quite an accomplished rider, and felt completely at home in the saddle. Recognising this, Sergeant-Major Jaye put me in the lead for exercising the horses, a great compliment. It meant taking two spare exercise horses with me, one on either side, so that we were three in line. We headed out of the barracks and into the scrub, and as usual the rough-riding sergeant-major urged his mount into a trot, then into a canter.

I was right behind, and my own horses followed suit. I was holding a set of reins in each hand, looped between my fingers as we had been taught, and gripping Sixie tightly between my knees. I only had two hands, but right then I could have done with three.

Off went the sergeant-major – and off went Sixie and Co.

His shout of 'Follow me!' floated back on the warm winter air, but we needed no second bidding. By then it was too late anyway. We thundered through thickets and brush like a runaway stage coach, whooping with exhilaration – until in front of me I saw the sergeant-major clear a five-foot bush at full pelt.

Sixie and our two exercise companions followed at speed. The horses on either side sailed over the thorny barrier as if they were auditioning for the role of Pegasus. But Sixie had different ideas. She dug her hooves into the ground and skidded to a halt. I went up and over, hanging on to the reins like a charioteer in *Ben-Hur*, arms stretched wide, clearing that bush by two feet before landing smack on my backside in the dirt. Then came the really painful bit, as I was dragged along for several yards before the horses finally pulled up.

In those few terrifying seconds I became the Regiment's first man in space. The rest of the group had seen it, and I could hear them howling with laughter behind me. Miraculously I was unscathed. Dirty, yes, with mud and sand all over my face and staining my uniform, but unhurt – though there would probably be a bruise later. The sergeant-major reined in and came trotting back. From the imperious heights of his saddle he looked down at me, trying to hold back his laughter. Finally he controlled himself, and leaned down. 'Tough little bastard, aren't you?' he said.

'Yes, sir,' I said. 'Thank you, sir!'

It was because of this that the sergeant-major got the idea of putting on displays. He obviously gave it a lot of thought, because nothing happened for a couple of weeks. Then, after a morning's instruction, he took me to one side.

'Do you think you could fall off a horse if we gave you a soft landing?' he said. 'We could put on a show for the garrison, a proper display. The Colonel might go for it.'

'Not 'arf,' I said, radiating enthusiasm. 'I'll do any kind of fall you want.'

The idea that I might actually hurt myself never occurred to me. I was hot stuff at gymnastics, my body was toughened and hard, and I exercised every day for at least an hour. In the well-equipped gymnasium I practised forward rolls, side rolls, front handsprings, back somersaults, even falling backwards off the wooden box horse on to the mat, and always bounced back without a scratch to show for it.

The sergeant-major and I worked it out together: he would lay out a bale of straw on the parade ground, and I would come along at full gallop and dive headlong into it.

'How about setting fire to it?' I suggested eagerly.

'This isn't a circus, it's a military display,' rejoined Sergeant-Major Jaye, sharply.

'Then how about firing a couple of cannons at it?'

'Don't be daft, lad. Besides, I can't afford to lose you. Bad for morale!'

Far away from prying eyes, in a field near the river where grass provided a soft landing, we chose a spot to rehearse. We rolled a large bale of straw into position, and I fell off my beautiful mare in every direction – front somersault, which was easy; back flip, which looked easy but wasn't; a sliding dive. After a week the sergeant-major said: 'I've had a word with the Colonel, and he's all for it. Everyone will be there.' That included the officers and their wives, and it meant we had the green light to put on a real show.

The secret of falling off a horse without breaking every bone in your body is surprisingly simple. Make sure both feet are out of the stirrups. If you are diving to the left, you lift your right leg back over the saddle so that you are dangling only a couple of feet above the ground – and just let go. For a front roll you tuck your head in, and hit the ground with your forearms in a straightforward somersault.

For a backward roll you lie back and put both feet up by the horse's ear. By the time you leave the saddle you will actually be only three feet above the ground, lying flat and hitting the turf with your shoulders and backside at the same time.

Either way you shouldn't normally get kicked. You will have launched yourself out to the side, and by the time you've hit the ground the horse has gone.

A month later we put on our first display before the entire regiment. There was a parade, a mock charge, and I did my stunt into the straw, disappearing into it as if I'd been fired from a catapult. I was cheered to the echo, and the icing on the cake was when the rough-riding sergeant-major walked across, pulled me out from the straw and publicly shook hands with me.

Of course Army life was not all sweetness and light. I had an appetite you wouldn't credit from my small stature, perhaps because I didn't have much to eat when I was a kid, and it was my stomach that got me into trouble one evening.

We were at camp, God knows where, but miles from the barracks. The trumpeters were due to sound a combined Officers' Mess Call, with all twelve of us, on the parade ground where the flagpole stood. Half an hour beforehand I felt the familiar pangs of hunger and reckoned I had just enough time for a plate of egg and chips in the canteen before reporting for duty. But the queue was longer than I anticipated – and while I was still half-way through my meal a glance at the clock showed me I was running late.

In a panic I rushed to join the line – only to hear the first notes as I clattered round the corner. I was still chewing a forkful of food as I slunk into the end of the rank, and the most fearful strangled sound came out as I tried to blow my trumpet. It sounded more like a constipated camel than mess call, and afterwards I was immediately put on a charge.

The CO dished me out seven days jankers, which meant I was confined to base and forced to carry out menial tasks like cleaning out the toilets, sweeping away leaves – and peeling potatoes again! On the first morning of my punishment the provost sergeant marched me to a remote corner of the camp, and marked out a square in the baked earth with a piece of chalk. Then he threw me a spade. 'Dig!' he ordered.

The provost sergeant was a huge man, and one of the least likeable NCOs in the regiment. But I thought: if I make a good job of this, maybe he'll go easy on me for the rest of the time. It's called wishful thinking! 'How deep, sarge?'

'Six foot long, three foot wide, four foot deep. Make sure you do a good job, Wisdom.'

'Yes, sarge.'

That ground was rock hard. It was so hard I had to get a pickaxe from the stores to chip away the surface, then use the shovel. But I went at it with a will. It occurred to me that it must be for something important, like a dug-out for a gun emplacement.

All day I toiled away under the broiling sun, keeping up a cheery whistling, slicing the spade into the earth until my hands blistered and bled and I thought my arms would fall off. The sergeant stood watching for a time, then went away, then came back again. The sweat poured off my bent head in rivulets, and my hair was soaked.

At the end of the day, with just a short break for a sandwich and a drink of water, that hole was perfection, neatly trimmed, the edges smooth, beautifully symmetrical.

I heaved myself out of it, and stood proudly to attention as the provost sergeant came striding up. He looked down into the pit, then looked at me. 'Well done, Wisdom.'

Then he produced a dead mouse from behind his back, tossed it into the hole and barked: *'Bury that!'*

Years later I saw almost the same scene in the war film *From Here to Eternity,* when Frank Sinatra was ordered to do the same thing at a US Army camp in Hawaii. This time the sadistic guard threw a newspaper into the pit. A dead mouse would have been better!

On most evenings we would play in the Officers' Mess, not the entire band but in a group of half a dozen. Piano, violin, drums, clarinet – which was where I came in. The officers were a race apart. They even talked differently from us rough lads down the ladder. 'Cerry orn, Wisdom! Good work, leddie!' Even their sense of humour was different, as I found out when I taught myself to tap dance. No particular reason – it was just something I decided to attempt, beginning with a soft shoe shuffle and graduating to proper heel-and-toe tap.

Soft *shoe?* Hard boot more like! The best place to practise was the washhouse. I would go in, shut the door, and start behaving like Fred Astaire. Everyone can dream, can't they? Facing the mirror I flailed away in my Army boots – and the sounds of the studs made an awful racket on the stone floor that everyone could hear. The other blokes thought I was potty.

One evening in the barrack room I was stripped down to my shorts and started to shadow box, just as I did every day in the gym. I pranced about, hitting an imaginary opponent while the other lads, lying on their beds, encouraged me as if I was in a real bout. To make it more realistic I started ducking away from my non-existent opponent. Now I heard loud chuckles. I jerked my head back, putting on an expression of bewildered surprise as if the invisible ghost had caught me a fourpenny one.

The room filled with laughter, and I went at it like a lunatic. I crashed down from a might swipe, and got up rubbing my jaw. I cowered and covered up. Finally I ran for my life, scuttling through the beds and finishing with a flying leap over a two-tier bunk to screams of laughter as I landed on the other side.

Thus was born part of the routine I would later use at the London Palladium, before royalty, and all round the country in my variety shows.

The lads were doubled up, some of them with tears running down their cheeks. I had no idea how I had managed it, but for the first time in my life I felt strangely fulfilled.

Soon after that, the band gave a concert in the Officers' Mess. I did a tap routine and the officers started to laugh. I wasn't too happy to hear them because it wasn't supposed to be funny, but the 'Orficers' were chuckling away over their gin-and-tonics fit to bust. I felt they were taking the mickey.

So I tripped, deliberately. They laughed even more. That really annoyed me – so I took a few steps, tripped again, and this time I purposefully fell over, smack on the carpet. And now they were in stitches. Why were they laughing, I thought, and then it occurred to me. I was in full uniform and army boots!

As I sat on the floor staring back at them, it suddenly dawned on me. That's it! Comedy.

CHAPTER FIVE

I became the camp jester. I was paid a shilling a day for being a bandboy, and nothing for being funny. Tripping the other blokes up while marching on the parade ground always enlivened the day. I'd get my toe round the ankle of the man in front, and he would stumble and almost fall, emitting a low cry of *'Bastard!'*

Oops! Sorry! Accident! The sergeant couldn't do a thing if he didn't actually see it. If you knew that little so-and-so Wizzie was right behind you and that it was only a matter of time before he was going to trip you up, you'd march with your head to one side sending nervous glances back over your shoulder to anticipate the moment – or try to. They would go cross-eyed trying to squint back. Sometimes a bloke would take umbrage, but the others were usually laughing so much that I was never actually walloped.

Another caper we used to pull was marching with the right arm going the same way as the right leg, which spread down the platoon like a rash until everyone was doing it, and all of us finding it a hoot – except for the sergeant. He would get quite apoplectic. 'Wrong arm! Wrong leg!' he would bellow. 'You load of bloody lunatics!'

A variation of that little teaser was to swing our arms completely at random, all over the place, nothing what-soever to do with the legs, which was one of the funniest sights you could ever hope to witness – and would send the sergeant spare.

But best of all was the shoulder arms routine. I learned to twist the heavy .303 rifle round so that it ended up on my shoulder with the barrel pointing down at the ground and the butt sticking up in the air, and the red-faced NCO screaming at me: 'You stupid *berk!*'

I would stutter: 'I'm s-s-sorry, sarge!' And lower the rifle in confusion until I was standing to attention with it – but the gun would still be upside down! I would carry it as far as I could before he put me on a charge or died of apoplexy, and somehow I got away with it. The lads started actually looking forward to the daily parade wondering what was going to happen.

I was always careful not to overdo it, but the trouble was that sometimes things would happen to me that everyone thought were deliberate, but weren't. One Sunday on church parade the band was to lead the regiment as usual. As we gathered our instruments in the music room, it turned out that the chap who was on cymbals had fallen ill.

The bandmaster's finger pointed at me. 'Cymbals, Wisdom!'

I had half an hour to clean them and get into dress uniform for the parade. This was always a spectacular sight, with the massed troops marching past the CO and senior officers before passing into the church. The cymbals were brass, and were inspected to make sure they shone like a second sun.

There was a leather thong through the centre, tied with a knot on the inside, that went round your hand to keep it from slipping. All I had to do was march along going *Ching! Ching! Ching!* and keeping in time. It wasn't hard – or shouldn't have been. But in my hurry to get into my uniform I omitted to tie the thong on one cymbal properly.

I assured them afterwards that it was not intentional, but I don't think anyone really believed me.

We assembled outside in the hot sun, and the order rang out. 'Quick . . . *march!*' And I went striding out with the best of them, my cymbals clashing to the strains of the regimental marching song, which believe it or not is 'The Merry Month of May'.

> In the merry month of May . . . (*Ching! Ching!*)
> . . . on a horn at break of day (*Ching! Ching!*)
> . . . forth I walked to the wood –

And that's when one cymbal took off like a flying saucer. It shot out of my hand and went trundling off under the feet of the marching troops with a dreadful clanging sound. Naturally I chased after it – and that brought more chaos.

The Regimental Sergeant Major was bellowing: '*Get back in the ranks!*' While Bandmaster Roberts was shouting: '*Get the cymbal! Get it!*'

They ended up both shouting at each other. 'He's got to get back in the ranks,' yelled the RSM.

'Don't you bloody talk to me like that!' retorted the bandmaster. Of course everyone thought I had done it on purpose. Somehow I talked myself out of being put on a charge, but it was a close call.

So, I found the blokes were starting to laugh with me. I carried the fun into their canteen with my tap-dancing, and would ask the bandmaster for a number like 'You Must Say Yes to Mister Brown' – a smashing song to dance to – and sing.

> You must say yes to Mister Brown,
> No 'more or less' to Mister Brown,
> He is the great white chief,
> So you must yes to Mister Brown . . .

It was a great Jack Buchanan hit, and that would be for starters. Then I would give them 'I Can't Give You Anything But Love' – and even fall down in the middle of the number to get a laugh.

When I was feeling particularly cocky I would tell a joke. One that went down well with the boys was about a chap who goes into a restaurant and says: 'I want two rotten eggs on two pieces of burned toast.'

The waiter says: 'What!'

The chap repeats his order. 'Two rotten eggs on two pieces of burned toast.'

The waiter is stunned. 'What on earth do you want them like that for?'

The bloke says: 'I've got worms. Anything's good enough for them!'

The idea of becoming a professional comic had still never crossed my mind. But it was blindingly obvious that the officers were more sophisticated than me and my mates in the lower orders, and I began to adjust my material accordingly.

The one pastime I took with deadly seriousness was sport. Soccer, cricket – I was a medium-pace bowler, and my favourite batting position was twelfth, cross-country running, but above all, boxing. I stayed in tip-top condition – or at least I thought I did, until one day I was in the middle of a hectic game of football (inside right as usual) when I found myself puffing heavily. I stood in the middle of the pitch with my hands on my knees, looking as if I'd just finished a marathon.

Luckily the physical training instructor, Pete, was in the team, and he came running over to find out what was wrong.

I gasped out: 'I'm right out of breath –'

Showing understanding if not sympathy, Pete said: 'I'm not surprised, Wizzie. Look at the pace you've been living at. Bands and comic turns in the evenings, drinking, smoking. And then you think you can come on to a field and race around for ninety minutes . . .

I said: 'Will that really affect me?'

'Don't be stupid,' he retorted. 'Of course it will.'

He was right. As a bandboy, which at seventeen I still was, I found that when we played in the Officers' Mess and at other dances they put up free drinks for us throughout the evening. They would ply us with anything from beer to spirits. I wouldn't say I was a heavy drinker, but more than once I woke up in the ditch not knowing how I got there.

From that moment on the soccer pitch I have scarcely touched a drop, and have rarely smoked. I may have a small glass of sweet sherry on a Sunday before lunch, or a glass of lager after a game of golf. Otherwise it's ginger beer or plain water. Sport was far more important than drinking, and if I had to give up one of them I knew which it would be. It was no contest.

But contests of another kind took place in the open-air ring they put up outside the gym where I trained every day. I found I loved boxing, and was winning respect with my sparring partners as a little 'un with a punch. Finally I felt good enough to go in for the Army championships as an eight-stone flyweight.

I fought at least a dozen times, and won every time. Men from other regiments were billeted in the camp, and as you might expect there was a great deal of rivalry. Finally I was representing the 10th Hussars, and felt like bursting with pride every time I climbed into the ring.

The bouts took place in the evening, when the suffocating heat of the day had subsided. The ring was set up under lights strung from the barrack roofs, and they would bring out rows of wooden chairs for the officers, while the rest of the lads would crowd at the back shouting encouragement.

The first time I heard them egging me on in a concerted

roar, my mind went straight back to another night and another ring – in Argentina. This time it was rather different. I wore a white singlet and white shorts, and on big nights there would be several bouts, all the way up to heavyweight. Being the smallest and lightest, I always found myself opening the show.

In my third year I became Flyweight Champion of the British Army in India. It sounds an incredible achievement, and I am still immensely proud of the title. Perhaps I had an advantage, because there were not too many blokes of my size in the Services. But I was still fighting weight for weight, and no-one can take that away from me.

They tried. I had to get through a dozen fights before being presented with the exalted belt. I was a southpaw, and the bouts were always three two-minute rounds. The night I became champion my opponent was a lively young kid who stood a couple of inches taller than me. He came from another regiment, so I was aware I was fighting for the honour of the 10th Hussars, and that spurred me on.

It spurred him on too. From the first bell we went at each other hammer and tongs, arms flailing. It was a great scrap. In the end I won on points, and I can still see myself standing in the middle of the ring with my arms raised.

Boxing can be a brutal sport, and I often asked myself why I enjoyed it so much. The reason is simple. Being so small, I was constantly a target for bullying. You can talk or laugh your way out of ugly situations – but sometimes the chips are down, and you have to know you can defend yourself. It was my way of getting even with anyone who tried to have a go at me. I had to endure my share of barrack-room bullies, particularly in the early days – the occasional clump round the ear for no reason, or a kick up the backside. But when they realised I would take anyone on, the bullying stopped.

I was always nervous before going into the ring – anyone

who tells you otherwise about nerves is telling porkies – but never frightened. It's the same with the stage. But I had the confidence of knowing I was good, and I never worried about getting hit or lost any sleep over it. I knocked out more than one opponent – but I was never K.O'd myself. Nor did I ever get a liver on – that's Army slang for losing your temper.

I wouldn't call it pain when you get hit. A thump on the head gives you a jolt and makes you dizzy, but that's all it does. It can be hard to stand up, but I just remembered to stay down until the count of eight, and then Dizzy-Wizzie usually had his senses about him.

I defended my title twice – and when I sailed for home in February 1936 I was undisputed champion. It was the final accolade. After five years in India my time in that vast, strange, romantic country was over.

Romantic? In that area I was what is generally known as a late starter. I was too busy enjoying myself in other fields, and between sport, music, horses and the discipline of Army life there was little time for other dalliances. But I did manage the odd foray into feminine company, the most memorable of which was a lovely young girl named Margaret. I met her at a sports meeting in Naini Tal, in the foothills of the Himalayas. I was playing in the band, and running in the mile. I came second – in the mile, I mean. As I walked away, a young lady shook my hand and said, 'Well done.' I think I just stood gawping, she was so lovely. Then, to my astonishment she said, 'Are you going to the dance tonight?' I said, 'I wasn't, but I am now!' And I did, at a place called 'The Centre', with my closest pal, 'Stinker' Headley, and she was there!

She had long dark hair, hazel eyes, and she was just eighteen – the same age as me. I watched her sitting at a table with some of the officers, and I was afraid to intrude and ask her to dance. But at the end of the evening she came up to me at the bar and asked coquettishly: 'Are you ignoring me?'

'I – er – N-no,' I stammered, completely thrown. In those days women were not known for doing the asking. It was too late to dance, but she lived in a bungalow a mile away on the far side of a hill and I arranged to meet her there at 1.30 a.m.

Margaret left around midnight with a couple of girl friends, while I hung on till the dance ended. Then as arranged I walked through the beautiful, moonlit night past a lake to the bungalow where she lived.

Margaret was waiting on the verandah, and I stayed with her for two hours – just a kiss and a cuddle, nothing more. I was a little shy in those days, a late starter as I say. And after all that – she left Naini Tal next day for England, and a budding romance burst like a soap bubble.

One last memory of India stayed with me as I leaned my elbows on the rails of the troop ship and watched the bustling quayside of Calcutta slide past three decks below. A group of kids went tearing by on rusty old bikes, keeping pace with us, and it made me smile as I recalled how we used to hire bikes ourselves and play bicycle polo around the barrack square, in the searing heat.

One day I found my machine curiously hard to control. It started to wobble, then the wheels got into some ruts and I fell off – and found the ground itself was shaking! So was I – because it was an earthquake. I could see the barrack square physically moving up and down, a weird unforgettable sight. A lot of damage was caused to the shacks in the poorer part of Lucknow, some of them reduced to splintered ruins, and I was just glad I was outside in the open air when it happened.

If you have ever experienced this phenomenon – and most of us haven't – then you will know the sheer helplessness and terror it evokes. It was a sensation unlike any other I had known. And it wouldn't be the last time I was brought face to face with the awesome power of nature.

I was nearly twenty-one, the Army had been good to me, but it was time to stretch my wings.

The five-week voyage to Southampton gave me an opportunity to think seriously about the future. I wanted to pursue a musical career in some way, even if the 10th Hussars had locked my clarinet and trumpet away in Lucknow for the next aspiring rookie.

I had kept in regular touch with Mum while I was in the Service, and there was a room waiting for me in the large house in Sherrick Green Road in West London where she had moved with her husband. They were both delighted to see me when I came marching in, tanned and fit, to find out what the world had waiting for me.

In India I had saved diligently, putting by as much as I could of the twenty-one shillings a week that was my final financial Army ration. After eighteen months I had been able to send £35 home to my mother to pay her back for buying me out in the first place. Now I bought myself out for the second time, and at the same price.

I didn't feel I was good enough to be a professional musician in a band, not yet. While I started looking around for a job, my mother gave me driving lessons in her car, a low-slung Riley, in the streets around Willesden. Soon I was proficient enough to apply for a job as a driver for a private car hire firm in Kilburn – like father, like son. The firm was called Speedy Service, and my fascination with cars dates from the day I walked in and was shown my first motor, a Wolseley, that I would drive.

My voice helped me get the job. Remember how we bandsmen were 'The Gentlemen of the Regiment'? Many of the said Gentlemen would put on airs and adopt high-tone voices, all lah-di-dah, which quite rightly resulted in a lot of mickey-taking from the other troops. But the undeniable upshot was that I lost all trace of my Cockney street accent, and came home speaking 'proper'. I regard it as a great compliment that today so many people think I must have had a good education. I also found I had the gift of mimicry, and could pick up any accent on the spot.

Mum was vastly amused to hear how my voice had changed. I had gone out to India as a Cockney lad 'talkin' like that'. I had come back sounding almost educated. The driving job was enjoyable, and I saw a lot of London. But I wanted to make more money. One day I took a lady in my taxi, and she directed me to the Willesden Telephone Exchange. I spotted a notice that they were looking for night operators – and I walked in to the imposing old red brick building by the Green, put on my best cut-glass accent, and to my delight I was accepted. They hired me as a night telephone operator, which was when I realised they had women operators by day, and men at night.

I was given a course at Clerkenwell Training Centre, and with my acquired mellifluous tones I was able to sound as smooth as silk on the switchboard. Of course, it was a manual one in those days, and the operator had to get the number for you.

When you sat at a manual switchboard with lights winking all round you in almost hypnotic patterns, it was like playing with a bowl full of coloured spaghetti – wires and cables criss-crossing everywhere. . . plug this one in, take that one out. 'Yes, sir, number please . . . *Can* I help you . . . ? Certainly madam, please hold on for just a moment. . . I'm sorry, the line's engaged' – pull the plug – 'Oh, Christ! I've cut her off'.

Politeness was the name of the game; 'courtesy in adversity' was what we were taught. The customers heard our syrupy tones – but what they couldn't see were the faces we'd be pulling that went with it!

On the early evening shift there would be sixteen of us, but later on into the night these were reduced to four. The only time I lapsed was when a lady said angrily: 'You've got me the wrong number' – and I replied without thinking: 'Yes madam, but don't you realise you're talking to a complete idiot?'

The phone company was very strict with its employees, and rightly so. After all, we were the sharp end, and it was drummed into us that the company would be judged by our attitude.

I would work three nights a week from dusk till dawn, then go straight to the hire firm. The other nights I started at 6.00 p.m. and finished at midnight. With the daytime taxi work it was a gruelling schedule, but I was fit and keen and I found I could handle it – and I never dropped asleep at the wheel, not once.

It was one year before the war, in the autumn of 1938, when an event occurred that I have never before revealed to anyone. I used to grab a quick supper at a fish-and-chip shop round the corner from the Telephone Exchange, and I would go there almost every evening before reporting for duty. It wasn't just the quality of the fish that kept me dropping in there – but the quality of the girl behind the counter who served it up in yesterday's newspaper.

She was a lovely girl, with a dazzling smile, blonde curly hair, and a vivacious manner that made it the brightest fish shop in London! Her name was Doreen, and I fell head over heels for her. I asked her out, and to my surprise she agreed. I would take her to the pictures, or go for drives around London in my Wolseley, and out into the country at weekends.

It took me a few months to pluck up my courage – and pop the question. Again to my utter astonishment she said yes. We were married in church at Willesden Green in the spring of 1939. I was 24, she was just 19. We found a small flat to rent close by, and I moved out of my mother's house and bought a few bits and pieces of furniture to start married life. We were young, carefree, with no ties, and it seemed like a huge adventure.

Then the war came.

CHAPTER SIX

The Telephone Exchange was on the top floor of the building under a huge sloping glass roof. Because of my job, I was exempted from call-up – the recruiting office called it 'a restricted occupation' though being perched up there under the blackout curtains with the bombs raining down over London was not exactly a recipe for the most secure feeling in the world.

When the air raid siren started its sinister wail, we sat and waited for the first *c-rump*. I would climb on to a desk for an illicit peek through the curtains, and recoil at a surreal vision of the night sky lit up around us like a great firework display. Often the building shook and the glass rattled in its frame. I kept thinking: 'Blow this for a barrel-load of monkeys!' My five late-night colleagues and I agreed that we felt like one of those targets that move ever so slowly across a fairground rifle range, just waiting to get picked off.

I stayed for eight long months, feeling totally frustrated. Emerging in the cold light of dawn to see the rubble and smouldering ruins, I felt that old people bombed out of their small homes were even more directly in the front line than I was, and I wanted to hit back. I was a fully trained soldier who knew how to handle a rifle, and here I was spending my time saying: 'Number, please!'

But some months into the war, I suddenly *was* catapulted into the front line – in a manner of speaking. For three days a week I was seconded, along with a chosen handful of other telephone operators, to a top-secret wartime communications centre, a basement bunker off the Edgware Road where Winston Churchill housed one of his key command units.

Our post was situated two floors underground, down a flight of stone steps from street level to a small office where I sat with other colleagues at a large switchboard. There was no clue on the heavy green-painted door next to us as to what was going on – but inside was the Strategic Command Room, the inner sanctum where Churchill would confer with his top brass. My job was to monitor calls and direct them to whichever part of the war theatre our leader needed to reach.

I found myself speaking to Montgomery, Ike in Washington, General Patton . . . I would call up the hot-line numbers, usually answered by an aide, and within seconds I would be talking to the top man. Our orders were to wait till we knew it was the person the PM wished to speak to in person, then plug in the appropriate line, press a button, and wait for Churchill's unmistakable growl: 'Yes?'

'General Eisenhower on the line, sir!' As long as we got the name and rank right, we were safe. Woe betide the man who got an underling by mistake. Churchill had no time to hang on, listening to empty space, either.

I met the great man on a number of occasions. You would hardly call it a social chat – 'See you round the corner for a drink, then?' sort of thing – but he got to know me by name as well as face.

Sometimes I would smell the fragrance of a Havana cigar, the kind rolled on a sweaty Cuban thigh, and then Churchill's huge bulk in khaki combat jacket or sporting the famous bow tie, would lumber out of the Strategic Command Room and tower over me. He would always utter the same words: 'Everything all right? Anything to report?'

On my first day when he appeared I tried to spring to my feet and salute, which isn't too easy when you are attached to a switchboard by a pair of headphones. Churchill motioned me back with a gesture. After that I stayed seated, staring up at the awe-inspiring figure who held the fate of a nation in his grasp. The man had such charismatic presence.

So I settled for: 'Everything is fine, sir,' in my best clipped, British Raj-trained accent.

I met Churchill again, just once, after the war when I was selected to perform at the El Alamein reunion at the Empress Hall in 1951. Six thousand men gathered in that huge vaulted arena to pay tribute to their leaders, and to their brothers in arms.

The place was packed. All of a sudden the lights went out, and a spotlight came bursting out of the darkness to focus on three figures standing in the doorway by the podium: and there stood Churchill, Ike and Monty. They strolled through the throng as if they were at a garden party, and the place went mad! The lads cheered them to the echo.

Monty and Ike were supporting Churchill by either arm – he had obviously had one or two snifters of brandy by then – and the boys were cheering and shouting as the two generals led him to the stage. It was an extraordinary scene, something I shall never forget. And so moving – I looked around at these heroes, all of them wearing their decorations, and I saw many of them with tears in their eyes.

I did my act in front of this wonderful crowd – the shadow boxing routine, where I get knocked off my feet by an imaginary opponent, and the sketch where I slide right over the piano and end up in a heap and at the end when I took my bow I have to say that it was one of the most marvellous receptions I was ever accorded in my life. I thought the roof was going to fly off!

I was in my misfit evening dress, and when I'd finished

and was still getting my breath back I was taken up on the podium to be introduced to the three guests of honour.

Ike pumped my hand vigorously, and said: 'That was one helluva show, young feller!' Monty simply nodded and shook hands.

Churchill studied me through a haze of cigar smoke. I waited for the accolade. After a lengthy pause he took the cigar from his mouth. In measured tones he pronounced his verdict: 'By the way you fall about, Mr Wisdom, if you had been blown up during the war you would certainly have escaped unscathed.'

To some remarks there is no reply. I could only say: 'Thank you, sir.' Then I thought: *why not?* And added: 'This isn't the first time we have met, sir.'

'Oh?' he said. One eyebrow raised a fraction.

'In the Edgware Road,' I told him. 'Your communications bunker. I was your switchboard operator. Er – we used to call it the bunk-up.'

Another pause. Another puff of cigar smoke filled my nostrils. Then Churchill said: 'So I gathered.' And his eyes twinkled through the haze of smoke.

In Willesden I kept on pestering the recruiting office – and at last a brown envelope dropped through my door. Her Majesty's Government had decided that Wisdom N. would be of greater use to the war effort in a more active role. In short, I was called up. And oddly enough, my first feeling was one of relief.

I immediately applied for the 10th Royal Hussars, my old regiment. But they were in the Middle East, fighting the desert war in El Alamein and other North African hot spots. Besides which, the recruiting office understandably felt that my telephone training would be better suited to communications.

Which is how I found myself in the Royal Corps of Signals.

I was stationed first at Cheltenham, and was able to find

a small flat where Doreen and I could live. I even got her a job in a local telephone exchange six miles from the base where I was stationed. So far the war was being very good to me.

The place was known as CNW – Cheltenham Network. It was another top-secret establishment, possibly the forerunner to the celebrated spy headquarters that would make headlines in the late eighties. I found myself talking over the airwaves to pilots homing in on bombing raids into Germany, as well as to Generals fighting the war on the ground. To Ike again – and to Churchill.

My job was simply to connect them up, announce: 'Mr Churchill for you, sir,' or words to that effect – then get off the line, sharpish.

I had spent four months seconded to the bunker. In Cheltenham, a new career was about to open out. Meantime I spent rather too many hours indulging myself on the sporting field. There were just so many opportunities – the base had all the facilities you could wish for, and I spent hours playing soccer, or cross-country running, or cricket and swimming – and, of course, boxing. Doreen was left alone – and the inevitable happened. She was an attractive girl, and she wanted to have a good time. My marriage foundered – but I must take my share of the blame. It had only lasted a few months, but I can't even call her a casualty of war. I just spent too many hours away from her.

I found out that Doreen had been seeing other men – and we agreed to call it a day. The divorce went through quite quickly, and I was single again. I moved out of our flat and into the Moray House Hotel which had been requisitioned by the Army to accommodate the troops.

I never saw Doreen again. She was a nice girl, but also I think too young to appreciate the seriousness of marriage. It was simply a wartime romance that went sour.

My rank was Signalman. And looking back, I can see that

this was the moment where my show-business career actually started.

Out of the blue, the Commanding Officer decided it would be a good idea to have a dance band. Splendid for morale. Give the company something to do in their spare time. A notice appeared on the board in the Mess: 'Anybody who can play music and is interested, please let me know.'

I knocked on his door, marched in and snapped off a smart salute. 'In response to your notice, sir, I'd like to apply for the post of saxophone player,' I said, briskly.

The colonel looked up from his desk and fixed me with a beady gaze. 'Oh really, Wisdom,' he said. 'Can you actually play the thing?'

'Certainly, sir,' I responded. 'And the clarinet too. I happen to like jazz.'

'Really,' he said, and leaned back in his chair. 'How good are you?'

'Good enough, sir, I assure you.'

'We'll see,' he said, toying with his pen. There was a pause. Then he looked up. 'All right. I'll trust you. I'll give you the money to go out and buy a saxophone and a clarinet. But for God's sake don't let me down.'

There was a music shop I had already spotted in Cheltenham high street, and I raced over to it. Sure enough, they had what I wanted. The alto-sax cost me £8, the clarinet a further £10. I got the receipts, and the Army paid up without a murmur.

I hurried back to the base, clutching the precious instruments, and burst into the CO's office. 'There you are, sir – done!'

'Good,' he responded. 'Let me hear you play them.'

I unpacked the instruments. 'You don't trust me, do you sir?'

'Just get on and play!' he said.

ᴠᴇ: The lads at St Luke's School – and 's me holding the ball.

ᴏᴡ ʀɪɢʜᴛ: The ladykiller – aged 14.

ᴏᴡ: Hullo, soldier!

LEFT: Trumpet at the ready.

FACING PAGE: First-ever professional appearance – at Collins Music Hall.

BELOW: Lean and mean – the Army flyweight champion.

TOP: Three clowns together – with Laurel
Hardy.

BELOW LEFT: With friend and agent Billy
Marsh.

RIGHT: A bear hug from Gracie Fields.

And another loving embrace from Spike.

Oh dear! they can't get in to see Norman – another full house at the *Palladium*.

Opening night at Leicester Square – 'gone to the pictures, back in ten minutes'.

LEFT: Knockout fun with my first straight man Eddie Leslie.

RIGHT: A ducking from director John Paddy Carstairs during my first film *Trouble in Store*.

James Bond was shaken *and* stirred when my film *A Stitch in Time* toppled *From Russia With Love* off its No. 1 box-office perch, but Sean Connery and I became good friends.

ABOVE: Family group, with Freda, Nick and Jackie.

RIGHT: A kiss from Mum.

Then and there I gave him an impromptu rendering of 'When the Saints Go Marching in', switching instruments in mid-tune with the dexterity of a conjuror producing a rabbit from a hat. My eyes were closed. Dimly I heard his voice. 'Enough, Wisdom, enough! Go and find the other musicians!'

The CO was a man of his word. Within two days he had found a trumpeter, a drummer, and a violinist. There were seven of us:

Dusty Miller on trumpet, Freddie Bridgewater on piano, someone else on guitar, another on clarinet. We were a very friendly outfit, and we all got on well even though we had never played together up to then. Slowly the band took shape. We started out by touring the local hospitals and bases, playing for troop dances and for the RAF at their airfields. I would play my sax – but I'd also fool around a bit, trying to make people laugh and cheer them up. Particularly in the hospital wards; I'd have them in stitches, laughing that is. The more I fell about, the more the patients roared – and I got bolder with every passing week.

One Sunday the band was asked to do a charity concert at Cheltenham Town Hall. That marvellous actor Rex Harrison was in the audience as part of a tour he was doing in the area, and afterwards he came round backstage as we were packing our instruments. He singled me out.

'Are you a professional?' he inquired, in that inimitable voice of his.

'No I'm not,' I told him.

'Well,' he said, 'If you don't give it a try, you must be utterly mad!'

My personal life, such as it was, kept in fourth gear. As a bachelor on the loose without any ties, I could afford to have a fling with some of the local girls. But after having my fingers burned I was in no hurry to get serious with anyone. The girl I fancied most was a lovely creature called Tricia who worked in a hairdresser's in town. She was nineteen, and she had the most glorious long black hair and voluptuous figure. My heart did a flip when I first set eyes on her.

I found I could make girls laugh – and I was halfway there! I persuaded Tricia to come to dances with me for several months as my steady girlfriend. Half-way through the evening I would put my clarinet down on its stand and take her for a whirl around the floor.

It was all very delightful and romantic. At least I knew the music would be good, and if I wasn't quite Fred Astaire, I was pretty nimble on my feet.

I bought myself a second-hand motor bike, and at weekends we would go buzzing off into the country lanes, with Tricia on the pillion clutching me round the waist. It was a typical wartime romance – we were both young, we liked each other, and I never knew where I might be sent next week. So we were living for the moment, not expecting anything from each other, and it was wonderful.

Petrol was rationed but that was no problem. At the Moray Hotel my turn to be on night guard would come round once a week. At 2.00 a.m., when all was quiet, I would creep round to the back where I had parked my motor bike – next to the colonel's staff car – and with a length of hosepipe I would quickly syphon out some of his petrol and fill up my small tank to the brim. It would last me the week, and the Colonel never noticed.

My closest mate on the CNW base was a tall young fellow named Patrick Dickinson. We were both sports fanatics and played in the Signals football team – I was a nippy inside right, he was a sturdy right back. After the war we lost touch with one another, but years later when I was on the bill at Newcastle he suddenly turned up backstage with a cheery 'Hi, Norman – remember me?' We've stayed pals to this day. He's now a retired schoolmaster and keeps himself busy writing scripts. A few years ago he wrote a book on famous people's school reports which raised £5,000 for the Save the Children Fund. I often nip up North, and we go to watch Newcastle United play, or have a game of golf. Sometimes I go along to the local People's Theatre, where Patrick is a patron, and he ropes me into being a steward and selling programmes. It's fun though. And Northumberland is such a beautiful county. I enjoy visiting those gorgeous seaside villages.

One afternoon I was walking down the high street on my way to pick up Tricia, when something gleaming through a shop window caught my eye. It was a cluttered second-hand store – but I stopped in my tracks when I saw what was behind the glass. It was a beautiful saxophone, an American Conn tenor-sax, inlaid with silver plating, and I just knew I had to have it.

I went in, picked it up, weighed it in my hands, and asked: 'How much?'

'Twenty pounds,' said the shopkeeper.

'I'll give you ten,' I said.

We settled at twelve – and that beautiful saxophone is still in my act today! I wouldn't have any other. I have always liked the tone of a tenor-sax better than an alto – it is deeper, more mellow, with a wonderful haunting quality that is like no other sound in the world.

After three years at the CNW base I was getting restless. Like a lot of the lads, I wanted to see some action. I kept applying for a transfer to be posted abroad, but with no luck. The top brass obviously felt we were doing more important work behind the barbed wire at Cheltenham.

But finally the CO called me in. 'All right, Wisdom, your application has been accepted. We're sorry to see you go – the entertainment won't be the same without you.' It was a generous farewell.

I left Cheltenham with a tearful kiss from Tricia and a

happy smile for the lads. The trouble was, I had left it too late.

First Stop: an Army transit camp in Norwich where I was billeted to await orders. I spent a month in a kind of limbo, wondering where I would be heading.

In the camp there was a sergeant-major who was loathed by everybody. There's always one, as they say – and he was it. Imagine a large, stout man with a tiny toothbrush moustache and slicked-down black hair, combining the qualities of being a bully, a braggart and a loudmouth to boot – except that nobody dared boot him. That was our sarge. His voice could carry across the whole parade ground, even in a high wind.

He was a strict disciplinarian, and would pick you up on the slightest provocation. A stickler for appearances, our sarge could not bear sloppy deportment – on or off the parade ground. Seeing any of his men slouching around was like a red rag to a bull. *'Take your hands out of your pockets!'* he would bellow in your ear from about two feet away, ensuring you were deaf for the rest of the day. The man was actually quite well-spoken, which somehow added to the overall effect.

I got the full brunt of his wrath practically every day. I just seemed to get in his way. After a week of it I evolved a plan to get my own back.

I was going to the outside bo, which was about fifty yards up the road away from the main NCOs' hut. I strolled past the windows, noticed a familiar bulbous face with its little moustache just inside– and quickly slipped both my hands in my pockets as I walked by, whistling.

Sure enough, a few moments and some twenty yards later came the familiar blast. 'Hey, you! Take your hands out of your *pockets!'*

I turned round and shouted as loud as I could. *'Pardon?'*

He bellowed back: 'I said: *Take your hands out of your pockets!'*

And I yelled: 'I'm sorry, I can't hear you from here!'

His face had turned a curious purple colour as he bellowed the same order in the same stentorian tones.

My voice was almost as loud: 'I don't know what you're saying,' I shouted. 'Can you come a bit closer?'

Now faces were appearing from everywhere, from underneath lorries, from windows, peering out of doorways, to watch the fun. They all knew I was taking the mickey – but he couldn't do a thing about it.

Sarge tried again – and this time I started to walk, very slowly, back to him, still with my hands in my pockets, still shouting, *'Please speak a bit louder!'* And I walked right up to him till our faces were almost touching, nose to nose, and both of us were still shouting at the tops of our voices.

All the blokes were laughing fit to bust. The sarge saw it, and finally dropped his voice to hiss in a virulent whisper: 'I said: Take your hands out of your f-ing pockets!'

At which point I dropped my own voice and said quietly: 'Oh, all right sergeant-major. But it's cold.' He bestowed a withering glare on me, before turning to stride back inside with a face like thunder – but he never shouted at me again.

All told I did seven-and-a-half years in the Service, and I have to say without any doubts whatsoever that I owe *everything* to the Army. Everything I am, or became. Self-discipline. Tidiness. Personal neatness – I still polish my shoes every day. My voice: enunciation and clarity of diction – and I don't care if sometimes it does sound a bit posh!

The Army taught me music. I was given the impetus to learn to play instruments: trumpet, clarinet, trombone, drums, saxophone, piccolo, xylophone, violin, banjo, piano, post horn. All right, I'll never be certain of a lasting place in the Royal Philharmonic, but I can hold my own in a tight musical corner. The sixteen bandboys all played different instruments, and if after a time you got fed up with just the one, it was accepted that you would be able to have a go on someone else's. That is how I had the incredible privilege of being able to learn to play so many instruments, and it would become a vital part of my future variety act.

But above all, friendship. How to treat people properly. The true spirit of camaraderie. Oh yes, one other thought occurs to me: I would like to take this opportunity to thank the Army for training a professional berk to make a good living out of it!

I had been in Norwich for just a month when the ultimate All-Clear sounded. I was actually hosing down a lorry beside the parade ground when it seemed as if every door in the barracks burst open and khaki-clad figures were running everywhere and shouting: 'It's over, it's all over!' I took the train with my mates from Norwich down to London, waving a fond farewell from the window to the barracks as we passed, and headed for Olympia to pick up our civvies. We were each given one civilian suit, two shirts, a tie and a pair of shoes.

My suit was light brown, and I remember joking to my pals:

'With my luck I'll get a jacket and two pairs of trousers – and then I'll burn a hole in the jacket!' The idea was that you would go out into the big wide welcoming world nicely dressed, and get yourself a job. The only problem was that there were hundreds of thousands of men all nicely dressed with the same idea.

Me, I went back to Mum. Sherrick Green Road was still there and so was No. 26. My mother welcomed me with open arms, and my old room was still there.

When I think back, it is amazing that I left home at the age of nine, now I was nearly thirty – and in all those twenty-one years I had hardly seen my mother at all, apart from the few weeks I spent with her before the war and occasional spots of leave when I had stayed for a couple of days.

In those days Willesden Green was a bustling suburb.

There was a corner shop that sold everything from marbles to gob-stoppers, and the Prince of Wales pub was the forum for local debate.

Mum's husband Sydney was a nice bloke. She had married well the second time around, and he was devoted to her. It was good to see her so happy. The first evening we celebrated my return around the kitchen table with a bottle of wine for them and ginger beer for me. Mum cooked me my favourite Shepherd's Pie, and we discussed what I was going to do for a living. The words of Rex Harrison came back to me. 'If you don't try for it, you must be utterly mad . . .'

I looked across the table. 'Mum,' I said. 'I'm going to try and get into show-business.'

'All right, dear,' she said. 'Whatever you think is best.'

And that, for me, was all the encouragement I needed.

CHAPTER SEVEN

Next day I presented myself at Collins Music Hall. Before I left home I gave my shoes a special shine, donned my brown civvy suit, and then took the No.93 bus to the Angel, Islington.

The legendary variety hall was known as the Chapel on the Green, and I suspect a load of prayers had been offered up over the years by hopefuls being given their first stab at fame. The foyer looked like a picture gallery, with framed photographs of stars who had appeared there lining the walls. It was the show-business cradle for future talent like Tommy Trinder, who sang there as a boy soprano, Arthur Askey, Max Miller and many more.

I rapped on the window of the ticket kiosk, and asked if I could see the manager. The girl behind the glass simply jerked a thumb up the stairs, where I found an office marked 'Manager'. Inside, Mr Lew Lake turned out to be a tall, authoritative figure in neat, grey pin-stripe with a receding hairline and spectacles, who rose from behind his desk, gestured to a chair, and inquired: 'What can I do for you?'

I said: 'I'd like to go on the stage, sir.

He said: 'What have you done, exactly?'

I tried to make it sound impressive, reeling off the details on my fingers. 'Troop concerts. .. charity shows. . .cabaret . . . India . . .'

He raised an eyebrow. 'Don't be bloody silly,' he

admonished. 'Do you realise there are dozens of stars coming out of the Army – established comedians and singers from ENSA, Stars in Battledress . . . You're lucky not to have been trampled in the rush. Go out and get yourself a steady job.'

The theatre seemed pretty quiet to me, but it was hardly my place to argue the toss. Instead I thanked him for his encouraging words, left the office, and walked down the stairs to the Stage Door, feeling disconsolate but determined. There was a notice board by the door, and a young fellow was studying the cards pinned there. I saw one that advertised: 'Rooms for Rent'.

We got talking, and he turned out to be a musician named Stan who had been hired for a season with the orchestra. We went over the road to a cafe, and over a cup of tea came to an agreement – we would share a room, and I would pay my whack as long as I was there, but I could move out any time.

We checked the address: it was just round the corner from the theatre, and the room small and uncomfortable – but who cared? With a couple of divans on opposite walls, it couldn't have been better for my plan of campaign.

We moved in, and from that moment I became Mr Lake's shadow. Everywhere he went – there I was too. Nodding good morning from the next table as he tried to eat breakfast in the local greasy spoon cafe. If he was in the long bar at the back of the stalls and he raised a pint of beer to his mouth, my head was under his arm.

I would wait outside the stage door after the show to nobble him when he came out, and beg in my most appealing voice: 'Please, just give me a chance!' And he would growl out of the corner of his mouth: 'Push off!' But I wouldn't give up.

I hung around outside the theatre during the day until he emerged to get a paper, and I'd follow him to the newspaper seller on the corner – and back again. 'I won't let you down,

Mr Lake. Just one chance. I know you're the bloke to do it, everybody says Collins is the place to start. . .' Persistence was my middle name.

When the poor man sought refuge in Lyons Corner House up the road, I would wait until he was seated with his lunch in front of him – and just as his fork was poised I would slip into the seat opposite. 'Come on – just one chance, that's all I'm asking!'

After three weeks of it, Lew Lake cracked. Over breakfast in the greasy spoon, he suddenly said: 'All right. If I let you go on first house on Monday and you're no good, will you promise to go away and *leave me alone?*' His voice hit an alarming high pitch.

'Absolutely sir, thank you. I won't let you down. You won't regret it.'

'I'd better not.' He unbent a trifle. 'If you last a week, I'll give you five pounds.'

The following Monday I went on, first house. The date was 17 December 1945, the time was 6.15 p.m. The night before was a sleepless one for me in my small bed-sit across the road. I only had one copy of the music required for my act – and when I walked into the theatre to meet the musicians I found myself facing a forbidding twelve-piece orchestra who would be backing me. They went by the name of Gaucho's Orchestra – 'The band you have been waiting for, a feast of music, melody, novelty and rhythm', enthused the programme.

I had only had £43 discharge money from the Forces, the grateful thanks of Her Majesty's Government, so I was nearly skint. In a panic I found a member of the band who seemed an amiable sort – and offered him a fiver to copy out the remaining eleven sets, on the spot. He was kind enough to oblige, just in time for rehearsal.

My dressing room was the smallest in the building, a tiny cellar hardly bigger than a cupboard – but it was enough. I was so scared that I just sat in front of the small mirror staring at myself in the glass and shivering uncontrollably. There is no feeling in the world like stage fright, and at one point I wondered if I would even be able to get to my feet, let alone walk out to face the waiting masses.

In fact the waiting masses at First House, 6.15 p.m. on that Monday were comprised of less than a hundred people who obviously had nothing better to do to pass a couple of hours. They sat individually or in couples occupying the first ten rows of the stalls. First House Monday is by tradition known as a 'Quiet House' – and my job was to make it noisy with laughter.

I was given what we call in the business the 'graveyard shift' – number two on the bill following the opening chorus of half a dozen leggy lovelies, called, with incredible imagination, The Girls. As a comic I was more warm up than stand up, but that cold December night I didn't care. Collins Music Hall was famous as the launching pad for unknown hopefuls. Agents would gather on the Monday night at the long bar which ran the length of the theatre behind the stalls, to drink and watch the acts at the same time.

My name appeared on the programme under a sexy poster of a Can-Can dancer, and indeed on the bill was Lisette Darnier, 'the Atomic Dancer', from the Folies Bergère in Paris. Other acts included George Burgess ('Just a Mug'), Ed Jackson and Dot Brown ('Doughboy meets Doughgirl') and Wendy and Brenda Georgia ('The Light and Shade of Variety').

I billed myself as 'The Successful Failure'. My act started with just one prop on stage: a piano. I was a clown let loose into a virtually empty arena, and somehow I had to fill it with mime, imagination and fantasy. I walked out in my misfit tails – baggy trousers ending three inches above my ankles, tie half undone, looking an absolute mess but trying to retain a shred of dignity – and bowed deeply to the orchestra.

Then, in a quavering voice, I would begin the 'I'll Walk Beside You' sketch that was to become an integral part of my most successful stage shows. I would get no further than the 'I'll walk –' before the orchestra changed to a new key and left me gasping like a stranded fish.

I would then rush from one musician to the other, plead with the conductor, finally race over to the piano . . . slam it down . . . get my fingers caught in the lid . . . ouch, ow! . . .

As I stood in the wings, feeling the butterflies in my stomach having a field day, Lew Lake came up. 'All right. You've got ten minutes, that's all.' He told the stage manager too.

But on that first night, where I touched fingers with history in the legendary music hall, I got so carried away with the heady excitement of just being there, sensing that the people out front were actually starting to like me, that I went way over my limit. I could hear the stage manager hissing from the wings: 'Come off! Do you hear me – *gerroff*!.'

The trouble was that I didn't know how I *could* get off. My act was all mime. It was purely visual, apart from the initial brief 'I'll Walk –' vocal. Shadow boxing, tap dancing, falling about.

Another major gag was my tap routine: I would collect a tap mat from the wings and with due solemnity place it in the exact centre of the stage. Then I started to tap dance my way around this magic circle as if I was striving to get on to it – but n-e-v-e-r quite made it.

It was silly, but it was fun – and by now the audience were laughing. Okay, it wasn't brilliant, and the sound was more like a few peas rolling around in a gigantic hollow pod, but I knew I'd got to them.

I've done it all thousands of times since, but that was my first ever professional performance in public, and it is something you do not forget in a hurry, if ever. But on that first night, the problem remained – how to 'gerroff'? In the end, I solved it with a hasty:

'G'night!' and almost ran off the stage as the lights blacked out on me.

The stage manager was standing in the wings with gritted teeth. 'If you do that again, I'll drop the curtain on you,' he growled.

I went back to my tiny cupboard below stairs, and sat and waited. Nothing happened. Nobody came in to say 'Well done' – but more important, nobody came in to say 'Get out!' There was no sign of Mr Lake. I could hear the Second House, at the curious hour of 8.10 p.m., starting to fill up – you would be surprised how noise filters in backstage in those old theatres – and the butterflies started to build again inside me.

The only way I could think to get rid of them was to get out into the fresh air and go for a run. And that is just what I did, slipping out of the Stage Door for a trot round the side streets, gulping in the night air.

The Second House went marvellously. The place was full for a start. They laughed. They rocked in their seats. Generous applause followed me off the stage and into the wings and all the way back to my dressing-room. And still no-one said anything. I stared at my reflection in the mirror again, and spoke aloud: 'Well, so far so good!' Until they threw me out, I'd just keep going back on that stage.

Two nights later, after the second show, a man appeared in the door and said without preamble: 'Do you have an agent?'

The thought had never occurred to me. 'Er – no,' I said.

'You have now,' he said, extending a big hand. 'The name's Peters. Here's my card. Are you doing anything next week?'

'Er – no,' I said again.

'You are now,' Mr Peters said. 'Would you like to do the

Portsmouth Coliseum for a week? Starting Monday. Ten quid. Get yourself digs. See you there, okay?'

'Okay,' I said bemusedly – and he was gone. But I made a phone call later in the week to check, and sure enough I was on the bill:

Norman Wisdom, the Successful Failure.

On the Friday night following the last house, just as I was packing up to go back across the road to my theatrical digs – that's how I had begun to think of the room I was sharing – there was another knock at the door.

A second new face presented itself. 'I'm an agent,' it said. 'Martin's the name. What are you doing next week?'

'The Portsmouth Coliseum,' I said grandly.

'And the week after?'

'Just a minute,' I said. 'I'll have to look in my diary.' I was learning fast. It's called Theatrical Bullshit.

I opened a small notebook, careful to keep the pages out of his sight, since they were totally blank apart from one small entry, and took my time poring over it. 'Um . . . ah . . . Let's see now. I think I can fit it in.'

'Good,' he said, radiating enthusiasm. 'The Grand Theatre, Basingstoke. One week. See you there.'

I was on my way!

On the Saturday between shows I went to draw the five quid I had been promised. It was Christmas Eve, and the season of goodwill was upon us. Lew Lake was bent over his cash register, totting figures. Then he straightened up, fished in the cash box, and carefully counted out five one-pound notes on his desk. 'Sign here!' he said.

Eagerly I put my signature in the margin opposite my name, and reached out for the money. But Lew was quicker on the draw. He snatched up the notes and popped them into his pocket. 'Commission!' he said, with what I can only call a triumphant grin.

It was the first time I had seen him smile, and I understood. He had taken a risk and given me my chance, and we both knew it. It was worth five pounds any day. 'Merry Christmas,' I said. The Scrooge of Islington shook my hand. 'Good luck, Norman. Perhaps we'll see you back here some time.'

'You never know,' I said. But I never did go back.

The idea of being billed as The Successful Failure was my own, just as all my material has always been original. It epitomised the stage persona I was building, even though I was still feeling my way and 'Little Norm' had yet to be fleshed out as a fully developed character. But it gave me the opportunity that I needed for a whole range of effects, from slapstick to the pathos that is a traditional part of a true clown's make-up.

I was thinking about these things as I sat in the fast train to Portsmouth, listening to the rhythm of the wheels. The South London suburbs turned into the green and brown patchwork quilt of the Surrey countryside. I was bound for my first professional out of town engagement! Was I worried? Yes, of course I was. Nervous? Who wouldn't be? With just one week's experience under my belt, I was bound for one of the biggest theatres in the country, a 3,000-seater, to do my turn in front of the gathered masses.

Oh dear – was I nervous!

I had packed just one small case with my gear in it. A change of shirt. A toothbrush. And my music sheets – all twelve of them. I wasn't going to be caught out again.

The first thing I did on leaving Portsmouth Station was search for digs. I made for the seafront and soon found a room with a view over the harbour. Later that day I reported to the Coliseum for band-call and rehearsal. It was a huge theatre built in the old prewar mould, a mausoleum of a place with a high domed roof and gloomy corridors lit by single yellow light bulbs.

This time I was a small cog in a big-wheeling variety

show, end-of-the-pier stuff with Teddy Brent as the star comedian heading the bill, and myself way down at the bottom. In fact my name was about the same size as the printer's at the foot of the poster. I was second in the running order, following the girl dancers, graveyard shift again. But I didn't care. I was earning a living.

The first douche of cold water came with a peremptory knock at the dressing-room door, and in walked the manager. He was a burly man with a flushed face that suggested he liked to prop up the bar during the interval, and probably at other times too.

He said: 'Mr Wisdom, we've got rather a crowded bill this week. Would you mind doing First House only?'

Even at that early stage in my career I recognised that I was being put out to grass before I'd had a chance to nibble the hedgerow. Obviously he didn't think I was good enough – and there would be fewer people in the First House to witness my shortcomings. I swallowed my pride, because I had no choice. 'Very well,' I said, quietly. 'I understand.'

All that week, every morning, I arrived at the theatre at nine o'clock on the dot. I walked out alone on to an empty stage, playing to an empty auditorium. It can get quite spooky, being all alone in a darkened theatre. And I practised hard. I worked my way right through my act again and again until shortly before six o'clock at night when the people would start drifting in for the First House. Perfecting my timing. Trying to get it right.

And finally I was satisfied.

I noticed the difference. As the week went by, my act got better and better. I knew it, even if no-one else did. The audience were seeing it for the first time, and wouldn't know. But I wondered if my fellow artistes had spotted it.

Mid-way through the week, I found myself up in the theatre bar before the show asking for a lemonade. Several of the cast were there. I found myself standing next to the star. Teddy Brent was a successful Australian comedian who spoke as if a piece of toffee was stuck to the roof of his mouth.

I just had to ask him: 'How am I doing?'

He said: 'You're doing fine, Norman.'

I pressed on. 'Er – is there any advice you could give me?'

Teddy looked benignly down at me from his lofty six foot height like an uncle about to give a favourite nephew a pat on the head. 'Well yes, Norman,' he said. 'Since you ask, I've got a good idea for you. You're a visual comic, aren't you?'

I nodded. 'Yes, I am.'

'Now, if you can get hold of a big iron ball, about so big' – he held his hands three feet apart – 'then paint it so that everyone thinks it's a balloon, see?'

I nodded eagerly. The others had gathered round, and were listening intently. Teddy went on: 'Then you throw it up, head it and catch it . . . roll it around . . . trap it with your feet . . . lift it high in the air and drop it – and it will go smashing right through the stage and leave a great big hole. Then you fall into the hole. I promise you, everyone will be screaming with laughter.'

The rest of the cast had turned their heads away, and were subsiding into giggles of mirth at my expense. I kept my expression deadpan, thanked him politely, finished my lemonade and left.

And I never asked anyone for advice about my act, again.

If people come up with ideas now, that is totally different. I have always welcomed anything creative, new gags, fresh situations, and throughout my career I have had people sending in scripts or ideas for sketches. I always read through them carefully – because you never know, one might be a gem.

But in those early days I invented everything myself.

Every word, every movement, every expression. Even my costume was chosen down to the last button.

I went through the week at Portsmouth doing First House only. The audiences were patchy, the theatre never more than half-full. On the last night, Saturday, I did the early evening show as usual, and I was in my dressing-room packing my small case before heading for the station. There was a knock at the door, and the manager walked in.

'Norman,' he said, 'I just came round to say good-bye, and to thank you for all your efforts. I must say you've improved enormously – I know you've been rehearsing hard every day, and it has paid off. Congratulations, I wish you luck!' And he turned to leave.

But at the door he stopped. Almost as an afterthought he said:

'How would you like to go on Second House tonight?'

'Cor!' I exclaimed. 'Do you mean it?'

'You're on,' he said.

I unpacked my misfit suit again and put it on, and sat listening to the familiar thunder of feet as the theatre filled up. The tremors were building inside me – not fright, but anticipation and excitement, and I felt the old buzz of the adrenalin starting to surge. No performer can go on without it, or he's dead.

The manager had put me on in my usual place, and the master of ceremonies gave me a special introduction. And this time I walked out to a sea of faces, a full house, row upon row of white blobs in the darkened auditorium fading back into blackness, apart from the single blinding spotlight shining . . . on me!

I gave it all I had. I fell over the piano, under it, round it. I tap-danced till I thought my shoes would fly off. I gave them the 'I'll Walk – in every key except Yale.

And at the end I was swamped by the first real applause I had ever known. I stood stunned in the spotlight, the sweat pouring off me, panting for breath, grinning from ear to ear like a Cheshire cat as I took my bow.

The First House at both Collins Music Hall and the rest of the week at the Coliseum had given me a nice response, but it was like the pitter-patter of raindrops compared to this thunderstorm around my head.

In that marvellous moment I realised why I had been toiling so hard and for so long. I had glimpsed the crock of gold at the end of the rainbow.

I would never give up. If applause is a drug I was hooked! And I wanted more.

Next stop in my busy schedule – Basingstoke! After that – nothing. My diary was blank. I went on First House, usual spot for the warmup comic. In the interval I was getting out of my gear when the manager suddenly appeared in my dressing-room. I thought: 'Oh no, not again. First House only. Here we go – instead he bestowed a friendly smile on me and said: 'You were very good. I was wondering – can you go on again and do a spot in the second half?'

Now, in the business we all know that the second half of any variety show is always more important than the first. And in the pecking order, more prestigious. It hadn't taken me long to tumble to it, even if I was still green round the earholes.

The pattern was as regular as a trip to the bathroom after last night's curry dinner. A gaggle of gorgeous leggy dancers to open the show, followed by your warm-up comic, then a group of jugglers or speciality acts like sword-swallowers or fire-eaters, and finally a singer to close the first half. After the interval, more dancers, more laughs from another comic, maybe some acrobats – and then the big star all the people out there have really come to see.

But second half was distinctly better than first. I appreciated the compliment. 'Delighted,' I said, and meant it. 'Er – but not tonight.'

He said: 'Oh – why not?'

'Because I haven't got the material.'

He looked crestfallen. Quickly I added: 'But I will have by tomorrow!'

'You will?' His eyebrows went up. 'Are you sure?'

'Dead certain,' I assured him. 'I'll sit up all night and write some.' And I did. I developed the piano sketch, adding more sight gags, and including some other instruments that I knew I could play like the tenor-sax and piccolo, which I still had at home. I worked through till dawn, snatched a couple of hours' sleep, and took the early train to Paddington to pick them up. I was back at the theatre that afternoon to go through it again and again. That night's hard labour would become the framework for my favourite act.

It opens with the curtain slowly rising to reveal me in my misfit evening suit, leaning on a grand piano, reading a newspaper and munching a sandwich, oblivious of everyone. When I realise in horror that I am being watched, I hurriedly try to conceal the half-eaten sandwich by stuffing it into the piano. Of course my hand gets stuck under the lid – and when I walk away I'm jerked back and end up on the floor.

I fool around on the keys, and suddenly launch into 'I'll Walk Beside You' – only to find the orchestra are playing in the wrong key, at least an octave too high. I start again, squeaking: 'I'll walk –' as if my trousers are too tight. Down goes the orchestra, and I sink into a frog-like croak: 'I'll walk –'

We rehearsed it until we had it spot on, and it worked a treat. I ended the act by picking up my tenor-sax and finishing with some jazz and a spot of tap-dancing for a bonus. On the last night I thought to myself: Whatever happens now, at least you can tell people you were the only act to go on solo in both first and second halves. That must mean something. What's more, my salary was increased by £2. 10s to £12. 10s a week.

It was on that Saturday night between shows that another agent came knocking at the dressing-room door, introduced himself as Mike Sullivan, and asked if I would like to join a touring revue called *New Names Make News* for impresario Will Hammer. I took it. They gave me two good spots, and a part in a sketch, and my money went up to £15 a week.

We started off at the Grand Theatre, Blackburn. On the last night of our week I was in the dressing-room that I shared with one of the other comics in the show, an elderly comedian named George Francis who used to do monologues. Out of the blue he looked at me with his watery old eyes and said: 'I want you to know something, Norman. One day you're going to be a star – and that day isn't so far off. I want you to have this –'

And he reached behind the door and produced one of the silver-topped walking sticks he used for his act, and handed it to me.

I pushed it away. 'I can't –' I began.

'Go on,' he said. 'One day you'll look back and think about how you started out. This will help you remember.' And I've still got it. I keep it in a special stand in my bedroom, and I see it first thing every morning. That was my first taste of the marvellous camaraderie you can find in the theatre, and it meant a lot to an unknown young knock-about comic.

Chapter Eight

Some people might have wondered why George Francis and I weren't rivals vying for the laughs. But we were all part of a team, and tried to help one another. In fact I was able to work up a sketch where I went out with him as his feed, playing a window cleaner who came to this old boy's house and landed into all sorts of trouble because of his clumsiness. Me, a straight man!

The money wasn't important, which was perhaps just as well. None of us starved, but we didn't exactly get fat, either. We stayed in classic theatrical digs, those small rooms with a gas fire that have been part of every aspiring entertainer's life. My world was one of dingy wall-paper, faded carpets, echoing stairs, and the smell of bacon and eggs for breakfast and beans on toast at dinner time when we came back after the show.

And I loved every minute of it.

There was a lot of laughter in those days because we were living for that moment, not the next one, and the hours were too precious to waste. A show out on the road is like a family, even if it's only a temporary one.

I shared digs with a dance duo named Louise and Leroy, with a pair of acrobats who called themselves the Jeffery Brothers – I'd refer to them as Jeff One and Jeff Two – and occasionally the soothing sounds of Johnny Farley and his 'Eight Strings in Harmony' would filter down the stairs.

It was a three-month tour in that summer of 1946, and it took me all over Britain. We travelled by coach, with our costumes and instruments packed aboard. Towns that had only been names on the map came alive for me. From the Bumley Vic to the Blackburn Grand to the Brighton Theatre Royal, I saw them all. TV had yet to reach out its tentacles and grab every home in the land, and variety was the name of the game.

Audiences varied from night to night, but that was the name of the game too. You could never tell until minutes before the curtain went up, and a peep through the slit in the drapes would show us whether the seats were filling – and give us an idea of what was in store.

Some, like the Glasgow Empire, a huge, forbidding building, had a reputation that preceded them. The Empire was notorious for its nickname of the Cockney Comics' Graveyard. The Scots would shout from the stalls: 'Aye, that's no' funny at all – will ye gi'e us something to laugh at!'

When the New Names revue finally made it north of the border, I stepped out onto the stage in some trepidation for the First House. I gave them 'I'll Walk Beside You', went into my patter, downed around – but the audience remained almost silent, and towards the end there was some heckling. They couldn't understand me, hence the Cockney Comics' Graveyard . . . and I was being buried in it. I strode back to my dressing-room smarting visibly. It was the first time I had not taken a curtain call.

Second House, I hitched up my baggy pants and my confidence, and went out to face the tough crowd once more. Only this time – not a word passed my lips! I did it all in mime. The piano sketch, the boxing, trying to eat sandwiches on a jolting train, making a call in a pay-phone. And they loved it! I called on all my old store of impressions from my Army days, including tripping the man in front of me on the parade ground.

Desperate situations call for desperate measure, as they say – and they don't get more desperate than a comic dying the death at the Glasgow Empire. With a stand-up comic, in the words of Frank Carson, it's the way you tell 'em. With me, it's the way you do 'em. Mime saved me that night, and all the rest of the week. But ironically I shall always be grateful to the Glasgow Empire – because I found a new dimension to my performing ability which later would play an important part in my films.

It was first house Monday at the Grand Theatre, Blackburn, that something else happened that shook me down to my battered size six boots. I had finished the first half, and although the audience had been a little quiet I had managed to get a ripple or two out of them.

I put it down to just one of those nights, and was relaxing in my dressing-room when the manager appeared. He didn't mince his words.

'I'm sorry,' he said with typical Northern bluntness. 'They don't like that sort of thing here. You'll have to do something different next house – or else.'

'Or else what?' I was too stunned to take it in.

'Or else you're out!' Like I say, they don't mince their words up there.

My mouth dropped. Change my act? To what? It was unthinkable after all the hours of rehearsal, the sweat and the sleepless nights that had gone into it. 'No – no I can't,' I managed to stutter.

He looked at me coldly. 'Well then . . . I'm sorry,' he said, and walked out.

It was going to be an early night in Blackburn for one New Name at least. Sullenly I started packing my case . . . and there, on the bottom, I spied two pages of sheet music I used as props on the piano. One was that lovely old number 'They Didn't Believe Me', the other was a Frank Sinatra song, 'Some Other Time'. I thought:

'Norman, this is the time to use your loaf!'

I hurried down the passage to the manager's office, and hesitated. Then I knocked at the door. He looked up from his desk in surprise. 'Yes?'

'Look,' I said, 'I've got to be truthful. I apologise for the mess up, but really I'm a singer. I've always been mad on comedy, and thought I'd try it out this week. But obviously it hasn't worked. So if it's all right with you, I'll go back to singing.'

The manager frowned. 'Why on earth didn't you tell me in the first place?'

'I was hoping I could make people laugh.'

'Well, obviously you can't,' he said tartly. 'Just get out there and sing.'

The second house was in full swing. My place, as the last comic on the bill, should have been to get the audience in the mood to greet the last act – a singer! Oh dear. It was only as I walked out to hand the pianist my sheet music that I realised this no-nonsense Northern crowd were going to be treated to not one, but two singers back to back – so to speak.

What's more, I would only have the piano in the pit to accompany me. As I walked out from the wings – inspiration! There was another piano ready and waiting – the concert grand I used on stage. Quietly I said to the pianist: 'Would you come up on stage and use that one?'

To my relief he agreed – and the effect was far more prestigious. I put all I'd got into 'Some Other Time', and followed up with the most soulful version I could muster of 'They Didn't Believe Me' . . . and I stopped the show!

I came off with my ears ringing, dazed with the reception. In the wings the manager touched my arm. 'That's better,' he said approvingly. 'You should have done that in First House.'

At which point the star of the show came storming up,

and hissed in the manager's face: 'What the bloody hell's going on? I'm supposed to be the singer around here. How am I going to follow that?'

They looked around for me. But, as the saying goes, I had already made my excuses and left. Quietly.

By sheer chance, an agent happened to be in the audience that night watching the Second House. Afterwards he appeared in my dressing-room, and booked me for a week at the Pavilion Theatre, Hastings, after the New Names run – as a singer! When I did get there I went on stage and opened with a song – 'Some Other Time' – then went straight into my full comedy act. Cheeky little beggar, I know. Immediately after the show the same agent came backstage and slapped me on the back. 'Hey, that was smashing!' he said. 'You could be a comedian.' I'd won!

The New Names tour finally came to an end, and following Hastings I returned to London and went back home to Mum. I was starting to earn a respectable whack – the £10 a week from the Portsmouth Coliseum had increased to £12 10s at Basingstoke, and the New Names paid me £15 a week.

That winter I got into pantomime at the Grand Theatre, Brighton playing the Mate in *Robinson Crusoe,* with Renee Houston as principal boy, and picked up £25 a week.

I still treasure my first major review by the critic of the Brighton *Gazette.* 'Every pantomime needs a really good comedian, and *Robinson Crusoe* is lucky to have such a mirthmaker as Norman Wisdom, whose versatile antics stole the show . . .' My chest swelled with pride when I read it.

Don't ever believe actors and entertainers who insist they never, but never, read their reviews. They may swear it on their grandmother's Bible – and next thing they'll be slipping into the nearest newsagent's disguised in wig and dark glasses to snatch up the paper for a sneaky look. And if it's bad, however long in the field and long in the tooth you are – it hurts.

But now, with one good review and a year of fun behind me, I suddenly found myself out of work. I was not too worried, I must admit. I knew I could earn £30 a week on the variety halls, which was good money even if it wasn't happening all the time. The average workman was getting about two and a half quid, so I was doing well!

To celebrate my return to London and home base, I bought a brand new AJS motor-bike for £35. I was feeling flush – and flash! The first day, I took a nostalgic journey, with a purpose. The nostalgia was Deal. The purpose was to find my brother Fred.

Sixteen long years had passed, and I'd had no word from him. Mum had somehow lost touch, and had no idea where he was living. The only clue was that I knew he had been employed at a coal merchant's along the Kent coast before the war, and I thought I might as well start at Deal. Hawksfield's, that was the name. Besides, it would be nice to see the place again.

I headed through the tangled South London suburbs and out through the hop fields of the Garden of England, feeling like the king of the road on my brand new bike. Finally I got to Deal, found the high street, and stopped on the street corner of Blenheim Road to get my bearings.

A young man was passing, and I called out: 'Excuse me, do you know Hawksfield's Coal Yard?'

The fellow, a nicely-dressed chap a bit taller than me said: 'What? Oh, yes. It's just round –' Then he peered closer. 'Norm?'

'Fred?' I said: *'Fred!'*

Incredibly, it was him.

Unashamedly, my long-lost brother and I embraced on that corner, laughing and shouting incoherently and slapping each other on the back like a pair of hysterical school kids. I've often wondered since what the odds must be on something like that happening. But on that sunny summer's afternoon in Deal, it did.

We had a lot to catch up on. Fred was married, but he had never moved out of Deal since the time we were both there as kids. He had become the area manager for a leading coal firm, with personal responsibility for the whole of South-East England. He was also the Southern Coast sculling champion, which surely proves that sport is in the Wisdom blood.

He took me to his house, introduced me to his wife, Christine, and we celebrated our reunion with – for me – a rare beer. I regaled him with my adventures in India, and with my other adventures on the boards back home. We filled in the lost years – and that day we vowed we would always remain close. And we did. I loved my brother, and made sure we saw one another frequently after that.

I was out of work for several weeks, but still not alarmed. I had my room at my Mum's in Willesden, I had enough money saved to keep me going, and I had my bike. And enough confidence in myself to know that sooner or late, I would be all right.

My pride received a slight dent when I answered an advertisement in *The Stage* newspaper, the Bible for out of work entertainers, announcing auditions for the Windmill. This was the celebrated 'Topless Tart' theatre in London's West End where shows would be repeated halfway round the clock from mid-day to midnight, the girls would dance bare-breasted – and the occasional nude would appear but have to stand absolutely motionless.

The shows changed regularly, and many star comics found their springboard to fame here, launched on a sea of disinterested male faces or even those that remained buried behind newspapers until the girls came out.

I never got as far as seeing this off-putting spectacle,

though Harry Secombe, who did, later told me it was enough to drive a comic to the nearest knacker's yard. By tradition, at the end of each hour the front rows would empty and amid a rustle of newspapers there would be a hasty scramble from the back to grab their place. But agents were always there on opening night, looking out for fresh acts.

Harry was there on that audition day, a rotund, jovial fellow trying out his shaving routine for the boss, Vivian Van Damm, who sat impassively in the fourth row of the stalls.

Harry pretends to shave, looking out at the audience as if staring into an invisible mirror, and talks to himself. Of course he gets soap in his mouth, and nicks his cheek. I thought it was hilarious, and so did Van Damm. Harry was hired on the spot.

No such luck for me. I wore a bright sweater instead of my ill-fitting tails, piped a tune on my clarinet, and fell about on the stage. The boss didn't. After less than four minutes, while I was still only halfway through, he waved an imperious hand from his seat. 'Thank you,' he said. 'Next!'

I slunk off, my head hung disconsolately. At the Stage Door I bumped into Harry – quite an easy thing to do, even in those days. He clapped a hand on my shoulder. 'Bloody shame!' he said. 'But never mind. You'll make it.

We still mention it occasionally when we meet on the golf course or at a charity concert. My one regret is that I never did get an eyeful of those topless tarts.

I went home and sat on my bed, and took a long, hard look at myself to see what lessons could be learned from that rebuff. I couldn't allow it to dent my confidence – that would be fatal. Then I brightened. The fact was that Harry was patter, and I was mime. They wanted patter. That must be it.

It's a funny thing about rejection. Some actors want to go off into a dark corner and cut their throats. Others get angry and fight back. For me, as long as someone explained *why* they didn't want me, and I understood it, I could accept it and get by without too much grief. It did not necessarily mean you were bad – just that you were in the wrong place at the wrong time.

But if ever someone thought I was no good – that made my hackles rise. It would double my determination. I would say to myself: 'He's a lunatic. I'll show him!'

This has been my attitude all through my life, it has stood me in great stead when the chips were down, and I reckon it must have been ingrained in me from the days when I was a barefoot urchin running loose in the streets.

The impresario and agent Bert Montague had been to the Brighton panto, liked what he saw, and at last a letter dropped through my door. Would I join another touring revue, called *Let's Make Hey!* This was my longest contract yet – fifteen weeks at a generous £45 per week. In addition, Bert became my agent.

I found I had enough in the bank to splash out £250 on my first car, a snazzy green 1937 Morgan, a beautiful little mover with loads of guts under the bonnet. She made me feel great at the wheel – and from the moment I slid into the leather bucket seat and looked at the mahogany dashboard, I was hooked on cars for ever. Real cars – not the mass-produced kind that roll off a conveyor belt like peas out of a pod, but the kind with character. And did my fiery little Morgan have character!

The girls fell for her charms too. I made the most of it when I first met a lovely young woman named Freda Simpson on the *Hey!* tour. She was a bubbly chorus girl with thick dark hair and a bright smile who also doubled as assistant to another comedian, Charlie Cameron, who shared a dressing-room with me.

Freda and I hit it off from the moment we set eyes on each other. Apart from being a wonderful dancer, she had a great sense of humour too.

The three of us would fool around for hours on end, making up sketches, telling stories, filling the tiny dressing-room with laughter. It was inevitable that I would fall for her and I did.

Quite honestly, I never did think of myself as good-looking or even particularly attractive to women. You could hardly call me tall, dark and handsome, though I suppose my hair was the right shade. But I had a positive outlook on life, and I did have the ability to make girls laugh – and cry, too! I had perfected the art of a trembling lower lip, which you may have noticed in some of my films when the going got rough!

But I was also as honest as I could be with anyone I took out. I didn't try to rush them into bed. I wanted to relax so that we both could be ourselves and get to know each other before anything of a more intimate nature took place. For me, affection and kindness in a woman have always come before sex. I suppose you would call it old-fashioned today, but that's the way I was – and still am. My early brief, disastrous marriage had been my first experience – and looking back I realised it had been infatuation rather than real love.

This time it was different. I felt I was very lucky to have such a lovely girl as Freda actually wanting to be chums with me – and perhaps be prepared to turn it into something more lasting.

My great advantage was that we were flung together by our work. Every evening I knew she would be there in the dressing-room, and the three of us were always chatting away about the show, about how to improve our acts, giving each other advice – and criticism too.

Eventually I plucked up the courage to ask her out, playing it as casually as I could. We were rehearsing in a church hall in Acton, in West London, and in an off-hand way I asked her if she would like to come for a spin in my sports car that weekend. She said yes. And on a sunny Saturday morning, with the hood open and the breeze in our hair, off we went in my jaunty green Morgan – all the way down to Bournemouth, where I ended up meeting her parents.

I'm not a speed freak, though I have been known to do the occasional ton. What I do like in a car is fast acceleration, and that car could go like a little firecracker! Most important to me, though, is a motor with classy looks and a beautiful bodyline.

Freda's parents seemed a little taken aback when we appeared out of the blue, wind-swept and pink-cheeked, on their doorstep for lunch. Three months later, after I had proposed and been accepted, they looked even more dubious at the prospect of having a comic for a son-in-law, and confused about the kind of act I actually did. But I was meticulously polite, and careful not to drop a single piece of crockery or fall over the furniture, and they soon mellowed.

In those fifteen weeks the show took in Derby, Liverpool, Brighton and even a holiday camp at Skegness. Finally we reached Bournemouth, and I decided there was no better place to pop the question.

I took Freda for a stroll on the pier, and as we leaned on the rail at the far end looking out to sea I reached in my pocket for a diamond ring I had bought the day before and said: 'Let's get married.'

Freda smiled back at me and said simply: 'What a lovely idea.'

We drove over to her parents to break the news. They were still unsure of what I actually did, so I felt it was time to come clean and show them. I arranged to have two tickets waiting for them at the box-office that night. That was when they saw me falling all over the stage, diving over the piano and crashing into the drums.

I said to Freda at the time: 'I'll be lucky if they ever let me back in the house. But at least they'll know exactly what I do for a living. Let me know if they laugh.' Luckily for me, they did.

It was on a Monday during rehearsals for *Let's Make Hey!* that the director, Hastings Mann, came to me and asked: 'Would you like to do a charity show?' I jumped at the chance, because I was after as much experience as I could get.

'Good,' he said. 'It's Sunday night, eight o'clock.'

'Where is it?' I asked.

He looked evasive. 'I'll tell you on Friday.'

I waited until Friday, then asked him again.

The answer stunned me. 'The Victoria Palace.'

No wonder he had been evasive – he didn't want to frighten me. My heart started pounding like mad. This was the biggest thing to hit me since I first walked out on that stage at Collins Music Hall what now seemed light years ago.

It was a Water Rats charity show, and I was brought in as a last-minute replacement for another comic who had gone down with laryngitis. My quivering nerve-endings were not helped when I arrived at the theatre that Sunday morning for rehearsals, and saw the list of names pinned up on the call sheet on the notice board inside the Stage Door. My mouth dropped open and my jaw nearly hit the floor as I read: Will Fyffe, Vera Lynn, Harry Tate Jnr, Clarkson Rose, Charlie Chester, Nat Jackley – and, top of the bill, Laurel and Hardy!

The stage doorman ran a finger down his list to the very bottom. 'Wisdom? Up there!' He jerked a thumb skywards, and I started the long climb to my dressing-room. It was somewhere up near the roof, but I would have changed in the lavatory if I'd had to. I took my music and went down those endless flights of steps and out on to the stage.

And there they all were, the biggest names in variety, standing around drinking coffee and chatting as if they were at a cocktail party. Nobody knew me, and I suddenly felt like Cinderella finding half-way through the ball that the fairy godmother's wand hadn't worked.

Will Fyffe nodded vaguely to me, Charlie Chester said 'Hi!' and they were all very polite. When my turn came I went through my routine, trying to hide my nerves, and even received a smattering of applause from the stalls where my peers sat. Coming from them, it made me feel better.

I was due to be the second act after the interval, following the girls, just as I had been back in Portsmouth and Basingstoke. A warm-up spot, getting the audience in the mood for the stars. But I had no alternative, and it was enough to be there with a black-tie audience out front, including many impresarios, agents and professional entertainers who would see me for the first time.

Twenty minutes before curtain up, Vera Lynn's pianist approached me. 'I've got a message for you,' he said. 'Vera has to catch a train, and she's worried that she might miss it. She would like to change spots with you. Is that okay?'

Vera Lynn was on immediately after myself. 'That's fine with me,' I said. Anyway, my piano was on the stage and it was just what she required, so there were no complications about shifting props.

That night I watched her from the wings with the butterflies once again knocking holes in my stomach. She was wonderful, of course, the Forces' Sweetheart at her best with that pure voice entrancing them with 'The White Cliffs of Dover' and getting everyone to join in with 'We'll Meet Again'. At the end the audience was so warmed up you could almost feel the heat!

My turn. I was caught up in the euphoria of the moment. Something took hold of me, and I stormed out like a miniature cyclone, poured out the gags, fell flat, tap-danced like a madman, crashed over the piano and thumped around the stage as if my life depended on it. At the end the house rose to me, and called me back for four curtain calls. I came off breathless and triumphant, with the other performers slapping my back and congratulating me – and there was Vera Lynn, giving me a big kiss on the cheek and saying: 'Well done, Norman!'

I finally caught my breath. 'But – I thought you had a train to catch –'

'Well . . . no,' she admitted. 'But I saw you in Brighton, and you were so good, that I thought this would be a wonderful opportunity for you.' She knew I had a tough spot, and she was a big star who would have no problems, so she volunteered to take my place. It was a wonderful gesture, and I've had my own special soft spot for that lady ever since.

Chapter Nine

Backstage I found myself under siege from a battery of variety agents. They had been part of the pro audience, and a group of them pushed their way unceremoniously into my dressing-room. If they weren't exactly waving blank cheques they all wanted to sign me up on the spot. It was very flattering, and did my ego no end of good. But I had to tell them: 'Sorry, but I'm with my new agent, Bert Montague.' However, I took the precaution of pocketing their business cards for possible future use – and it would make an enormous difference to my life.

Top of the bill in *Let's Make Hey!* was an American comedy-singing trio hired to give us 'international appeal'. Forsyth, Seaman and Farrell made a big impact in British music halls over many years, and were a treat to watch. Forsyth was a fat man, Seaman was a fat woman, and little Betty Farrell was a pocket-sized dynamo of a ballet dancer who could pirouette around the entire stage on the tips of her toes like a tiny whirlwind.

Bert booked us around the country for three months. But after four weeks, Forsyth, Seaman and Farrell had to fly back for other contractual engagements, and the star act was replaced by Alfred and Elsie Price, two experienced performers flown in from Canada to bolster the troupe when we opened in Manchester and keep the international flag flying high.

I had never heard of this pair, but they were obviously tops in their country. At any rate, they kept telling us so. They did a fast-moving comedy, dance and singing routine. Alfred was slightly overweight, with chiselled good looks while his wife Elsie was a blonde.

The problem was from the word go, I was doing better than they were in terms of audience applause, and I watched them growing more and more peeved as the first week proceeded.

On the third night, just when I had reached my important pathos scene, who should walk on to the stage but Alfred Price. It was a crucial moment as far as I was concerned, carefully constructed between the pratfalls and the verbal comedy to balance the act as a whole.

He waved me to silence. Then he addressed the packed house. 'You're gonna like this bit,' he proclaimed. 'It's so sad, you'll feel really sorry for the little guy. Sometimes I can't help crying myself.' Then he turned and strolled off.

I could hardly believe what I had just heard. The audience didn't know whether I was spoofing or not, and it was impossible to get my timing back.

A few minutes later, just as I was getting into a spot of miming, there was Alfred again. 'Hey, this bit's real funny,' he shouted, jovially. 'You'll laugh until your stomach aches . . .' And off he went. I was left standing there like a lemon. He'd killed me stone dead.

During the interval I went to their dressing room, and faced him. 'Please don't do that sort of thing, you're ruining my act,' I said.

His retort was brusque. 'I'm the star. I'll do as I please.'

It happened several times more during the run, and finally I appealed to George Hollis, the touring manager. 'You've got to stop this,' I pleaded. 'Look what they're doing to my act!'

'I can't do anything about it,' he shrugged. 'They are the

stars. They will do as they wish.' He was a bluff fellow who liked throwing his weight about, and from the start he had ingratiated himself with the two names at the top of the bill. There was nothing I could do, except seethe. Throughout the next nightmare eight weeks I lived in a cold sweat of uncertainty. Alfred would not appear every night – only if it was a good house and I was doing well. If it was average, he didn't bother.

The final night was at the Metropole Theatre in the Edgware Road, a legendary music hall steeped in Victorian variety. It was one of the great venues in Britain, a kind of Mount Olympus for any entertainer anxious to carry the torch of his talent to the top. A place you could look back on with pride, and one day tell your grandchildren: I was there!

The First House was quiet, and nothing happened. I began to think it might be all right. But just to make sure I knocked on the door of the star dressing-room between shows, and stood just inside as they put the finishing touches to their make-up in the mirror. I said: 'Look, be fair. Don't come out tonight. All-right? It's our last show together.'

Elsie turned her head. 'Push off, you little creep!' was all she said, and there was venom in her voice. I caught Alfred giving her an approving 'That's telling him!' wink. Then he looked at me in the mirror.

'You heard the lady. Get out!' Then, ominously: 'I'll see you later.' Sure enough, I was two minutes into my act – when out bounced Alfred. 'Hey, it's funny – it's really funny. You'll split your sides!' He gave a wide grin, and pranced off the stage – only this time I followed him into the wings.

'Oi!' I called, and tapped him on the shoulder. 'It's sad, too!' And as he turned I belted him with a right-hander to the jaw and laid him flat on his back, out cold!

Then I ran back on stage with a broad smile as though

nothing had happened, and broke into an exuberant tap dance which ended in a crescendo of applause. And this time no-one came out to interrupt me.

Out of the corner of my eye as I carried on clowning I could see a lot of activity, with assistants helping Alfred to his feet and persuading him to go back to his dressing-room. I finished my act, took an extra few bows to celebrate, and went off one way as Elsie led her partner – now rather less bouncy than usual – on stage the other side.

In the wings George Hollis confronted me. His face was livid with rage and disbelief. He seized me by both lapels, lifting me almost off my feet, and snarled: 'This is the last time you'll ever work in this theatre! And if I get my way it will be the last time you work in *any* theatre –'

I pushed him off. 'In that case I've got nothing to lose, have I?' I said – and belted him too.

My last sight of the touring manager as I made my way back to my dressing-room was of a pair of eyes bulging in disbelief as he toppled back into a welter of backstage scenery, ladders and props. No-one tried to stop me, and I must say I felt a whole lot better.

On 7 October 1947 Freda and I were married at the Methodist Church at Shirley, near Croydon, in Surrey. Her wedding dress was pale blue silk, with an embroidered neckline. She carried pink roses and wore a blue orchid in her head-dress – and looked like a princess. Our honeymoon was ten days in Brighton.

I was now beginning to spend quite a lot of time out of work and had been advised to find a new agent. I had almost decided to do this when suddenly Bert booked me for a new show called *Piccadilly Nights,* to be staged at the Alhambra in Brussels. For my first international appearance I was promoted to principal comedian at £50 a week! At least I was heading in the right direction: onward and upward. Freda was also taken on, and our spirits were sky-high as we sailed on the ferry to Ostend and then took the train to Brussels for the grand opening at the Alhambra.

There was one slight hiccup: I had to learn my words in French, and somehow it didn't sound right to start my act with: '*Mesdames et Messieurs . . .*' But I did my best, learning it parrot fashion. Luckily you can fall into a piano in any language and still get a laugh.

We were booked for two weeks. Unhappily there was a problem over money, and we were never paid. Rather than hang around arguing in an expensive foreign country we begged and borrowed enough for our return fare and headed back home. But out of that minor mishap there was one grain of comfort: Laurel and Hardy were booked to follow us, and in our second week both legendary figures turned up to see us.

They remembered me from the charity concert at the Victoria Palace. Ollie was very amiable. 'We're sticking to English. Let 'em use sub-titles if they want!' he joked. While Stan would come in every night to sit in my dressing-room and chat about everything under the sun.

It was the start of a friendship that would last until his death in 1965. Our characters had a lot in common – both of us life's victims who would never let it get us down, and I almost found myself on stage with this marvellous visual clown.

Part of the show was a wallpaper sketch I was trying out for the first time. One night my partner fell ill and was unable to perform. To my amazement Stan Laurel offered to take his place – and it was only the small print in his contract that prevented him doing so. Now *that* would have been something to treasure!

My mother now decided to buy a house in Deal, where she would be nearer to Fred and his family. By this time Freda and I had rented a flat in Willesden, and Mum made sure we had our own room waiting for us in Deal whenever we wanted it. I spent many weekends down there, relaxing and just pottering about, with a spot of fishing from the jetty to laze away the hours. But I was never totally still: something in me was always driving me on to create new ideas, songs, gags or sketches. I would keep a note pad and pencil constantly with me in case an idea came out of the blue. And I would rehearse in front of the mirror in my bedroom upstairs, while Mum, Freda and possibly my brother Fred and his wife Christine were watching TV downstairs.

It was during one of those impromptu rehearsals that I frightened the life out of the window cleaner. Many years ago I had discovered the enjoyable art of pulling faces. It really is quite easy, and the more you practise, the more you can manipulate your skin into all sorts of monstrous looking masks.

In the army I became a positive India Rubber Man, mainly to take the mickey out of snooty officers and sadistic sergeants. I could pull the most horrendous faces behind their backs – and lapse into child-like innocence when they whirled round to find out why everyone was laughing.

On this particular summer's day in Deal, I was upstairs by myself, 'working out' in my first-floor bedroom. This meant twisting my face into all sorts of gorgon-like expressions, some of which frightened even myself.

Unbeknown to me, my mother had arranged for a window cleaner to go over the house. I was happily prancing around as the Hunchback of Notre Dame in front of the wardrobe mirror when I was aware of a movement behind me. I turned sharply, all twisted and horrible – and found myself glaring malevolently at another face peering through the window, a very frightened face in a cloth cap.

The poor chap was totally transfixed for a second, before he let out a yell and vanished down the ladder and out of sight. He obviously thought there was a lunatic locked away upstairs. The rattle of a bucket being kicked over came to my ears, then he was gone. Mum had to phone him and explain her son was in show-business and was just rehearsing his act. 'Tell him he frightened the life out of me,' said the cleaner. 'I'll come back when he's gone.'

During the times I was out of work I established a pattern. The most important thing was not to lie around in bed moping or waiting for the phone to ring. The second was to keep practising my instruments and rehearsing my act. The third was not to lose faith in myself.

Being out of work gives you time to think. As I've said before, I wasn't desperately happy with Bert Montague, and one day I came across the half-dozen business cards I had collected after the famous charity night at the Victoria Palace. I had kept them in a drawer, and now I took a long, hard look at the names. Then I did the rounds. One of the last few was Billy Marsh, at London Management Agency.

Without an appointment I simply went along to Jermyn Street, climbed the stairs to the second floor, knocked on the door and walked in. Billy sat behind a large desk with a cigarette between his fingers. From the fag ends in the ashtray it was apparent he smoked a lot – in fact he was a chain-smoker, a habit he never gave up.

Billy was small and dapper, with keen features and huge glasses behind which his dark eyes gleamed shrewdly. He nodded in recognition, gestured me to a chair, and said: 'All right, tell me about it.'

I sensed an immediate rapport. 'I'm signed to Bert Montague, but I can't seem to get any work,' I said. 'I've been round all the other agents, and it's hopeless.'

Billy was a good listener, and was on my wave-length instantly. 'I'm not surprised,' he said. 'There's only one way round this.' He got up and picked his coat off the peg. 'Let's go and talk to Bert Montague.'

I let them do the talking. At Bert's office in Soho what are known as 'delicate negotiations' took place. In the end they did a deal on commission, agreeing to split it fifty-fifty – whichever of them got me the job.

That was the start of an association that has lasted to this day. Billy became a friend and confidante, and I felt totally safe in his hands. That first evening we chatted long into the night, discussing my act and my future, and swapping backstage tales. I told Billy how I liked to think of my audiences as my friends. But of course sometimes I used to get heckled, too – particularly in the early days before they got to know me.

You can't avoid it – and it would be very strange indeed if over the years I had not had that familiar, usually slurred voice from somewhere in the darkness shouting at me. A lot of comics have a built-in script of responses, and they automatically go into overdrive.

You know the kind of thing: 'Oh, I know you: weren't you born in a village on the other side of Wedlock?' Or: 'Promise me you won't drink any more Long Life beer!' Or: 'Hold your head back, sir. You're spilling it!' And the classic: 'The last time I saw a mouth like that, it had a hook in it!' I heard one comic up north in a club being heckled by a woman, and he told her: 'Be careful, madam, or I'll go round to your house and switch off the red light!'

Comedians are only too aware that if they start answering back it can get out of hand, especially in a club where drinks are flowing and maybe someone is trying to show off to a girlfriend or some of the lads. Worse, it can upset the audience, and when that happens you might as well walk off the stage.

Me, I do it another way.

I have only one response to hecklers, but it never fails. I wait for them to finish, then look in the general direction of where the noise is coming from, give them my biggest smile and say: 'Hullo, whoever you are!' – then I pucker up my lips in a big juicy kiss!

That's all it takes, and everyone falls about because what I'm saying is: 'You're *lovely!*' And there's no reply to it. The only theatre I would never try it out is the Glasgow Empire – well, I may appear a bit stupid sometimes, but I'm not suicidal! That was the place, remember, where the saying went that they had specially long intervals so that the audience could reload with tomatoes!

Some comics say that you walk a tightrope every time you go out and face the public. I know what they mean, but I don't see it that way. I treat them all as chums – rather like Morecombe and Wise did, and Tommy Cooper too.

Ten days after I met Billy Marsh I got a call from him. It was Monday, and I had just finished lunch. 'Listen,' he said. 'Could you get down to the Brighton Hippodrome and take the place of A. J. Powers, who has fallen ill? It's in the Moss Empire chain, and will do you a lot of good.'

'Sure,' I agreed. 'When do I go on?'

'Tonight!' he said.

Strewth, I thought! That means no band call, no rehearsal, no time to get to know anybody. I would see how the stage was set for the first time just before I went out.

But I tore down there, breaking all records in my Morgan, and was out on stage, comic warm-up immediately after the girls, in time for the First House. Between shows the manager came round and shook my hand. 'You were so good that I'm putting you on in the second half for the rest of the week,' he said.

The Second House went even better, and I tore them up! That's the saying we have in variety for really winning an audience over. The manager appeared again. 'I think you should know that I've just phoned Val Parnell, and told him he's got to come and see you.'

For me that was like hearing someone had been on the

hot line to God. Val Parnell was king of the variety shows in Britain, and for an aspiring comic he could be the difference between fame and oblivion. And on Tuesday night, sure enough, the manager came rushing round in a high state of tension. After all, his head was on the chopping block too!

'He's out there!' he cried. 'Third row, aisle seat. Give it all you've got.'

I gave it all I'd got. And afterwards there was a summons to see the great man in the manager's office. I thought I should try to make the right impression, and in those days I smoked. Parnell was sitting behind the desk while the manager hopped from foot to foot by the window. I took out a packet of ten Capstans and with a casual gesture offered the big man one. 'Cigarette?'

Parnell simply smiled, raised his hand and pulled out a cigar that must have been a foot long. I thought: it's no good trying to swank. But he was looking at me shrewdly, and finally he said: 'Sit down.' He lit up his cigar, and through a cloud of smoke his voice came:

'I'd like to make you a star!'

Faintly I said: 'You would? Oh – thank you, sir.'

'You'll go on at the Palladium,' he said – and by now I was wondering if I was hearing properly. He paused. Then: 'There's only one thing. I want you to sign on with an agent of my choosing.'

This put me in a dreadful spot. I found myself stuttering: 'Well . . . but if it hadn't been for Billy Marsh I wouldn't be here tonight, and you wouldn't have seen me.'

Parnell considered me for a long moment. Then he said coldly:

'Show business is like that.'

'Not for me it's not,' I countered, rather more quickly than I intended. 'I just can't do that to Billy.'

'Very well,' said Parnell. 'Now listen carefully. I am going away for a week's holiday. I hope you will reconsider, and let me know on my return.'

The interview was over. I realised I had probably burned my boats, but I wasn't going to budge. Even if it meant turning down the offer of a lifetime: a season at the world-famous London Palladium.

Next night Billy came down on the train to see me. I told him about the conversation – or confrontation – with the great Val Parnell, and he was very touched. Between shows I spotted him on the public phone by the stage door, and he was talking into it urgently. He had called Bernard Delfont, who ran the London Casino in Soho in cut-throat rivalry to the Palladium.

Parnell booked in huge American stars like Danny Kaye, Bob Hope and Betty Hutton, while half a mile away in Old Compton Street, Delfont came back at him with acts like Hoagy Carmichael, Sophie Tucker, and the Inkspots, lavishly presented shows with that vital international flavour.

Billy told Delfont what had happened. How Parnell wanted me, and what I had said. 'You've got to book Norman for the Casino,' he declared.

Delfont was on the next train to Brighton. He caught my act that night, and though he had to hurry back to the station for the last train to Victoria without seeing me, Billy came backstage to give me the thumbs-up. 'You're on!' he said, excitedly..

Loyalty had always been a vital constituent flowing through the bloodstream of the three Grade brothers – Leslie, Lew and Bernie. I knew I had been given my chance on that ticket alone, and I was still billed as 'The Successful Failure'. But I was walking on air, because I knew that in only two years I had reached my goal of a 'legit' spot on a West End stage.

I duly reported for rehearsals on the Monday morning,

my heart thudding as I marched through the Stage Door off Greek Street and gave my name to the keeper in the little glass booth. He ran a finger down the list of 'artistes', and stopped somewhere near the bottom. 'Right, sir – in you go!'

Sir? Cor blimey, things were definitely looking up.

Allan Jones was top of the bill. Two decades later his son Jack Jones would become an even greater singing star. After the overture from the Casino Orchestra and the leggy delights of the Casino Girls to put the audience in the right mood, would come The Six Edwardos, billed as 'hand-springing acrobats' who bounced around the stage as if they were on invisible springs. Bennett and Williams were a pair of cross-talk BBC funny men, then came Maurice Rocco, the tremendously versatile 'Boogie-Woogie Pianist-Dancer'.

Then it was my turn, in at Number 6 and now billed as 'The New British Comedian', hardly the most imaginative welcome mat to be laid out – but who was I to complain? It seemed I had kissed goodbye to the Successful Failure.

Following me were 'America's Greatest Dance Stylists' Harrison and Fisher. And after the interval: Bing Crosby hits from the orchestra heralding more acts. Twin girl contortionists. The loquacious George Doonan ('The Life and Soul of the Party'). A trick cyclist named Marie Wilson who did extraordinary things on a unicycle that would have had me speaking in a high voice for weeks.

And the legendary Wilson, Keppel and Betty with their comedy Egyptian 'sand-dance' routine – the fellows in striped sheets, hands flapping, and Betty (naturally) gyrating in the obligatory belly dance – before Allan Jones came on for the big star climax.

We gathered on the stage, and were introduced to the musical director, Harold Collins, who would conduct the Casino Orchestra. He consulted his notes on the board he was holding, and finally got to me. 'Right, Norman. Let's see – you've got eight minutes.'

That threw me. My act was fourteen minutes, minimum, and often over-ran if the audience wanted more. I looked past him into the stalls, empty apart from half a dozen figures in a small cluster watching the rehearsals. I recognised Bernard Delfont's bulky figure.

When the right moment came and other acts were being put through their paces, I nipped round the side and slipped into the row behind him. 'Excuse me, sir?' It was the first time we had actually met.

'Ah, Norman,' he said affably. 'Welcome to the West End!'

'Thank you,' I said. 'But there's just one thing: they're only going to see eight minutes of me.'

'No,' Delfont said. 'Six. I'm really sorry, Norman, but we've got a very crowded bill.'

I told him: 'But my act is fourteen minutes. I can't possibly cut it down.'

'Well, you're going to have to,' he said, not unkindly but firmly. I could sense the steel behind the smile, and knew better than to argue.

Instead I went back to my dressing room and sat down and stared at myself in the mirror, trying to work out the options. If I did six minutes and it went down well, they would keep me on for the month's run, and maybe the tour after that – but for only six minutes. If I flopped, they would give me the push anyway.

But if I went on and did my full fourteen minutes and wowed them, I might get the chance to carry on with my proper act. I don't mind admitting that I have always tried to be a perfectionist, and I just didn't want to give anyone half measures.

In the end, after an hour of agonising, I thought: I'll chance it!

I went back to the stage and found Harold Collins. 'Ah yes,' he said. 'You're down to six minutes. What are you going to cut?'

'None of the music,' I assured him. 'That can all stay in. But I'll have to cut the dialogue right back.'

'I'll say you will,' he said, studying my script closely. 'You'll hardly get a word in.'

The date was Monday, 5 April 1948. I was shivering with fright as I climbed into my well-worn misfit evening suit, a bootlace for a tie, the trousers cut off short to reveal bright yellow socks. These were genuine first-night nerves made all the worse because I knew I was going to step right out of line that night.

I also knew the Fleet Street critics were there – not to see me, but because Allan Jones was a big name in a big show. They always came to the First House so that they could get their reviews phoned through in good time for next day's paper. The place was packed.

The applause for Maurice Rocco's rockin' rhythm died away, and the maestro boogied off past me into the wings, his face flushed and perspiring. He nodded at me: 'They're okay,' I heard him say, before the stage manager clapped me on the shoulder. 'You're on,' he said. 'Have fun!'

I go out ahead of the curtain. Behind the thick drapes I can hear the animated, expectant buzz of an audience between acts. I walk quickly over to the grand piano, and start biting into that enormous sandwich, just as the curtain goes up.

A voice announces: 'Ladies and gentlemen. We are proud to present Britain's gift to the operatic arts'. I am oblivious to everything except the sandwich. My hair is slicked down, and parted in the middle.

I look like a slightly mad opera star, caught with his vocal trousers down, blissfully unaware of the audience. Slowly the dreadful realisation dawns that I am not alone. I glance furtively round at the audience – and they're laughing already.

I grin bashfully, try to hide the sandwich. First in my trousers, then in the piano, passing the whole thing off with airy, grandiloquent gestures as one of life's little mishaps. Furtively I drop the sandwich into the piano, close the lid, start to walk away – and end up on the floor.

Now I move into my routine of 'I'll Walk Beside You' – in different keys, chasing the orchestra up and down the scale. I can even see Harold Collins grinning up from the pit as he waves his baton madly to keep just out of my reach. Now comes the moment where I lead the audience into an Oriental song – in total gibberish. And the shadow boxing that ends with me flat on my back on the boards.

I did the whole fourteen minutes, and probably over-ran even that. And at the end the audience rose to me. I was called back *three* times for curtain calls, bowing each time to the three different corners of the theatre, right, left and finally centre. They wouldn't let me go, and my heart felt as if it was literally bursting with emotion.

When I came off for the last time I saw the large dinner-jacketed figure of Bernard Delfont standing impassively in the wings with his arms folded. 'Oh Gawd!' I thought. 'I'm in trouble here!' But the echoes of applause were still hanging in the air. I knew I'd gone too far, broken the ground rules – but surely he wouldn't . . .

Delfont looked at me for a long moment. Then he stuck out a hand, took my moist one in its grasp, and said: 'Well done!'

That was all. He never said another word. Nor did anyone else. The Second House came, and nobody told me to stick to six minutes – so I gave them another fourteen, and again it brought the house down. Backstage afterwards Billy Marsh was in a ferment of elation and apprehension. 'This is all very odd,' he said. 'No-one saying anything.

What do you think?'

'I think I'd better keep going till someone tells me to stop,' I replied.

No-one ever did – because the early morning papers came through, and with them the first reviews.

For me, that night turned into a dream come true. The *Daily Mail* critic wrote: 'He has joined the star comics'. The *Daily Express* did a follow-up on me next day, sending show-business writer David Lewin round to my home in Willesden to interview me.

With him came a photographer who pictured me pulling faces with my props of the doormat-sized sandwich and musical instruments. The headline simply said: 'A STAR IS BORN'.

In a national daily newspaper that would put my name on breakfast tables all over the country, what more could I ask?

CHAPTER TEN

That second night, drama at the Casino! The trick cyclist Marie Wilson had her amazing balancing act ready – but when she got to the theatre she was told she had been cut down from six minutes to just ninety seconds! It was obviously because of me. Other acts, too, had been pruned by a couple of minutes here or there to make room for the new star in their midst – and suddenly I felt terrible. What had I done? But the show had to end promptly at ten-thirty so that people could catch last trains home, and the management didn't want to over-run.

In the circumstances everyone was very nice about it. 'That's all right, Norman. We can cut two minutes,' said Maurice. But when I heard what they'd done to poor Marie, the lovely lady on the unicycle, I felt worse than ever. I thought: Oh God, what is she going to think of me?

I plucked up the courage to go round to her dressing-room, and hesitantly knocked on the door. 'Look, I've come to apologise –' I began. 'I know you're normally six minutes, and now you're down to a minute and a half, and it's all because of me.'

Her face lit up in a big smile. 'Don't apologise,' she beamed. 'There's no need. Actually you've done me a big favour.'

'How's that?' I asked, bemused.

Her voice dropped to a whisper. 'Promise not to tell anyone – but I'm pregnant!'

I couldn't believe it. I mean, fancy riding a unicycle when you're in the family way!

Meantime Harold Collins called me over and said: 'We're putting you in the second half. It's called promotion!' And as I left the theatre, there was a long line of people stretching up to the Stage Door with autograph books in their hands.

I walked over with an expectant smile and took the nearest book from a young girl. 'Who's it for, dear?' I asked smugly, fumbling for a pencil.

But she grabbed it back. ''Ere,' she cried. 'Wotcha think you're doin'?'

'Don't you want my autograph?' I asked, lamely.

'Who do you think you are?' she retorted. 'We're all waiting for Allan Jones!'

Oh dear! I crept away down Frith Street and into the bright lights of Soho, hoping no-one had overheard.

On the third day I got a call at home. Billy Marsh was on the line. 'You won't believe this,' he said. 'But Allan Jones has gone down with laryngitis. You're top of the bill.'

Allan never returned to the show. I stayed on the top spot for another three weeks, and at the end Billy booked me straight into the Golders Green Hippodrome, another highly-sought venue – top of the bill at £100 a week. I have never been less than top ever since! The exceptions are charity shows or royal variety shows where everyone is considered equal, and going on last doesn't necessarily mean you're the top act. You could easily find Bob Hope, Tom Jones and Shirley Bassey on the same stage – and of course each of them could fill a theatre for weeks.

My professional career was blossoming, but I still stayed in modest digs in Willesden. In that heady summer of 1948, I was starting to earn good money – enough, as I used to say, to allow me to suffer in comfort! But success was always much more important to me than money. As long as I could enjoy life, I was happy.

It was at this point, with offers flooding in, that I sat down with Billy Marsh in his Jermyn Street office and told him bluntly: 'Look, it's marvellous what's happening, and I appreciate what you're doing for me, and getting me big money – but I really don't think I know my job well enough yet.'

He looked at me. 'What on earth are you talking about? I've got dates coming up for you all round the country.

I said: 'No, I don't want all this chopping and changing. I want to get a real act together: sketches, comedy routines, singing, dancing, even a monologue. Somehow I want to build up a character that is quite unique. I can't keep on being the "new British comedian" for ever.'

Billy thought about it for a long moment, tapping his blotter with a pencil as he deliberated my future. At last he said: 'Well, there is something that you might like. Summer season in Scarborough. The Spa Theatre, a show called *Out of the Blue,* in its third year. You'll be able to experiment and work with other people –'

'Say no more!' I told him. 'That's for me.'

'There's just one thing,' said Billy. 'You'll only get £35 a week. I can get you three times as much anywhere else.'

'I'll take it,' I said.

With all the moving about, Freda and I talked over how a travelling comedian should live. One solution sprang out: a caravan. We bought an old second-hand Vauxhall, drove around various caravan sites in the Midlands, and finally settled on a neat little two-wheeler.

When the salesman hitched it to our car, I suggested a test drive as I knew that towing can produce some unique driving problems if you're not used to it.

He agreed, and I set off with Freda leaving the salesman standing on the kerb watching. Everything was fine for a few minutes. Then I noticed through the offside driving mirror that we were being overtaken by another caravan. I pulled sharply in to the left, and then realised with some alarm that I had seen the overtaking caravan before. 'Look out, it's ours!' I shouted, just as the caravan pitched forward into the road, digging its towing bar into the ground with a dreadful screech. We left the car and caravan to be fixed up properly, and came back for them next day.

We found a site off the Barnet by-pass north of London which became our base for the first few days of our new nomadic existence. On the way up the Al to Scarborough, dusk began to fall – and I found our car lights weren't working. In something of a panic I drove the car out of the traffic and up the banking. There she stalled, and refused to come to life again.

We had no choice but to spend the night there. The caravan was so lopsided that if a tin of soup had been put on the lower shelf the whole thing would have toppled over. For some reason we chose to sleep with our heads at the lower end, and I kept waking up in the night, wondering why I felt so dizzy. It was a most uncomfortable experience. I was glad to see the dawn, and get our temperamental old banger going again with the starting handle.

At Scarborough we found a pleasant site near the sea, parked the caravan on its jacks, set out the Calor gas containers and our dustbin, and made it our home for the next three months. All we had for entertainment was a small battery radio. But with the fresh sea breezes blowing in through the windows, we both felt a great sense of freedom, and although it was small we were able to invite friends from the cast to dinner and generally have a high old time.

Scarborough was to prove one of the best moves I ever made. I found myself sharing a dressing-room with a conjuror, and the company had to do a different show each week. Apart from my own act I had to sing, dance, go into sketches – the lot, week after week. By the fourth week it was getting tough, but the challenge meant we had to write new material all the time – and somehow we did it.

We were doing four different shows in the month, so that holiday-makers could come and see us over and over again if they wanted. Maybe the weather was a bit unsettled, or the North Sea was cold that summer – but we were packed every night.

The conjuror was having problems finding material in the fourth week, so he said to me: 'Norman, let's try something different. I've got an idea – when I invite someone out of the audience, you come up and help me out. We might get some laughs together.'

I said: 'That's fine by me. I'd better get myself a suit.'

I went into town that afternoon and wandered around looking in all the clothes shops. Finally, buried away down a side street, I came upon a second hand shop that sold clothes as well as a whole lot of other knick-knacks. There was a rack of old suits along one wall, and one caught my eye: a scruffy check suit.

It looked a bit small, but the owner let me try it on in a dressing-room the size of a telephone box. I was right. It was at least two sizes too small – but it was perfect.

I eyed myself in the mirror. It felt a bit tight, but I could breathe and move. I stepped out into the shop.

'How do I look?' I asked.

The owner was middle-aged with thinning hair, an apron over his paunch, and an eye for a soft touch. But even he baulked at the sight of his customer parading around the shop in a check strait jacket.

'Er – isn't it a trifle small, sir?' he inquired.

I kept my face straight. 'Certainly not. It feels fine.'

'Oh,' he said. Then he beamed. 'Well, in that case – a splendid choice, if I may say.'

'You may,' I said. 'How much?'

'Er – it's thirty shillings.'

'Done,' I said, wondering if I had been. 'Now I need a cap to go with it.' There was a shelf full of hats above the rack, and I picked out a matching check peaked cap, priced at a shilling. 'Ah, just the job!'

As I strolled out into the Scarborough sunshine, the summation of sartorial elegance packed into a plastic bag under my arm, I glanced back to glimpse his face peering through the window. There's one born every minute, his expression said. In this case he was right. It was the Gump.

That night I changed into the suit, waited till the conjuror was about to go on, gave him a nod and a wink, then quietly slipped out front into an empty aisle seat.

At the right moment he called out for volunteers, and I was up there like a shot. We 'ad-libbed' the act, though we had rehearsed it earlier – and to our delight it worked so well that the audience were in hysterics. Word got back to Bernard Delfont, who took the next train up to Scarborough, saw the show – and booked us both on the spot for the London Casino as a double act at the end of the season.

That was how the Gump was born.

The conjuror's name was David Nixon, whose bald head, friendly smile and brilliant tricks would make him a fireside favourite across the land. The act was deceptively simple. David wheeled on a large cabinet in which I was supposed to disappear. I clambered into it with apprehension written all over my face – only to dart clear when he closed the curtains as if I was scared. 'I'm not going in there!' I'd cry out. 'It's too dark.'

David then explained patiently and at great length what I was supposed to do. I just stood with my mouth open, not comprehending a word of it. Finally he said: 'Look, I'll show you. It's perfectly safe.' And in he would climb. That was when I pulled a lever, a pistol went off – and Hey Presto! He'd vanished!

It sounds pretty obvious – but it worked a treat. So much so that soon David was helping me get laughs instead of the other way round. We developed other tricks and routines. Cards, disappearing braces, broken watches – he would make me smash mine with a hammer, then miraculously bring it back intact. In my little Gump suit I sensed that audiences felt more sorry for me than they had in the past when I was milking the Successful Failure for all he was worth. I began to play it up, laying on the pathos to see how far I could stretch it. Sometimes I overdid it, and laughs would come where I had not intended them. But now at last I felt I had hit upon a unique image.

This little fellow was someone I would get to know. He would grow with me. And hopefully he would touch a chord with people everywhere.

David and I got on famously. He was a brilliant conjuror, and often in the dressing-room afterwards I would plead: 'Come on, show me how you do it. Just one trick. Any trick.'

He would produce a pack of cards, say: 'Take one,' and I'd take the five of diamonds. He would guide me through how he was fooling the victim – and then I'd turn the card over and it was the ten of clubs! In all that season, he never let on how to do one trick. The closest he came was saying: 'I'll tell you later' – but he never did.

One fine Sunday the boys and girls all decided to pop over for the day to Ravenscar and use the really splendid open-air swimming pool there. I went all coy. 'I think I'd rather not. I'm . . . shy. You see, I can't swim.'

'Come on Norman,' said David. 'What does it matter? We'll have a nice day out.'

'No,' I said firmly. 'I'm going to stay home and read a book.'

David got really mad at me. 'Any fool can learn to swim if he really puts his mind to it,' he raged. 'Look – I'll teach you.'

I told him that numerous people had tried, and failed, over the years. 'I'm a natural non-swimmer, David.' I looked at him pathetically. 'I – I . . . just sink –'

David gripped me by the shoulders. 'I guarantee to have you swimming in six lessons,' he declared. 'Now come on, we're holding the others up.'

I gave in reluctantly. 'I'll try once more,' I said, bravely.

They got me into the water at the shallow end. David worked hard and patiently, with one hand under my chin, encouraging me every foot of the way. 'Trust me Norman, and you won't sink. You can't! Kick out, sweep your arms wide, I've got you. You're doing fine –' He took his hand away, and I went down like a stone.

He tried again, same voice, same exhortation – same result. Wild floundering from me, with frantic gasps, bubbles everywhere as I sank under the water.

Finally, after fifteen minutes of it, I stood up. 'Now do you believe me?' I demanded in a choked voice.

'Norman, I think I do,' said David.

'Well, I'll have one more try,' I said, the hero to the last. 'Thanks so much for your patience.' And with a thrashing of water I set off up the pool in a crawl that would have shamed Johnny Weissmuller. At the end I looked back, and there was David still standing up to his waist, shaking that bald head of his in disbelief.

The summer came to its end, and I bade farewell to the sea breezes of Scarborough with that sadness we in vaudeville inevitably feel at the end of a season.

It was back to London, and for Freda and me, back to our caravan site near Hendon while I went into a double act with David Nixon at the scene of my earlier triumph, the London Casino. This time he would be my straight man. It worked well enough, but we both decided a double act was not for us. After the initial month's run, we agreed to go our own ways.

It was on 22 November 1947, that I made my first appearance on television. Saturday afternoon, 3.00 p.m., live. I took the long drive out to North London and the unwieldy sprawl of Alexandra Palace to take part in a BBC show simply called *Variety*. It featured Gwen Catley (soprano), Frank Raymond (another comedian). Dennis Forbes (conjuror), the Southern Singers (a Negro choir) and myself. That lovely blonde comedienne Joy Nichols introduced it, and I spent most of my six minutes trying not to crash into the cameras. It was all very fraught, but a lot of fun, and I was rewarded with a fee of £15. Don't knock it. In those days that was big money!

My first actual TV special in the title role was called *Wit and Wisdom*. It was a 45-minute variety show that went out from 'Ally Pally' at 3.00 p.m. on 18 October 1948, and my guests were Dorothy Squires and Billy Reid, with the resident BBC baton-swinger Eric Robinson and orchestra. We repeated it again two nights later at prime time viewing – 8.30 p.m.. You could probably count the watching viewers in tens rather than thousands, but it certainly set the adrenalin running.

The *Radio Times* billed me: 'New Comedian – his props consist of no more than a comic baggy dress suit, an old shirt and stringy tie, and his clarinet.' That was all I needed. We spent our time avoiding the furniture, and somehow managed to get through without knocking over a camera.

CHAPTER ELEVEN

Now came my first ever pantomime. Norman Crusoe, the character they dreamed up, was an ideal role for me. The long-lost brother of *Robinson Crusoe* took his bow at the Alexandra Theatre, Birmingham, in the 1948-9 Christmas season. The impresario Derek Salberg signed me for four consecutive pantomime seasons, and it would be the start of so many fun costumes in pantos, from the tattered rags of Billy, to the page-boy outfit of Buttons, the ill-fitting togs of Simple Simon in *Jack and the Beanstalk*, to *Aladdin*. But always I kept a spot where I would appear as Norman in a tight suit and cap, to give the people the knockabout routine they expected.

Crusoe was played by Betty Huntley-Wright, and that exuberant twelve-week run introduced me to Eddie Leslie, who was cast as the Dame. We hit it off straight away. Eddie proved to be a natural foil, a man who would go along with my most outrageous ideas. He was built like a bouncer, with a face carved out of granite – and it stayed that way despite all my efforts to 'corpse' him in rehearsals.

For a gag Eddie once took on the undefeated ju-jitsu champion Yukio Tani at the London Palladium – and was thrown about so much that afterwards he claimed to have seen the theatre from more angles than anyone else in show business. Instinctively I knew that something could come of us as a team.

This feeling was encouraged by the review I got in the *Birmingham Mail* after the opening night. 'This quaint and highly original comedian sets his signature on his part, endears it to us and makes it peculiarly his own.' I should have framed it. Eddie waved a copy of the first edition at me as we sat in the bar of our hotel in the early hours and demanded: 'Are you sure you didn't write this yourself?'

The pair of us had already been booked for a repeat the following year at the Grand Theatre, Wolverhampton, this time with Lorna Dean playing Robinson Crusoe. Billy Marsh also found me weekly variety spots at the Swindon Empire, the Bolton Grand, the Dewsbury Empire, the Folkestone Pleasure Gardens, the Clapham Grand and the York Empire. I was getting to see a lot of the country that year.

In 1949 I made my first film. Not too many people remember it, probably because not too many people saw it! There were still six years to go before *Trouble in Store*. The title was *A Date with a Dream,* and it was more important for the career of another rising hopeful named Terry-Thomas, whose unique gap tooth and cigarette holder were giving valiant support to Sid Field in *Piccadilly Hayride.* You'll see me if you're quick – a thirteen-second excerpt of my shadow-boxing in rehearsal for the show, nothing more.

But now came a major blow to my pride. I had been looking for a full-scale West End revue to take me another step up the ladder, and in 1949 I got it. The impresario Cecil Landau put on *Sauce Piquante* at the Cambridge Theatre, with an impressive roll-call including Tommy Cooper, Bob Monkhouse, Douglas Byng, Moira Lister, Peter Glover and the wonderful black singer, Muriel Smith. Alas, it ended up as *Sauce Malaise.*

My own act gave me the lot: I sang, tap-danced, played the clarinet and drums, appeared in sketches, and had three solo spots: The Boxer, the Singing Lesson and Soho

Soliloquy. I was also able to branch out with my impressions, such as a skit on an Italian tourist in London where it rained every day. You can't ask for more than that. The only thing that worried me was that the director John Fernald – later to become the boss of RADA – insisted on decking me out in a fifty-guinea dress suit and patent leathers for a slapstick routine, and wouldn't allow me to go anywhere near my little suit and cap. 'I'm building a class show, Norman,' Fernald said heavily. 'That suit won't work.' And – my mistake – for once I didn't argue.

But despite the massed talent – and the appearance in the chorus line of a young dancer named Audrey Hepburn – the show flopped. There were just too many people trying to do too much.

There was one scene where I was going to dance with Audrey. We practised for hour after hour, whirling round the stage together, then blending into a tap routine and a soft-shoe-shuffle. But poor Audrey just couldn't get the hang of it, and we kept slipping out of time or losing the rhythm. She was a lovely, lissom creature, at least five inches taller than me. Perhaps it was because she had never danced with someone my size before – but it threw her. And in the end the producer said: 'Sorry, you two. We're going to have to drop that number from the show.'

For me, it didn't matter too much. I had plenty left on my plate. But it was Audrey's one chance to shine, to be taken out of the chorus line and dance on her own. A little while later I was passing her dressing-room, and put my head round the door to give her a cheery word. The room was empty apart from a lone figure sitting at the end of a row of stools, staring at herself in the long mirror. Tears were coursing down Audrey's cheeks.

I hurried over, and put my arms round her. We stared at our reflections. 'Oh Norman,' she sobbed. 'I'm sorry.'

'So am I, darling,' I said, gently. 'But I'll tell you

something: you've got what it takes to be a star. I know it. You know it. You've just got to make sure *they* know it. Never lose faith in yourself.'

She gripped my hand tightly. 'You really think so?' The huge gamine eyes searched mine doubtfully. I felt as if I was looking at a doleful Bambi.

'Course I do. I wouldn't say it otherwise. Now – you go out and show 'em!'

The headlines on the day after opening night did the rest. They didn't rave about the show – but they did pick on an unknown girl from the chorus who stood out like a beacon on a dark night, and they wanted to know more about her.

It's nice to be around when a star is born.

I shared a dressing-room with Tommy Cooper – another conjuror who kept me in stitches but never showed me how to do a single trick! That man was unique, and there can never be another like him. It was a laugh a minute from the moment that huge, lugubrious face appeared round the door with its Hallowe'en pumpkin grin to the final curtain. Tommy of course had that inimitable laugh of his that he must have patented – and his timing was perfection. I'm just glad I never had to be his straight man – I would have cracked up in seconds.

The only problem with Tommy was that his feet smelled like rotting fish – something horrible! Their malodorous presence filled the dressing-room, and whenever his size 12 shoes came off, I would swish a newspaper frantically around, and moan: 'Phew – Tommy! Your feet!'

'What's wrong with them?' he'd demand, his six-foot-four bulk towering over me threateningly.

'Cor,' I'd say. 'Didn't anyone ever tell you about Lifebuoy soap?' But I'd been in the Army, so I was able to take it – just. 'At least it'll keep the mosquitoes away,' Tommy rejoined.

We had a dresser called Charlie Fenton. He was even

ABOVE: Meeting the Queen at a Royal Variety Show.

LEFT: 'You little tinker!' said the Queen Mum.

ABOVE: It looks like I'm conducting Noel Coward and Jerry Desmond in a chorus – of *Smoke Gets in Your Eyes*?

BELOW: With Tony Fayne, my marvellous straight man and friend for more than twenty years.

ABOVE: The horrendous *Lessons in Rhythm* machine with 'biffer' and 'bonker', aided and abetted by Tony Fayne, making life a pain for me.

LEFT: I hope I was using a warm spoon: the office party scene from *Trouble in Store* when I inadvertently plop ice-cream down Joan Ingram's cleavage . . . and, being a perfect gentleman, naturally try to scoop it back . . .

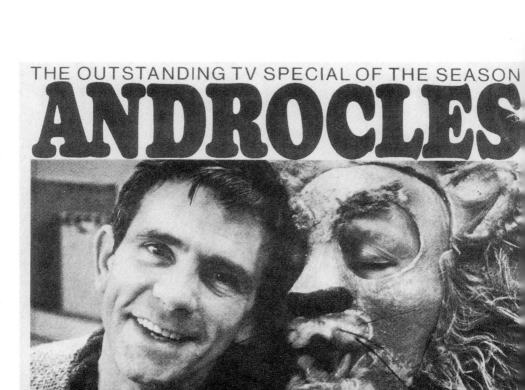

Androcles – one of my proudest moments, but I had to go to America to get it.

That's me *Walking Happy* on Broadway.

Having a laugh with the troops in Red Square.

RIGHT: Me and my chum, Bob Hope.

BELOW: *The Night They Raided Minsky's* – with Jason Robards and Britt Ekland.

My one weakness – cars . . .

. . . Oh – and yachts. This is the *Conquest*, which I designed myself, and that's my son standing with the proud owner at Venice.

At home on the Isle of Man.

On your bike, Norman!

smaller than me, about five feet tall, and in his younger days had trodden the boards himself for a while as a comic. He was a lovely little fellow, but I have to say that we did find him a trifle full of himself. And he just loved compliments.

Tommy knew this too. 'Norman,' he said to me suddenly one day. 'Who does Charlie remind you of?'

Charlie, busily giving one of our costumes a last press, perked up. 'Er – I'm not sure,' I said.

Tommy regarded the diminutive dresser long and hard, then nodded slowly. 'Yes,' he said. 'It's a film star.'

Charlie brightened perceptibly. 'Yes?' he said, eagerly. 'Who?'

Tommy said slowly: 'Well – he's American, he's tremendously good-looking. A little taller than you, and more filled-out. You're the smaller image of a big handsome Hollywood movie star – By now Charlie had forgotten about the ironing and was staring at himself in the mirror with rapt attention.

Tommy shook his head in frustration. 'It's his face,' he said. 'But not all of it. It's the bit from the bridge of his nose and his eyes – *here* – to the top of his head . . .' Charlie turned towards us, positively crying out for the answer.

Tommy took off one huge sweaty sock and wrapped it round Charlie's face so that it covered the little man's nose and mouth like a mask, stretching from ear to ear.

They stood like that for a long minute. Charlie's eyes bulged, his breathing came stentoriously through the sock, and finally he snuffled: *'Whnnnf ift it?'*

'Who is it? That's what I'm trying to figure out,' said Tommy, patiently.

'Sorry I can't help,' I put in. 'I know who you mean, but –'

Eventually Tommy took his sock back. Little Charlie, grey around the gills, looked at him hopefully.

'I'll think of it,' Tommy assured him. 'Don't you worry. It'll come to me.'

Sadly, it never did.

Bob Monkhouse was young, brash and brilliant. All I can say is that I wish I had his brain! He didn't have a solo spot in that show, he just took part in sketches with myself and Dougie Byng.

My favourite was a railway sketch where the three of us were in Army uniform – Bob was a lieutenant, Doug was a colonel and I was a private. We were all going 'home', but the gag was that I turned out to be a lunatic who was going into a home. The laughs grew as I slowly became more and more unhinged, and the whole carriage grew more chaotic by the minute.

Opening night went well enough, but we felt uneasy. We had all done our best, but with some shows you sense that first cold draught of impending doom like a shadow hovering in the wings – and that shadow was there at the Cambridge.

But we put our bravest faces on, and at the final curtain as I lined up with the others to take our bow I suddenly heard a voice shout above the applause: 'Norman Wisdom! Norman Wis-dom!' A woman's voice.

'At least you've got one fan out there, Norm!' Tommy Cooper observed out of the side of his mouth. I grinned as modestly as I could, and waved in the general direction of my vocal supporter.

The voice would not be denied. It grew more insistent. 'Norman Wisdom! Congratulations, Norman *Wisdom!*' it cried.

Finally Cecil Landau himself strode out from the wings. The white-haired impresario singled me out, and led me to the front of the stage. His teeth were noticeably clenched, but it was my moment, not his. I swept a courtly bow to the voice, and the theatre gave me resounding applause.

Backstage after the show the doorkeeper rang through to my dressing-room. 'There's a lady to see you, sir.'

'Send her through,' I said. I couldn't wait to meet my new number one fan.

There was a knock on the door, and it swung open. A woman stood there, smiling proudly. 'Well done, Norman,' said my dear little Mum.

Sauce Piquante went into the waste bin, despite the fact that all the cast took voluntary cuts in a last-ditch effort to save it. I agreed to drop my own salary from £100 a week to £15 – oh, the pain! But nothing could save that show.

Licking my burned fingers I turned back to the bread-and-butter safety of TV, where I was now making a name for myself. *Music Hall* on 8 July 1950, with The Merry Macs and the Music Hall Maids, and another *Wit and Wisdom* the following month, with Sonia Rook and Veronica Martell, were both directed by the go-ahead Richard Afton, a man I was to work with a great deal in the future.

More important, I was getting extraordinary reviews – the kind that would turn my head if I had somewhere else to look. The *Observer* declared: 'Television has discovered a clown so prodigally endowed with talent that he might become another Grock if someone will take him in hand.' Crikey, I thought. That's telling them. Louder, louder . . .

What did I do? *Sauce Piquante* had closed, and with the West End such a hard nut to crack, I cashed in my meagre savings and flew off to New York to try my luck in the States.

I must have been nuts.

I landed in New York, found a cheap room in a cheap hotel off Broadway, and started plodding around the New York agents. With one accord, they gave me a universal reception – the order of the raspberry.

Nursing my sore feet in the hotel bar, my eye caught the TV screen in the corner. A show called *Toast of the Town* was in full swing, packed full of international variety acts hosted by America's top presenter, Ed Sullivan.

I thought: 'Hullo, that looks good. It could be just right for me.'

Next morning I located his agent Mark Leddy, and called him up. 'You don't know me,' I said without mincing matters. 'But I'd like to go on the Ed Sullivan Show.'

There was what I can only call a hiss of indrawn breath. Then his voice rasped: 'Listen, we choose our artists. They don't choose us.' And down went the phone.

I sat on my bed and looked at the receiver in my hand. My money was running out. I had nothing to lose. I found out where Ed Sullivan lived, and took a bus to his apartment at the swish Delmonica Hotel on Park Avenue. It was 11.00 a.m. on a bright morning in Manhattan.

I marched up to the receptionist with a confident swing in my stride, and looked him straight in the eye. 'Mr Sullivan, please,' I said in my most clipped stiff-upper-lip British accent. 'I have an appointment.'

He almost sprang to a salute. 'Yes, *sir!* Ninth floor. Suite 901.'

'Thenk-yoh!'

Suite 901 was at the end of the heavily carpeted corridor. My heartbeat made more noise than my feet as I approached it, but I was going to go through with it, whatever the consequences. I rang the bell. A manservant in black coat and pinstripe trousers answered. 'Sir?'

'I have an appointment with Mr Sullivan,' I lied. 'Mr Norman Wisdom, from England.'

'This way, sir.' He led me into the hallway, which was about eight feet square, with a couple of chairs in it and a snow scene from the Rockies on the wall, and vanished. After five minutes a large burly man suddenly appeared through the double doors, wearing a silk dressing-gown over silk pyjamas. Ed Sullivan. His normally amiable expression was furrowed with a frown.

He said: 'Excuse me, I don't think –'

'I'm sorry, Mr Sullivan' I said. 'You're right. I've gate-crashed your apartment. I'd like to be on your show.'

He regarded me for a long moment. Then he said: 'What do you do?'

'I'm an English comedian. I saw your show and I'd just like a chance –' I blurted out.

Ed Sullivan lowered his bulk carefully into one of the chairs, sat back and said: 'Show me!'

And in that tiny hall I went through my routine. I told jokes, I did some eccentric dance steps, fell on his carpet, sang. 'And when I tell them . . . how wonderful you are . . .' The sounds and thuds reverberated through the apartment.

Ed Sullivan let me go on for about four minutes. Then he raised a hand. 'I'm sorry,' he said. 'I don't use that sort of thing on my show.' He paused, then added: 'But I want you to know that I admire your initiative.'

I shook his hand and said: 'And I want you to know that I appreciate your courtesy. You're a gentleman.'

On my way back to my hotel from the Ed Sullivan fiasco, I passed a large bar on 45th Street called the Floral Hall. I was keyed up, the adrenalin was still flowing, and the bar inside was crowded with lunch-time patrons and seemed a friendly sort of place. The people looked smart and glitzy. The room was at least sixty feet long, with counters running down two sides of the room creating a huge space in the middle. There must have been 150 people packed around the bars drinking beer and martinis, and the hubbub could be heard through the windows and into the street.

I eyed the space in the middle, and thought: why not? Nothing else has worked. There must be *somebody* here who's in show business. What have I got to lose? If this doesn't work – finish! My money had almost run out, and all I had was my return air ticket home.

I pushed through the door, and edged my way in through the throng of noisy New Yorkers to the centre of the floor. I took off my overcoat and hung it over a chair. Then, without preamble, I went straight into my act. I tap-danced and sang and shadow-boxed with an imaginary opponent. I even told a joke. 'There was this bloke who had a dog with no legs. He used to call it Cigarette – because at night he'd take it out for a drag! What about that, then?'

Nobody took a blind bit of notice!

The barman went on polishing the counter and serving up beers. The figures hunched at the bar briefly turned my way, stared briefly, and then turned back again, shrugging at the obvious nutter in their midst.

New York is like that. Finally I gave up, left the bar and took the first plane home.

At least I had something in the pipeline to welcome me back – Derek Salberg's pantomime, *Cinderella,* at the Alexandra, Birmingham, with me as Buttons – who else? – and a lovely bubbly blonde named Betty Leslie-Smith as Cinders. Freda and I were still ensconced in our caravan, now parked in its site off the Barnet bypass.

That most gentlemanly of producers, Henry Hall, came to see me backstage, and invited me to join his summer show at the Grand Theatre, Blackpool, called *Buttons and Bows.* 'Donald Peers is top of the bill,' he said. 'You'll finish the first half. How do you feel about that?'

Wonderful! I was thrilled at the idea. It would be my first taste of the legendary seaside town where every major performer had played. Then a thought struck me. 'But he's a singer. Surely there's a risk he won't want me to sing as well?'

Henry's eyes twinkled reassuringly through the famous spectacles. 'Don't worry. I assure you that you will be able to sing,' he said.

It turned out just as I feared. My spot before the interval was second only to the star himself. By now I was actually rather proud of my voice. I was no Caruso, but I enjoyed it, and I usually got the applause I wanted after a soulful number like 'They Didn't Believe Me' – the one I'd warbled for Ed Sullivan.

Donald Peers didn't like the sound of that applause at all. After the first night he came to my dressing-room and said: 'Cut out the singing!' As brusquely as that.

I protested: 'But I'm doing well with it. I like it. Why should I?'

'Because I'm the singer,' he said. 'You're here to make them laugh.'

I stood my ground – and next day he went to Henry Hall. 'I want Norman Wisdom to stop singing. Or I quit.'

This put Henry in a dilemma. He was a pleasant, quiet-voiced man who hated trouble and backstage bickering. He called me into his office. 'I just wish this wasn't happening, Norman. But I'm keeping my word.'

I went on singing – and two weeks later Donald Peers left the show. The official reason on the publicity handout that went to the Press Association and thence to every major newspaper in the country was a 'recurring bad throat' that needed immediate and prolonged rest. I often wondered about that. But in came a breath of fresh air and the fastest ukelele in the land in the shape of George Formby to keep our fingers tapping and the show swinging.

It was here that the word Gump came into being. I didn't invent it. I knew it meant 'fool'. Also it had a connection with 'gumption', which means 'resource' – and let's face it, even Norm at his worst had that going for him. Actually I owe the Gump to a stage hand behind the scenes at Blackpool called Pete.

I came out of my dressing-room in my check outfit, and Pete called: 'Hey, Norm, I like the Gump suit.' Somehow it stuck, even though the odd thing is that I have never been introduced from the stage by that nickname or heard it mentioned in a film.

So – thanks a lot, Pete!

Chapter Twelve

Christmas 1950, and I was playing Buttons at Birmingham. In the interval one evening there was a knock at my dressing-room door – and there stood my old friend Henry Hall. He introduced the man with him: Claude Langdon, one of the country's top impresarios.

Langdon didn't waste words. 'I think you're very visual, and very good,' he said. 'We'd like you to consider doing our summer ice show *London Melody* at the Empress Hall. Big spectacular. What do you think?'

'Sounds fine to me,' I said enthusiastically.

'We'll see you in six weeks then,' said Henry. As they turned to leave he added: 'Oh by the way – er, can you skate?'

I allowed my jaw to drop in a show of surprise and indignation. 'Can I skate?' I repeated. 'Of course I can!'

'Oh, good,' said Henry, meekly, leading the way out. 'Just checking.'

Well, of course, I'd never been on skates in my life. But every morning from that day to the end of the panto I went off to the local ice rink, hired myself out a set of skates, and tottered and fell around the ring for hour after solitary hour. I learned a couple of painful lessons: one, ice is as hard as concrete. While I could fall on wood without hurting myself, concrete was a different matter. Two, I bruised as easily as the next man.

Finally, black and blue but determined not to be beaten, I got the hang of it. I even bought myself a pair of skates. Why didn't I hire a tutor? It just wasn't my way: somehow I felt it would have taken months to learn under a critical eye, and I'd always taught myself everything I knew, anyway.

By the time my six-week deadline was up, I was as ready as I'd ever be. We arranged my 'audition', and I duly presented myself at the Empress Hall, my gleaming new skates tucked under my arm, and found Henry Hall and Claude Langdon waiting for me in the massive, empty amphitheatre. The Empress Hall always reminded me of a huge aircraft hangar, big enough to house half a dozen Jumbo airliners. It had a roof of curved cylindrical glass, and towered up out of the maze of small terraced houses in Fulham like a concrete mountain. But it attracted the big shows, and made its name as an ice palace.

Henry and Claude sat in the front row, huddled in overcoats and scarves, two lone figures amid row upon row of empty seats. 'Ah, Norman,' Henry greeted me. 'We know you can do the funny stuff, so don't bother about any of that. But do you think we could just see you skate?'

'Of course,' I said airily, tying my laces with a flourish on the seat beside them. 'Mind you, I might be a bit rusty. But I'll soon pick it up again.' And off I went, head high, a beaming grin of joy and confidence stitched to my features as I circled that huge arena. I even managed a couple of spins without toppling backside over elbow.

At the end I skated up to them, leaned an elbow casually on the safety barrier, and said: 'Blimey, it's amazing how you forget it! But we've got a couple of weeks to practise, haven't we?'

They both chorused: 'No, Norman, that was fine!' And Henry added: 'We'll see you at rehearsals.'

Falling on ice is an art in itself. Unlike wood, you can slide, and it's as easy as pie to fall without actually hurting yourself

once you know how. The faster you're going, the easier it is
to fall without too much of a thwack. But if ever I bruised
myself, I'd just think of the money and I was alright.

The star of the show was Belita, a beautiful ice-skating
actress with close-cropped chestnut hair and a smile that
would blind you right across the arena. She had made a
small name for herself in Hollywood, but her real love was
the live ice-stage.

A huge cast had been assembled for this elaborate folk-
tale of high passions in the high Alps, mostly set in various
hotels with characters like Brita Hales as Gisela and Markby
Ryan as Napoleon skating on the thin ice of romance
weaved around an even thinner plot. I played a Cockney
waiter – somehow given the name of Angelo – and for me
the high spot was being able to sing, with the marvellous
backing of the Empress Hall Orchestra conducted by Harry
Rabinowitz, one of my own compositions, 'Beware', which
later became a modest hit.

That show was tinged with drama from the outset.
During the first week we were rehearsing an important
sequence where a man in a gorilla suit chased me through
the arena, starting on the ice and taking off up the aisles and
into the audience, even running along the rows of seats.
That would get them squealing!

The idea was that the gorilla would appear from the roof,
hurtling down on a rope from the iron girders to land on the
ice and go after me. The actor they gave the job to was a big
fellow, over six feet, and not a young man either. He had to
clamber out above the ice along a steel girder, grab the rope,
and shin down it.

But something went terribly wrong. We saw him grab at
the rope – miss it, and plunge 150 feet to the ice in front of
us. He was killed instantly.

The shock waves went right through the cast. Chorus girls
broke down in tears. The ice was cleared and rehearsals

suspended for the day. Thinking of that crumpled figure in its gorilla suit lying sprawled on the ice twenty feet from me still makes me feel queasy today.

They kept the sequence in, but found a younger, fitter man – and had him coming in through curtains at the side. I used to enjoy that part of the show most, running through the audience. I'd stop and chat and shake hands, and quite often some of the women wanted to kiss me.

My skating improved by the hour! The saving factor, of course, was that every time I fell over they all thought it was part of the act and just laughed. Eventually I was confident enough to try turns in mid-air.

Princess Margaret came to see the show one night, and sat in the front row in the VIP box with the red plush seats. I attempted a particularly daring mid-air twist – and fell flat on my back right in front of her. The whole party were doubled up. As I struggled to my feet I looked straight at her and said ruefully: 'I didn't mean that one!' The entire arena of ten thousand people picked it up from my lapel microphone, and the place convulsed.

Afterwards I met her at a small reception backstage, and she held out her hand, smiled broadly and said: 'It's a wonder you're not black and blue all over.'

'Actually ma'am,' I responded, 'I am. I'm just a glutton for punishment.'

'I think you must be,' she said. 'I'm surprised you look so happy.'

Opening night was one I will never forget. For a start the word went round: Gracie Fields was in the audience. She was in a box directly across from the stage, with Henry Hall on one side of her and Claude Langdon on the other. Every seat in the ten thousand-strong auditorium was taken.

It was obvious we had a monumental hit on our hands. The place was buzzing from the word go, and it was the kind of extravaganza for the whole family that would have people flocking in from all over the country. In the end that show ran for nearly three months, and was seen by more than a million people.

On opening night the applause at the end nearly lifted the roof, and we were one big smiling group, eighty-strong, as we gathered on the platform to take our bow. Or almost one smiling group.

I was aware that Belita seemed a little resentful that I was getting such good applause. Here was a beautiful girl, and a wonderful skater, but she was making it obvious to us that she was the star of the show.

On that opening night I was relishing the applause. I knew we'd earned it, and I could count the bruises to prove it. But in the finale, as we jostled on the stage to be introduced and take our individual bows, Belita had somehow lined up the cast in front of me so that I was well and truly hidden. She then stepped forward with that dazzling smile to drink in the applause.

Henry Hall came to the stage and took the mike for a speech of thanks. He finished: 'May I give a special welcome to our guest of honour tonight, Miss Gracie Fields!'

People were shouting her name, 'Sing us a song, Gracie,' and she rose and carefully made her way across the ice to the stage. Henry thought she might sing, and handed her the microphone. Instead she cleared a path through the cast – until she reached me. She took me by the hand and led me to the front, kissed me on the cheek, and said into the mike: 'In a couple of years this lad is going t'be the biggest comedian in Britain!'

She started to make her way back, and held out her hand to me. Henry Hall jerked a thumb. I scurried down and walked that lovely lady back across the ice to her seat. 'That was really kind of you,' I said.

'Don't worry,' she said. 'I'm an old professional, remember? I saw what was going on . . .

The sequel came the next night.

Towards the end of the run, Billy Marsh called me at the theatre one morning while I was practising on the ice. 'Lew Grade wants to see you. Get over right away!' I dashed over to Lew's sumptuous offices in Mayfair wondering what all the excitement was about, to find Lew shrouded as usual in a haze of cigar smoke behind his desk.

He said: 'I saw your show last night Norman, and it was great. More important, I had a friend of mine with me from America and he thought it was great too. He wants you on his show.'

I said: 'Oh, marvellous!'

Lew said: 'He's a gentleman called Ed Sullivan, and he wants you for one night only. What do you say?'

'Fine,' I said. 'Just tell Ed it will cost him £2,000 for one show.'

'*What!*' Lew nearly bit through his cigar. 'Two thousand pounds! You must be mad.'

'I'm sorry, Lew,' I said, firmly. 'It's either that or not at all.'

'I'll phone him,' said Lew. He put the call through straight away to Ed's hotel, sucking on the cigar between sentences. When he mentioned the figure there was a long silence. Then the glow on the cigar brightened, and he put the phone down and beamed at me. 'You've got it,' he said.

The £2,000 came through, and I used it for expenses – and an air ticket for Billy Marsh, which is why I'd asked for it all along. The only drawback was that Billy hated flying: he was always as stiff as a board from take-off to the moment the wheels touch down. I'm afraid on that flight I wound him up a bit from the moment we took off – the plane juddered, as often happens, and he squeaked: 'What's that?'

'That's nothing,' I said, grimly. 'Just wait till we get out over the Atlantic.'

Billy reached for the first of many miniature Drambuies,

and knocked it back in a gulp. I poured a few more Drambuies into him, and hoped the night flight would pass without incident.

We must have been half-way across the Atlantic when I looked out of the left-hand window and noticed flames pouring from the port engine. Most of the passengers were asleep, including Billy who was snoring happily in the seat beside me. I was going over my script for the show. I had seen a spot of activity up front on the flight deck, with the steward and one of the officers actually running down the centre aisle.

But seeing the engine on fire I felt it might be time to draw someone's attention to it. I gestured at one of the stewardesses as she hurried past. 'Er – excuse me,' I began, and waved a thumb at the window.

The girl simply nodded, and put a finger to her lips to shush me. I said: 'But you can't keep a thing like that a secret, surely?'

She hurried off. Minutes later the plane banked steeply to starboard, and the Captain made an announcement. *Emergency landing in Reykjavik!* As the plane nosed down through the clouds towards Iceland we were instructed to bend forward with our faces buried in pillows on our laps.

Billy was by now wide awake, extremely sober, and with a face fraught with disbelief and terror. He buried his face in his pillow, and I heard muffled moans issuing from his lap. As we came in, I saw below us a fleet of waiting fire engines and ambulances roar into life, racing down the runway alongside us in a blaze of headlights. Our wheels scraped the tarmac, and the plane lurched to a stop. Hosepipes sent plumes of water bouncing off the wing – thank heaven, they put the fire out in minutes, and we didn't even have to use the emergency exits. But we were stuck in the terminal for seventeen boring hours until another plane arrived to rescue us and take us on to New York.

The show was on a Sunday night, beamed live across

America. I gave it all I'd got.

I was in my misfit evening suit, and I downed around, tap-danced, did my falls, and finished with my one-man band routine. That's the one with a washboard, a cymbal on each knee, a loofah under my arm – *Honk-honk!* – a raspberry blower, and a leather strap with little bells strapped round my head, and more bells strapped to my ankles. The audience loved it.

A delighted Ed chatted with me afterwards. 'Great show, Norman, great show.' It was obvious he had no recollection of our meeting six months ago.

I was just putting my jacket on. 'You don't remember me, do you?' I said, smiling.

'Er –' Ed's brow furrowed.

I said: 'I'm the bloke who came to your flat and did an audition in your hall – and you told me you didn't have that sort of thing on your show.'

Ed stared at me. I watched recognition dawning on his face. Finally he managed: 'Jesus Christ! So it is.' And he enveloped me in a massive bear hug. I would do another show for him some years later when I was on the 'chat circuit', appearing twice with Johnny Carson, and with other TV hosts. But Ed never forgot that first meeting in his apartment.

Back at the hotel that night, tired but triumphant, I found a message waiting for me. Paramount Pictures. Would we go to their offices at 11.00 a.m. next morning to discuss a screen test? Would we! Not 'arf!!

At five minutes to eleven we presented ourselves at the reception desk nine floors above the cacophony of Park Avenue. The only sound in the carpeted interior was the receptionist filing her nails behind the potted plants. She said: 'Please be seated, gentlemen,' and gestured us to well-sprung sofas by the water fountain.

At 11.15 a.m., Billy said: 'Right, that's it. Let's go!'

'Go?' I said. 'Are you crazy?'

'No,' he said. 'They've got to think we're important. They're not going to keep us hanging about like this. Trust me!'

We went down the elevator and out into the street and flagged down a Yellow Cab. Inside it Billy said: 'I'll lay a bet with you. By the time we get back to our hotel there'll be a message waiting for us. And they'll want us back.'

Sure enough, there was the note in my pigeon hole. Billy got on the phone, and I heard him say: 'No, we can't. We're too busy.' It was Monday, and the week yawned emptily ahead of us.

'When? Let me see –'He rustled a newspaper down the phone. 'Um . . . how about Thursday?'

It meant we had to kick our heels in New York for two days with nothing to do. I took Billy to the Floral Hall and showed him where I had sung and danced my heart out only a few months ago. 'Not any more,' he said with a tight smile. That day I bought him a beer in the bar, and we drank to better times ahead.

On Thursday we were back at Paramount at five to eleven. Same potted plants, same girl, same fingernails. At eleven on the dot a smiling secretary emerged from one of the many doors, and ushered us into the boardroom. Inside three men in dark suits and crew cuts sat at the long oval table. One said: 'We saw you on the Sullivan show. We'd like you to go to Hollywood and do a film test for us. We feel Mr Wisdom has the makings of a star.'

'Sounds good,' Billy agreed.

'You'll stay in the Beverly Wilshire Hotel,' one of the executives said. 'It's nice. And we'll get the air tickets sorted out for you.'

Immediately Billy held up a hand. 'If it's all the same to you, gentlemen, we'd rather travel by train,' he said. 'Wouldn't we, Norman?'

Anything for my friend. 'I'd like to see a bit of the country,' I nodded. 'I've always wanted to go through the Rockies.'

No problem. They booked us on one of the great overnight sleepers, with a first-class cabin to ourselves, an observation car and a marvellous restaurant. As we slid out of Grand Central Station, Billy sat back, put his feet up, and visibly relaxed. He opened up a paper, allowed himself a smile of contentment, and said: 'Now this is what I call travelling. It's the only way.'

Half an hour later he looked out of the window – and his face changed. 'Good God! What on earth's that?'

I followed his gaze. And there, strewn across the far tracks and up the banking, was the wreckage of what had obviously been the most horrendous train crash. Cranes with lifting gear were laboriously shifting broken carriages. Men in helmets were standing around in small groups. It must have happened quite recently.

Billy paled. I rang the bell for service. A beaming black face appeared around the door. 'Steward,' I said. 'A large Drambuie. And make it quick!'

Our hopes for a scenic run through the high spot of the trip – the Rockies – were thwarted because we went through at night, and didn't even see a rock! But as the arid red wastes of the Nevada Desert gave way to the first palm trees of outer Los Angeles, my spirits rose. I was about to walk out into the sunshine of the very cradle of movie-making. The great express steamed into Union Station after breakfast, and I found myself staring open-mouthed at what has to be one of the great stations of the world, with its huge vaulted ceiling, echoing tile floors and shining mahogany benches that spoke of another, elegant era, of the Great Gatsby, or William Randolph Hearst.

A huge Cadillac was waiting for us, and a uniformed chauffeur to help us with our luggage. The drive along

Wilshire Boulevard took us through the Downtown area
and on through Hollywood itself to the imposing bulk of the
Beverly Wilshire Hotel, run by the ebullient Mexican-born
Hernando Courtright, one of the legendary hoteliers of his
time. Every film star worth their salt has stayed at the
Wilshire, and Warren Beatty even kept his personal suite,
No. 1000, unlisted in the lifts, as a permanent base for many
years.

I was like a schoolboy with a new toy, scurrying around
the huge suite they had given us with its leather Mexican
furniture, chairs like saddles, opulent drapes. The fridge
was stocked full.

But Billy was frowning. His nostrils were twitching,
always a bad sign. 'There's something wrong,' he said. 'I
don't know what it is. But I just feel there's some sort of
nonsense going on here.'

I couldn't see it myself, but I've always trusted Billy's
instincts. 'What shall we do?' I asked.

'Nothing,' he said. 'Just wait.' At that moment there was
a knock on the door, and a bellboy stood there with a
message: *A car will pick you up at 11.00 a.m. tomorrow to take
you to Paramount Studios. Meantime, please enjoy yourselves.*
Americans are always terribly polite.

Billy read it twice. 'Right,' he said. 'We've got the day to
ourselves. Let's make the most of it. At least we can tell
them back home what you're up to . . .

So far, not a lot. But we took a cab and set off downtown
on Billy's mission. In the no man's land of mean streets
between Sunset Strip and Vine Street he found what he
wanted – a photographer's studio, not much bigger than a
postage stamp.

Billy marched in, pulling me after him, and leaned
conspiratorially on the counter. 'I want a big, tall, busty
model,' he muttered. 'The biggest, tallest, bustiest girl
you've got.'

The sallow youth behind the counter smirked knowingly, and winked back at him. Consider it done, fellas. Leave it to me.'

'Let's see the options,' Billy demanded.

The photographer produced a dog-eared album filled with fading beauties who looked as if they had seen better days. We pored over it. In among the dross were a few violets. Billy made a choice: 'That one.'

It took one phone call, and an hour later I was staring up at the voluptuous acreage of a girl who seemed to go on for ever. Her name was Veronica, and her figure was like an egg-timer with all the sand in the top. But she had a sense of humour, and happily went along with Billy's idea.

She changed into a bikini, and posed nonchalantly beside me with one elbow resting on my head – and she wasn't even leaning over. That's how tall she was. It looked like a glamour session taken in a major Hollywood studio. Billy got the pictures processed in a hurry and raced round to the Associated Press offices in the city. They were on the wire that evening, with the caption: 'NORMAN WISDOM SAYS EVERYTHING'S BIG IN HOLLYWOOD'. Next day every popular newspaper in Britain ran it.

At 9.00 a.m. the big wrought-iron gates of Paramount Studios swung open. The guard put a face through the window, gave me a nod of total non-recognition, ticked off our names on a list and gestured us through.

I looked around at the pink walls of the buildings and the towering sets of one of the true Hollywood landmarks, unable to suppress a shiver of anticipation. The thought of the names who had passed through these portals was enough to make me blink. I thrust away Billy's doubts, and prepared myself to meet the Vice-President who would set up the screen test that could be my first step on the film ladder.

We were ushered into the office of a man called John

Littlejohn. He was a craggy six-footer with slicked-down black hair, an expensive suit, and a loud tie. He rose from behind the biggest desk I'd ever seen, shook our hands and gestured for us to sit in two seats at opposite corners of the desk.

Then he turned and gave Billy Marsh a piercing gaze, and said without preamble: 'We think you're a very funny man.'

Billy's eyes glazed behind their glasses. The vice-president turned to me. I said quickly: 'I have to tell you that my artist is going to be very expensive.'

Billy saved the situation from deteriorating further by quickly explaining who was who. To his credit, Mr Littlejohn was overcome with embarrassment.

'Oh gee, fellas. I'm so sorry. I don't know what to say. You're not offended, are you?'

'Oh no,' I said reassuringly. 'No, no' – 'If we did ask you to do a movie, you wouldn't refuse, would you?' he pursued.

'Oh no,' I said eagerly. 'No . . . no . . . no!' Billy was later to use this No-no-no as a publicity press item.

The film they wanted to discuss was a project tentatively entitled *Pleasure Island* – and tentative was the operative word. It became immediately obvious that the most I could hope for was virtually no more than a walk-on. We didn't even bother with the test.

In the car on the way back to the hotel Billy said: 'I told you it was a load of nonsense. But let's make something out of it while we've got the chance.' He smiled quietly. 'I've got another idea.' And he got busy with the cables to Fleet Street.

We were due to fly home the next evening, and I made the most of the intervening hours.

My all-time idol had to be Charlie Chaplin. To be compared to him, as I was later on in my career, was the most incredible compliment. But there was only one Chaplin. Although our pathos touched similar chords and our knockabout comedy touched similar funny-bones, his genius was his own.

I felt I could not go through Hollywood without at least making an attempt to meet him. Chaplin was filming *Limelight* at his own Fillmore Studios in downtown Hollywood.

'Wouldn't it be smashing if we could get to him?' I said over breakfast on our last day.

Billy was doubtful. He made a number of calls, and his face lengthened even more. 'It's no good. He's just not seeing anybody. It's a closed set, and nobody can get to him.'

Well, I thought, there's nothing like the direct approach. I called up the studio. 'I'd like to speak to Mr Chaplin, please.'

'Who is it calling?' said an impersonal voice.

'It's Norman Wisdom, a British comic. I'm over here from England, and I would like to speak to Mr Chaplin.'

Next thing, there was a click. And Chaplin's high-pitched, rather nasal voice said: 'Hullo, Charles Chaplin speaking.'

I nearly dropped the phone. 'This is Norman Wisdom, Mr Chaplin. I – er, I – I really would like to meet you. I –'

He interrupted: 'You may be surprised to know, Mr Wisdom, that I have heard of you. Why don't you drop by this afternoon?'

'Cor,' I said. 'I'll be there.'

We took a fast cab to Fillmore Studios, which unlike other studios which trumpeted their very existence was approached by a quiet road away from the bustle of Sunset Boulevard, with a small timbered bungalow at the entrance. There were no receptionists, luxury sofas or potted plants, and a Mr Crocker, an assistant who came to escort us, was at pains to point out: 'Don't expect anything fancy. It's amazing that he's seeing you. In the past six weeks he has only had one visitor – a Chinese schoolmaster who brought some little Chinese boys to California to learn the American way of life!'

But Billy and I finally met the great man with old boots and cane. We were shown to two canvas chairs where we could watch him direct Claire Bloom in a scene with meticulous attention to every detail. He spent ten minutes showing another actor how to put a pair of gloves down on a chair.

Afterwards he joined us, and over the next ninety minutes, between interruptions from various assistants, I was able to have a long chat with this living legend. Chaplin, affable and loquacious, was anxious to hear all the gossip from home. This was the last film he would ever make in America, before he was black-listed in the McCarthy witch-hunt for 'Reds under the beds' and retreated to his home in Switzerland.

After an hour, I plucked up my courage and said: 'Do you think I could see you doing your walk for me?'

He looked at me with those brilliant blue eyes, and chuckled. 'Only if you do *your* walk for me, Mr Wisdom!'

Nothing loth, I sprang to my feet. And side by side we marched up and down the set, Chaplin twirling his cane, me doing my jerky urchin's stride that I still use as an introduction to my act today. At the end, as the technicians gave us a spontaneous round of applause, Chaplin murmured in my ear: 'Young man, one day you will be following in my footsteps!'

I never told anyone, not even Billy Marsh, what Chaplin said that day. But I walked on air when we left – and it was all of five years later that I read the following words in an interview Chaplin gave:

'Norman Wisdom is the comedian who will follow in my footsteps.' I still treasure that cutting as if it were gold-dust. Well, it is – isn't it?

Next step: back to Paramount and the set of *Road to Bali*,

the sixth in the hilarious *Road* romps with Bing Crosby, Bob Hope and Dorothy Lamour. Bing was fast asleep in his deck chair, and our guide understandably baulked at prodding him awake to introduce me. I believe that would be classed as a firing offence. Bob Hope was with eight people standing around him in a semi-circle. They turned out to be his scriptwriters. Our guide poked a tentative head through the wall of flesh. 'Mr Hope, I'd like you to meet an English comic from Great Britain –' Without pause Hope turned, stuck out a hand, said 'Hi!' and turned away again.

Ten years later the pair of them did the last *Road* movie, entitled *Road to Hong Kong,* at Shepperton Studios at the same time that I was filming *The Girl on the Boat,* from the P. G. Wodehouse novel. On this occasion they came to see *me.* I said: 'Last time we almost met, you were having a kip, Bing, and you, Bob, were busy with a mob of scriptwriters. You don't remember me, do you?'

They looked at one another. Bing gave his wry shrug. Bob raised an eyebrow. Then they both said: 'Right you are. We don't. But we will do. Come and have a drink,' and we headed off for the bar laughing our heads off. Oh, they were a prize pair of gagsters!

We flew home that night, with Billy stocked up on Drambuies. When we landed at London Airport next morning I was astonished to be surrounded by a score of newsmen and photographers, clamouring for stories of my Hollywood adventures. Flash bulbs popped. Microphones were thrust at me. Billy pushed a newspaper into my hand. 'Here, you'd better read this,' he shouted above the hubbub.

And there in inch-high headlines above my picture was the story: 'NORMAN WISDOM SAYS NO, NO, NO TO FILM IN HOLLYWOOD!' Clever Billy had done it again.

Clever? Naughty? A bit of both, perhaps. All I know is that it made me look like a British star who was being feted and chased by the moguls of Hollywood – and the publicity was so enormous that it persuaded Bernard Delfont to sign me next day for what was to be one of my most successful shows.

I had checked into a hotel in Kensington to relax for a couple of days before heading back to my caravan. I was lying back on the settee with my feet up reading Billy's audacious story and chuckling at his cheek, when I heard the crash of a phone being slammed back in the next room. Billy appeared in the doorway, his pale face unusually flushed. He banged a fist on the frame. 'Norman, we've done it!' he shouted. 'We've *done* it!'

'Done what?' I asked in bewilderment.

'Bernard Delfont wants you to star in his new revue at the Prince of Wales – all because of the publicity you've got. Top of the bill. It's going to be a winner, the biggest thing you've ever done.'

If Billy got excited, which wasn't often, then I could afford to get excited too. *Paris to Piccadilly* was due to open in April, and would mark a milestone as my first ever West End solo star billing. I had Eddie Leslie as my straight man, and back-up acts like Bobby Tranter, Mini Gerrard, and Medlock and Marlowe leading up to my own spot, which lasted almost an hour.

First there was a panto stint at the Grand Theatre, Wolverhampton – I was Buttons again in *Cinderella*, with Ruthene Le Clerc as Prince Charming and Jean Inglis as a Cinders with a lovely lilting Scots accent.

But in those eight weeks I found it impossible to keep my mind off what lay ahead. This was my big chance. I had to make it work.

Before the curtain even went up, that show hit a crisis. The director was the experienced Dick Hurran, a small-boned, wiry veteran of countless shows who knew just what he wanted. The trouble was, so did I.

The day before we were due to open he called us together

for a full rehearsal. We spent the day going through the band call. The chorus girls did their bit, so did the speciality acts. Then it came to me. Dickie was in the stalls. I had thirty minutes to myself, and I started off with the piano lid trapping my fingers, then the shadow-boxing, then a few falls. Then I picked up the clarinet.

I heard a voice from the stalls. 'Whoa! Whoa! Whoa!' Dickie's voice. 'What's this?'

I said: 'I'm playing the clarinet. It's part of my act.'

'Oh no you're not,' he called up. 'We've got twenty-two musicians. We don't need another one. Stick to the comedy, Norman.'

I put the clarinet back, went on with a spot of comedy, and turned to my tenor-sax. Again came that voice: 'Whoa! Whoa! Whoa! What do you want that bloody sax for?'

'My act,' I said. 'It's important.'

'Look, we've got two altos, a tenor and a base saxophone. We don't need another one.'

I was feeling pretty upset by now, but I went with it, and laid my sax back in its rest. Finally I reached the climax of my act, where I break into song: . . . . And when I told them, how wonderful you are they didn't believe me.'

'Whoa! Whoa! Whoa! We don't need singing–'

'But I finish my act on it,' I protested.

'We've got professional singers in the show,' he said. 'Just give us the laughs.'

There was a long silence. The band stared at their instruments. I stared at the director. Finally I said: 'Dickie, I'm going for a cup of tea. When I come back I'm singing in my act, I'm playing the saxophone and I'm playing the clarinet. If you don't want it, then I've signed the wrong contract – and I'm out!'

As I walked out of the Stage Door, Eddie Leslie caught me up and slipped a hand under my arm. 'I'm coming with you, Norman,' he said. 'I could do with a cuppa.'

We sat in a nearby cafe in silence. At last I said: 'I know I'm right, Les.'

'So do I,' he said. 'You stick to your guns.'

We went back – and there in the stalls was Bernard Delfont. The director had summoned him to deal with the situation.

'Norman,' Delfont began, patiently, 'you've got to listen to what the director says.'

'I know,' I said. 'I have great admiration for him, but he's wrong about my act. It just won't be anywhere near as strong as it should be if I played it his way.'

'Just do what he says,' Delfont ordered.

'I'm sorry,' I said. 'You've got the wrong bloke. You'll have to leave me out.'

That's when they picked up the hot line, and summoned Val Parnell. The band were sent away for a half-hour break, and looked quite glad to get away from the tension.

Parnell strode down the centre aisle and thrust himself into a seat. He crooked a large finger at me. 'Norman, come down here will you please?'

When I was sitting with him he said: 'Listen, we know what we're doing. We've got to balance the show.'

'I know what I'm doing too, sir,' I told him. 'And the fact is there's not enough left for me to give a class act if you take the singing and music away.'

They went into a huddle at the end of the row. Then Parnell came back. 'All right, Norman,' he said, heavily. 'We're opening tomorrow. Do it our way – and then the next night you can do it your way. If it works, we'll keep it in for the whole run. If it doesn't, it's out. Is that fair enough?'

I said: 'I think I've got a better idea.'

Parnell stared at me. 'Jesus Christ!' he exploded. 'How can we get through to you?'

'I'll tell you what,' I conceded. 'I'll be fair. I'll do it my way on opening night, and if it doesn't work I'll do it your way for the whole run. How about that?'

'Bloody hell,' said Parnell. 'All right. Just get on with it.'

The show opened on 12 April 1952. All I can say is that I got a standing ovation – and as I came off after my third curtain call, soaked with sweat, Dickie Hurran was there in the wings with a towel. He wiped the perspiration from my face, gave me a kiss on the cheek, and said: 'Get back out there. They want you!' And he pushed me back.

No-one ever mentioned it again, and I kept the instruments and the singing through the next seventeen months as the show went on to become one of the West End's legendary hits.

The *Daily Telegraph* reported: 'As a spectacle it eclipses all the previous Folies Bergere shows seen in London,' adding: 'Wisdom's well arranged musical turn really captures the house.' Which was what all the fuss was about in the first place . . . I'm just glad I stuck to my guns.

In fact the confrontation was done calmly, without raised voices or a hysterical slanging match. That was something I never needed. Our profession is full of people who scream and yell to get their way, but in my whole career I can honestly say I never shouted at anybody in anger. I've had numerous creative conflicts, certainly, where I wanted to do things my way and others didn't. Always these were resolved somehow, even if one of us had to bite the bullet and give way.

Another of my idols as I grew up was the great Sid Field. He had been a virtual resident at the Prince of Wales, including one stint when he was there for four years on the trot. I had seen him in my Army days, watching him in uniform from a seat up in the gods that cost me ninepence.

Ironically, Sid's straight man was Jerry Desmonde, who would later join me as both stooge and friend. Who can ever forget the classic golf lesson sketch, 'Address the ball', and all the lunacy that followed?

Jerry: *Skip it! What are you jumping over the ball for?*
Sid: *Well, you said 'Skip it!'*
Jerry: *No, no. Get behind the ball.*
Sid: *But it's behind the ball all round. What a performance!*
Jerry: *Come on, square up to that ball.* (Sid starts to box). *No. Not like that, silly. Keep your eye on the ball.* (Sid kneels down and does so.) *Get up! Address the ball.*
Sid: *Dear ball –*

They don't write 'em like that any more.

Sid died in the spring of 1950. And now here I was in his dressing-room! Thirty minutes before the curtain was due to go up on that opening night, there was a knock at the door and a messenger handed in a telegram.

I opened it – and my hands started shaking. It read: 'IF ANYONE CAN TAKE HIS PLACE WE THINK IT'S YOU. EVERY SUCCESS. SID FIELD FAMILY.'

I couldn't help it – but all at once I found my eyes streaming with tears. I had to shut the door and lock myself in for several minutes while I recovered my composure. It's strange how unexpected things can trigger off a reflex reaction – but that telegram coming out of the blue did it for me.

Today it has pride of place above my desk in my study in the Isle of Man. And to this day I have never opened a good-luck telegram before a show. Afterwards, yes. But never before.

CHAPTER THIRTEEN

A straight man is as vital to some comics as their daily bread or monthly cheques. What I needed was someone, preferably an actor, with clarity of speech, a sense of timing, the ability not to laugh, and a person I could get on with after the show. I found it in Eddie Leslie, and I was lucky to find it again in both Jerry Desmonde and Tony Fayne.

As far as the public is concerned, the stooge simply has to take it on the chin and not move a muscle, whether he's getting a custard pie in the face or a car running over his foot. It isn't easy to train yourself not to laugh. I know actors who get stomach-ache trying to control it when the comic they're supposed to be feeding gets under their skin and they crease up. Laughter is highly contagious – that's what makes it so wonderful and healthy. But not to a straight man.

But we have had our moments when we 'corpsed', I must admit. If you ever see the film *A Stitch in Time* that I made in 1963 when Jerry Desmonde was my straight man, you will see a scene where Jerry, as top surgeon Sir Hector, is giving me a lesson in dentistry that inevitably goes dreadfully wrong.

For some reason Jerry started 'going', as we say in the business, and he couldn't look at me without breaking up. The camera was pointed over my shoulder, so I wasn't in the shot when Jerry got the wobblies. He disguised it brilliantly, and only I noticed his knuckles were white as he struggled to control himself.

'You – you imbecile! You will never be allowed in here again – you – you –' he spluttered. The director Robert Asher said: 'Cut!' And looked at Jerry: 'That was very good Jerry, nicely over the top,' he declared. He didn't notice that Jerry's eyes were watering.

David Lodge is another actor who is a terrible one for cracking up. That man has made literally hundreds of films, and apart from being a one-time King Water Rat with the famous variety artistes' association, he is also one of the funniest men I have ever met. In *On the Beat* he was cast as Superintendent Hobson, a stickler for playing it by the book. My favourite scene is where rookie constable Norman Pitkin (that's me) keeps blowing his police whistle to referee an impromptu kids' soccer match on a bombed-site. Soon the streets are full of policemen rushing everywhere, all blowing their whistles. David was tailor-made for his role – but he only had to see me standing by the camera in my ill-fitting uniform to burst out laughing. Sometimes it took several takes to get a scene into the can, and eventually Bob Asher had to shift me out of David's eye-line to get it done.

I once corpsed on a memorable occasion, and Eddie Leslie was entirely to blame. We were at the Wolverhampton Grand in the 1949-50 pantomime *Robinson Crusoe,* with myself as young brother Norman Crusoe and Eddie grandly dressed up as the Dame. One of the numbers we sang together was the golden old 'un 'There's a Hole in My Bucket', with slight differences to adapt it for a desert island.

We got to the line: 'With what shall I fill it, dear Norman, dear Norman –' when Eddie stuck two fingers through the holes in the bottom and waggled them at me, out of sight of the audience. That got me going. He then varied the fingers in a complete routine – and I doubled up with laughter. The trouble was that I got the giggles too, and it spread to the orchestra. Soon the whole pit was convulsed, the music ground to a halt – and it was so out of control that Eddie and I actually had to totter off the stage, holding our sides and weeping with laughter.

The director, William Summers, was understandably not amused. He called us to his office afterwards and read us the riot act. 'One more trick like that,' he said, darkly, 'and your wages are stopped on the spot, and you'll both be reported to Equity [the actors union]. People have paid good money for you to make them laugh, not indulge yourselves in messing about.'

Suitably chastened, we behaved ourselves for the rest of the run, though it wasn't always easy.

Over the years I would be Norman Crusoe in that pantomime no fewer than nine times in different seasons and different theatres, with various cast changes. That's how popular it was. But it was at the Palace Theatre, Manchester, in 1959 that corpsing took on a new meaning . . . when lovely Pat Stark, playing Polly Perkins, found herself on stage eating an apple – with a maggot in it. Well, half a maggot, by the time we noticed it. We were sitting on a piece of driftwood on Crusoe's island, and I had given her an apple as usual as part of Norman's romantic Garden of Eden approach. Pat had her mouth full – when I spotted the little black legs sticking out of my half of the apple. The rest was still in Pat's mouth. She gazed at me pleadingly. I stared back blankly. Brave girl – *gulp!* She swallowed it. I didn't hear the last of it for the rest of the run.

Life backstage is another world. Most performers have superstitions of one sort or another, little personal foibles they use to hype themselves up before going out to face the public. Mine? Nothing beforehand. But if a show has gone with a particular buzz, I'll kiss the wall of my dressing-room! It's a ritual: turn out the lights, kiss the wall, shut the door on your way out. The only mascot I've kept with me over the years is a large glass ashtray inside a rubber tyre, which I've had ever since I first appeared at Collins Music Hall. I don't smoke any more, but it goes with me everywhere.

It was on the dressing table at the Prince of Wales, and stayed there for the whole run. *Paris to Piccadilly* won some marvellous notices. It also became the show that celebrities wanted to see. One night there was a flurry of excitement, and a stage hand said to me:

'You'll never guess who's out front, Norman – Laurel and Hardy!' And there they were, four rows back in the stalls. I did something extremely rare that night: I asked permission to go out front during the interval and chat with them – and the whole audience cheered us to the echo! Stan and Ollie stood up and took a bow, and then Stan said to me: 'Bit different from Brussels, eh?'

'Not 'arf!' I agreed. 'How did you get on there?'

'We survived,' said Ollie. 'By the seat of our pants.'

Another very happy memory in connection with *Paris to Piccadilly* concerns an event that took place a week after the opening. When in the Royal Corps of Signals at Cheltenham I had been batman, servant, to a Captain Lowe. I had to look after him as if I had been his slave.

One night as I was getting changed after the show, a message came from the stage doorman that a bloke wanted to see me from my old Army days. I said okay, but make it quick. Just a few minutes later there was a knock at the door. I said come in. The door opened slowly, and a head poked round, smiled at me, and said, 'Can I clean your shoes, sir?' It was Captain Lowe.

The only break in that long seventeen-month run came with a commitment we had to a pantomime at the Coventry Hippodrome, signed and sealed before we realised *Paris to Piccadilly* would run so long. It was *Jack and the Beanstalk* – and no prizes for guessing who played Simple Simon! A young unknown beauty with a voice like pure silver featured as Princess Bettina. She was eighteen years old, she had a freshness about her that was totally captivating, and her name was Julie Andrews.

She would come into my dressing-room every afternoon between shows for tea – and knowing what a stickler I was for neatness, she would deliberately spill cake crumbs all over the carpet. Despite the meaningful looks I cast at the carpet, the crumbs kept dropping!

On stage we sang and danced together – she was a lovely little mover, and we made an incongruous couple as I whirled her around in my pieman's costume of ragged trousers and apron. That girl also had a mischievous sense of humour. One dance ended with Julie taking a running jump on to my back.

I could carry her weight – though I staggered a bit. But as the panto wore on I noticed she was jumping harder and harder on to me, and getting even higher before she landed. In the end my knees buckled one night, and I actually collapsed under her! After that Julie was as light as a feather – though a little bird told me later that she had a bet with another member of the cast that she would get me on my knees!

'Right, my girl,' I chastised her later. 'No more cakes for you!' In fact Julie was down to earth, full of fun – and *determined* to be a star. People have called her both an English Rose and the Iron Butterfly, and both descriptions fit.

I left the London show to do panto for twelve weeks in Coventry, stand-ins took our places. Leslie Randall, Archie Robbins, David Hughes and Patterson and Jackson kept the curtain up, and the spectacular costumes and opulent numbers meant good houses – if not packed ones.

As soon as panto finished, it was back to the Prince of Wales. I had the star dressing-room, while Eddie Leslie was on the floor above, sharing a dressing-room with Bobby Tranter. It so happened that this dressing-room had an iron fire escape that led directly down to the stage. One night after the show was over I went up to see how he was getting on, and found three or four of the cast there having a drink and a chat – and Eddie clowning around wearing only a jock-strap and socks, with a top hat on his head and a cane under one arm.

He doffed the topper to us, put the cane over his shoulder, said:

'Goodnight, all,' and sauntered out to the fire escape. That was when I shut the door on him. We switched out the lights, ignoring the banging and threats that ensued, and scarpered down to the stage to see what he was going to do. But in the wings we pulled up short at the sight of the stage manager showing a party of VIP guests over the theatre. Dimly I remembered something about the Lord Mayor of London and a private party being there that night to see the show.

It was too late to do anything. We froze in the shadows as Eddie Leslie suddenly appeared, strolling across the stage from the foot of the stairs behind the far drapes clad only in a jock strap and top hat, twirling his cane like Fred Astaire, while a dozen civic dignitaries stood in stunned silence.

It was mid-way through the second half of the run that Billy Marsh burst in through the door of my dressing-room without even knocking. 'Norman,' he said. 'I don't know how to tell you this – I've got terrible news –'

'Oh Lord,' I groaned. 'What is it? Is the show closing –?'

Billy smiled like a contented Buddha. 'All right, I'll spare you the agony.' He paused for effect. Then: 'The Rank Organisation want to sign you to a seven-year film contract!'

'*What!*' I couldn't believe my ears. There had been the odd whisper over the months, an occasional rumour, but never anything concrete.

Billy spelled out the details. Apparently Earl St John, the big boss of Rank, had seen me on TV in a *Christmas Party* seasonal special, along with Petula Clark, Vic Oliver, Terry-Thomas, Jimmy Jewel and Ben Warriss. He called Billy Marsh, who cannily dropped a hint that Rank's great rivals ABC, the Associated British Cinemas group, were also after me.

That did it. Within twenty-four hours Billy had negotiated a deal where I would film exclusively for the Rank Organisation for seven years, and moreover guaranteed me three films in the first two years for the first of which I would be paid £5,000. In these days of megamillions, it doesn't sound a lot. In 1952 it was big money.

They had no films lined up for me. No story outlines. Nothing. They didn't even want me to do a screen test until after I'd signed the contract. By which time if I'd turned out to have a stutter and a nervous tic every time I saw a camera lens pointing at me it would have been too late.

I was bought up by Rank at what can only be described as a sensitive time in their fortunes. They were the victims of a political row that had erupted in the late forties between the British Government and the Americans. Waving the age-old banner of greed, our lot smacked a 75 per cent tax on all foreign films coming in to the UK – and came a cropper when the understandably miffed Americans refused to show any of their films here in the face of this enormously unfair levy. Our producers were encouraged to fill the gap with home-grown product, and Rank announced a huge programme of forty-seven films to be made at a cost of £9 million – again, a fortune in those days.

Next thing of course, the Government had performed a U-turn, patched up their differences with the Americans, and suddenly we were overwhelmed with a glut of Hollywood films swamping our market. In 1948 the Rank profit and loss account showed overdrafts adding up to £13.5 million, and an accountant named John Davis was brought in as a trouble-shooter to cut costs – together with a few throats – and get the ship back on course.

This was the scenario I entered, in all innocence, in May 1952 when the company was buoyant once more, with only £8 million in debts – and tiptoeing its way very carefully through the financial minefield back into the black.

All the board-room back-stabbing meant nothing to me. It was way over my head. All I knew was that one day the phone rang and a female voice said: 'This is the production office at Pinewood Studios. Would you report here for a screen test on Monday morning, at 11.00 a.m.'

'Okay,' I said. 'What sort of screen test?'

'We'll tell you when you get here,' said the voice.

By then I had bought myself my first real car. That Monday I drove the two-tone Continental Bentley through the leafy heart of the Buckinghamshire countryside to the gates of Pinewood Studios in a state of high optimism. I was on top of the world. The West End show was a sell-out. I was in demand everywhere. Two big studios had been clamouring for my signature. The test would be a piece of cake.

They had prepared one of the smaller studios for me, roping off an area with a backcloth tarpaulin of pale blue, and a table set for two in the foreground. The director who was in line to make my first film was the experienced Ronald Neame, an outstanding cinematographer *(In Which We Serve, Blithe Spirit)* turned director *(The Card,* with Alec Guinness, and *The Million Pound Note,* with Gregory Peck).

At 11.00 a.m. I was ushered into the make-up room. At 11.30 a.m. I was led on to the set – and who should be waiting for me but Petula Clark! Neame, a burly authoritative figure, handed me a page of dialogue. I looked at it, and read:

Norman stares deep into Petula's eyes, and takes her hand.
Norman: *Your eyes are as light as gossamer . . .*

I thought: Hold on, this is a funny line for a comic. Funny as in odd. 'Turn left, turn right, just say the lines,' ordered Neame as the camera whirred. I gazed into Petula's eyes and did as I was told, but despite all my TV experience I felt like a fish floundering on the bank, gasping for creative oxygen.

The whole thing was a fiasco. I had no rapport with Neame, and no chance to explore any kind of comedy acting with the lovely Petula. The upshot was that they paid me off for the first film – and cancelled it! Broad hints were dropped about 'buying me out!' altogether, which would have meant no films at all. I was adamant, and so was Billy Marsh. We had a deal, and it would have to be honoured.

The Press got wind that all was not well behind the scenes. In August 1952 *Picturegoer* told its readers: 'It has been three months since the perky little clown with the clever line in poignant comedy signed his first film contract. Now decision time is at hand. After months of worrying about Norman Wisdom's debut, the Rank studio chiefs have reduced the field to three or four possible scripts. But let's be blunt, the odds are dead against him in his new venture . . .

I didn't like the sound of that. It seemed to me that in the eyes of the powers-that-be I was a dead duck before I even had a chance to take wing.

But finally, more out of desperation than anything else, something did happen. Earl St John, as senior production executive, hired Jill Craigie – the wife of the future Labour leader Michael Foot – to write a script specially tailored for me. After six weeks incarcerated in her Hampstead home, she came up with the goods. I loved it – but Rank were dubious. Jill called it 'a satire on a big store in a

Chaplinesque vein, with plenty of scope for slapstick.' I found it uproariously funny, and before I had even finished the first draft I was elaborating some of the scenes to stretch the ideas to the limit.

Fortunately the plan to get me off the launch pad was put in the hands of John Paddy Carstairs, a prolific writer and director who had made his name with thrillers like the original screen version of *The Saint* and *Sleeping Car to Trieste*. He had a sense of humour like mine, and thank heaven he could see the ridiculous side of everything. Along with another well-known writer, Ted Willis, and a new producer, Maurice Cowan, he worked on the script and turned it into something that was a joy to behold. They even gave it a new title: *Trouble in Store*.

The plot was simple. My character, just called Norman throughout, is a lowly stockroom assistant in a posh West End store named Burridges. My ambitions are to become a window dresser – and win the heart of Sally (played by Lana Morris) who works in the record department, and is quite oblivious of my existence. But I fall foul of the arrogant new Chief (brilliantly played by Jerry Desmonde) with the result that I'm continually getting the sack one minute and being reinstated the next.

There are so many favourite scenes in that film that it's hard to know where to start.

The opening, for one. Here's the new Chief apparently sitting side by side with me in the back of his open Rolls Royce at the traffic lights. Both of us are looking straight ahead. The only difference is that he is immaculately dressed in a charcoal suit and tie, while I look a bit scruffy in my tight Gump's jacket and cloth cap.

When the lights turn green we see why – the limousine pulls smoothly off, and there I am pedalling furiously away on an old bike. But I catch him up at the next lights, and casually lean my hand on the car. The Chief, without looking, takes a swipe at my hand with his glove – only for me to shift it at the last minute. For me it becomes a great game. For the Chief, it's like swatting an irritating fly.

Without a word being spoken, everyone knows exactly who we are. But possibly the best scene comes when I am summoned to the Chief's office without realising who he is. He wants to meet 'the lowliest member' of Burridge's staff. To me, he is just a stranger – and we can have a bit of fun in the boss's absence. So I put my feet on his desk, swan around, help myself to his cigars – 'Go on, 'elp yerself, nobody'll notice!' – and have a high old time . . . until the enraged Chief shouts for his personnel officer (Moira Lister) and fires me on the spot.

It was wonderful stuff, thanks to the magic pen of the three scriptwriters, and the fact that Paddy Carstairs allowed me to ad lib, and push the character to its limits. And with Jerry Desmonde, we had one of the world's great straight men, someone who could keep his dignity intact even when being soaked with a soda syphon – as he was at the end of that scene in his office.

Funny thing about Jerry. He was as fastidious about his appearance in real life as his acting persona would suggest. Always immaculately attired, with his shoes polished like mirrors, he could have stepped out of any of his screen roles. Jerry was forty-five when we first teamed up for *Trouble in Store,* which would mark the start of an association that continued for over twelve happy years, with six films and countless TV and stage appearances together.

The greasepaint was in his blood – he had been on stage from the age of eleven with his family before teaming up with his brother Jack as the Desmonde Brothers in a song-and-dance act. Jerry found he enjoyed being a feed, and gained his experience with Scots comic Dave Willis before joining forces with the incomparable Sid Field in shows like *Piccadilly Hayride* and films like *London Town* and *Cardboard*

Cavalier in the late forties. After Sid's death, Jerry found himself in the 'most wanted' category to be straight man to Arthur Askey, Nat Jackley and even Bob Hope.

He branched out into other fields as host of the TV game show *The 64,000 Question* and popped up regularly as a panellist on *What's My Line?*

It was two years after we made our last film together – *The Early Bird* in 1965 – that Jerry sadly and inexplicably took his own life. It was a tragic loss to the business – and, for me, the shattering loss of a dear friend.

But in 1952 the Rank Organisation were still unsure of me. To cushion any possible disaster, they surrounded me with the cream of British acting talent, headed by the formidable Margaret Rutherford, who played a canny shoplifter, a titled lady who actually gets the staff to help her carry her ill-gotten booty out to a waiting taxi. Then there was Derek Bond, as the handsome leading man rivalling me for the lovely Sally's affections, and a row of stalwarts like Megs Jenkins, Joan Sims, Michael Ward, and my old mate Eddie Leslie, playing the villain out to rob the store.

Eddie was much more than just my stooge. Together we wrote numerous TV and stage shows, and collaborated with Jack Davies on five of my major films: *The Square Peg* (1958), *On the Beat* (1962), *A Stitch in Time* (1963), *The Early Bird* (1965) and *Press for Time* (1966).

In those early days of shooting, everyone was as tense as a bowstring, from the director down to the clapperboy. The atmosphere on the set was electric. I don't mind admitting that I was scared stiff every time I stepped out there, especially in the first week – though I wouldn't let anyone see it. I was given dressing room No. 8 – my lucky number – and I would insist on it for every film I made at Pinewood afterwards.

On the first morning I walked on to the set, shook hands with Carstairs, and said: 'I've got to tell you, Paddy, I'm really nervous.'

'If it's any consolation to you, Norman, so am I,' he rejoined – and I felt a little better.

Paddy was about the same size as me, an intriguing mixture of gentleness and explosive rages. They were over in seconds, once he'd let off steam. But when he was doing it, everyone ducked! He wore a variety of hats during the fourteen-week shooting schedule, and more than once I saw him whip his hat off in rage, hurl it on the ground, and actually kick it across the set.

The first time it happened was only three days into the picture. The sequence was the scene where Norman is mistakenly given a crate of crockery to set up in the show-window, and is about to achieve his lifetime ambition.

Naturally it is only a matter of minutes before the whole place is smashed to smithereens as I become locked into a contest with the official window dresser – played by a marvellously bitchy Michael Ward, who first throws a tantrum and then starts throwing crockery!

Paddy wanted me to play it straight. He felt there was enough slapstick when the mayhem really starts. I felt differently.

'Norman would want to do it his way, and that means hanging a cup from the teapot spout, sticking a spoon in the kettle, arranging the layout in an off-beat, eccentric way . . .' I explained my feelings at length. Finally the inevitable happened. Off came Paddy's hat, and he flung it on the ground and booted it right across the set. Then he stormed off.

I wondered if perhaps I had gone a little far. After all, it was only my third day. A bit early for a head-on clash with one's director. Ten minutes later Paddy was back, dusting down his hat.

'Right, Norman, are you ready to do it my way?' he demanded.

'Yes, Paddy,' I responded. Then added quickly: 'As long

as you're prepared to do it my way too. At least we can then look at them both in the rushes and you can decide which you like best.'

'Um,' he said, thinking about it. Then, with some reluctance: 'Oh, all right. Let's get on with it.'

Michael and I did the whole scene Paddy's way, then reshot it my way. Michael, incidentally, would get his own back later by throwing a bucket of water over me when I inadvertently set fire to myself at the office party!

Word had got round about the difference of opinion, and at lunchtime next day an uncommonly large crowd filled the screening room to see the results. There were some chuckles as I put the crockery in place and stared haughtily through the window at the crowds thronging the pavement. Then the other version, with the cup on the spout, the spoon in the kettle and me pulling faces at the onlookers. And the place rocked.

The lights went up. Paddy looked at me. 'That's the one,' he said. Then he shook my hand. 'From now on,' he said, 'we talk.' Those few minutes sealed our friendship.

Paddy got his own back a few days later. One of the scenes was where Lana Morris and I are feeding the ducks by a pond in the park. At the end I wade into the water, and get soaked. Paddy called for repeated takes, and I dutifully obeyed, rushing back each time to my trailer to get out of my wet clothes and into a fresh suit. After the sixth time, I started to smell a rat. Sure enough, Paddy had removed the film from the camera after the first take, and it was turning on empty! With the crew falling about, I charged at Paddy, swept him off his feet, and carried him bodily into the pond where we both got a ducking!

The fun and games helped to get us through a gruelling schedule. 'I like working with you, Norman,' Paddy said, as the tensions eased. 'You're the only one I can look straight in the eye!'

In fact I was being stretched to the limits. Every night I was due at the Prince of Wales for two performances of *Paris to Piccadilly*. Curtain up at 6.15 p.m. Finish the second show at 11.00 p.m. Back on set at 8.00 a.m. next day.

A car would be waiting outside the set at 5.00 p.m. with a driver at the wheel. I would dash out, dive in, and we would take off at speed, belting down the A40 to Shepherd's Bush, and on to Oxford Circus, before heading down Regent Street to Piccadilly Circus. It was a nerve-racking run, and I daren't think about the speed limits we must have broken. But only once did I almost miss the show. That was when we ran into heavy rush-hour traffic at Marble Arch, and everything ground to a halt. It was just after six. After sitting fuming for two minutes, I said: 'This is no good!' And I leaped out of the car in my little Gump suit and cap, and pelted off down Oxford Street.

People cheered me on. Shouts of 'Good old Norman!' pursued me through the West End until I arrived, panting like a carthorse, at the Stage Door with one minute to go. The orchestra was already going into my introduction as I staggered out through the wings and on to the stage – and of course everyone thought it was part of the act!

For years I had toyed with song-writing, penning the odd rhyme or drafting a few lines of poetry. My first real song was one I sang in *London Melody* – 'Beware', which was published by Chappell's in 1951. The same year I had 'Cinderella Man' with ATV Music Ltd.

Half-way through *Trouble in Store*, when we could see the first speck of light at the end of the tunnel, I had a word with Paddy. 'What are you doing about music?' I inquired.

'Funny you should ask,' he said. 'We've just added a spot where Norman sings to his beloved Sally by the record booth. All we need is the right song.'

'Well,' I said. 'I've got one!' And indeed I had spent several hours over the previous Sundays getting a song down on paper while I tinkled on my piano at home. I was rather proud of the result. 'Do you want to hear it?'

'Don't be daft,' said Paddy, who was not given to mincing his words. 'You're the star of the film, you do your own stunts, you'd rewrite the entire script if we let you – and now you want to do the music as well.' And he waved me away.

Next day I took my song with me to the studios. During the coffee break I nipped over to the music room where a number of musicians were practising various scores. It was a large studio with a raised stage, a podium for the conductor, and a screen at the back where they would run pieces of film for the orchestration.

I spotted a young pianist I knew and went over to him. 'Do me a favour, Mike,' I said, thrusting the song-sheet at him. 'Take a look at this, run it through so you know it. Then put your own name on it and take it over to Paddy Carstairs on Stage Seven. Tell him you understand he's looking for a song for Norman Wisdom – and that you've got one. And see what happens . . .'

That afternoon Paddy came over, his face alight. 'Norman,' he said, 'I've got a song for you. Come on over to the music room and we'll play it.'

'What's it called?' I said, keeping my face wooden.

'It's a new one, specially written for you,' said Paddy. He waved my song sheet at the pianist. 'Go on, son, let's hear it.'

The lad played it. Paddy turned to me. 'Well?' he demanded, excitedly. 'What do you think?'

'Um,' I said, with a dubious shrug. 'Sort of . . . I don't know –'

'Well I do,' he said. 'You're bloody singing it – and that's final.'

'Oh, all right,' I succumbed. 'Let's have another look at it.

I didn't tell Paddy the truth until we had recorded it and

the song was safely in the bag.

In fact, I had sung it once at the Prince of Wales to close my show – but only once. Charlie Stone the manager was furious. 'Cut that out, and go back to "They Didn't Believe Me",' he stormed. 'We're not having you trying out new material on this show.' That was the only airing it got before the whole country was humming it when the film went on release. It's not quite in the same league as the man who turned down the Beatles, but I suspect the emotions were similar!

The name of the song was 'Don't Laugh at Me'.

It would reach Number One in the charts, stay there briefly – then drop to Number Two where it would remain for several weeks. After that it stayed in the Top Ten for a record breaking nine months.

The secret of its success? It touched the hearts of lonely people everywhere, and there are a lot of them about. I just wrote what I felt.

Back at Pinewood the film was over. They flicked off the lights for the last time, we wished ourselves luck at the 'wrap' party in the Green Room overlooking the lawns behind the mansion, and Paddy took the cans of film off to the editing rooms.

The Rank bosses had no idea whether they had a hit or a disaster on their hands. But one thing was sure – they were sweating buckets.

CHAPTER FOURTEEN

To get an idea of audience reaction the Rank Organisation held a sneak preview on 25 November 1953 at the Gaumont, Camden Town, in North London. The cinema was full of people who had come to see Bernard Braden in *Love in Pawn* and found themselves watching me instead. I stood by myself to one side of the foyer waiting for the big noises from the film company to arrive. The two back rows had been reserved for the Rank executives, with a seat on the end for me.

John Davis – who by then was carving a name for himself as a ruthless cost-cutter – walked in with his lovely wife Dinah Sheridan. He nodded to me formally. 'Evening, Mr Wisdom,' and walked on. She flashed me a smile that might have been encouragement or sympathy. I was too keyed up to tell. Earl St John strode in, gave me a quick look, and muttered: 'Um, good luck' before stalking to his seat. Several other top executives passed by, with similar brevity. I felt as if I'd got the plague.

'Strewth,' I thought to myself. 'They can't 'arf be worried.'

The lights were already down. I fumbled my way into my seat, but I couldn't look at the screen – only at the faces around me. Then a gale of laughter swept through the cinema. It was the first sight gag with aristocratic Jerry Desmonde in his limousine and little Norman being left behind on his bike.

And in that moment I knew we were home and dry.

Afterwards it was all so different. The audience cheered and clapped at the end – and then gave me a standing ovation when they spotted me at the back. I slipped out to the foyer where I had stood before, and the Rank chiefs and their wives clustered round to pump my hand. Beaming smiles lit up the entrance like fairy lights.

'Oh, you were absolutely *wonderful* . . . What a brilliant comedian . . . marvellous . . . hysterical . . .' It's called the bullshit of show business.

Christmas week. They decided against a West End showcase opening, opting instead for a blanket release on the huge Odeon circuit around the country. All I can say is that in London alone, that film broke every existing record in fifty-one out of the sixty-seven cinemas where it played.

As for the critics, they reached for their pens – and out came honey and cream. I wish I could have framed every one of those reviews. Like the *Daily Mail:* 'What rich deep joy it is to find a master of really top-grade slapstick. Norman Wisdom hits the bull in one and gives the impression that he was born for the cinema.' Well, thank you, *Daily Mail!*

And the *Evening Standard:* 'It is impossible to avoid comparisons with the early Chaplin, for there is much in common between them. It establishes Norman Wisdom as potentially the greatest living comedian of the screen.'

I spent a few happy hours pasting up my press cuttings book. Whoopee! They liked me!

The final accolade came when I received the British Film Academy Award for Most Promising Newcomer. The ceremony took place at the Odeon, Leicester Square, and I was one of five nominees. I turned up in my best bib and tucker, but I didn't have to contrive to look surprised when my name was read out. It really knocked me back in my seat. It was the first big acting award I ever achieved – and for my first film, too! Can you blame me for rushing out to buy myself a new size in hats?

The fifties saw me reach a peak where the air was heady and rarefied. My career was getting better and better. In the middle of that marvellous *Paris to Piccadilly* run, I achieved a further ambition when I was asked if I would take part in the Royal Variety Performance at the Palladium before the Queen and the Duke of Edinburgh. The date was 3 November 1952, and, as usual, Val Parnell and Prince Littler had assembled a glittering array of stars, every one of whom could top a bill in their own right.

In those days it was mainly British, before it 'went Transatlantic', but they still pulled in Howard Keel and the Deep River Boys as part of an awe-inspiring line-up. The singers were headed by Gracie Fields, Vera Lynn and Josef Locke – but the emphasis was on comedy, and I found myself sharing a dressing-room with Tony Hancock, Vic Oliver, Terry-Thomas, Jimmy Edwards, Arthur Askey, Max Bygraves, Rob Murray and Ted Ray. In the far corner the Crazy Gang were getting into their togs. It was cramped, but it was fun – and I knew I would have to be good, or I'd get lost in the crowd.

I was delighted to be part of such an august occasion – even if it was November! The event was lavishly staged, and covered by TV, and we were all aware that there would be a huge audience looking in. To my delight, I found I was actually first on: normally the warm-up spot is heavy going, but with such a massive overkill of funny men this was the place to make your mark.

The curtain rises to show four tramps in the shape of myself and the comedy trio Jo, Jac and Joni, all of us dressed in rags, busily sweeping the stage. The others rush off in panic leaving me unaware of being watched – until slowly the penny drops and I realise I'm trapped on the stage in front of a VIP audience and some rather special people in the box above my head.

It gave me the chance to do one of my favourite routines – where I struggle with a harp and nearly strangle myself in its rubber strings, get my hand caught in the piano lid, fall all over the place, and finally warble 'They Didn't Believe Me'.

From the stage the royal box is in semi-darkness. But I had a glimpse of white gloves clapping as I bowed low, and I felt I wasn't quite ready for the Tower yet. In the presence of British royalty, strong men traditionally go weak at the knees, and the most powerful moguls in Hollywood have been known to need a reviving brandy after shaking the royal mitt.

During the interval Howard Keel cornered me. 'Gee, I'm shaking from head to foot,' he groaned. 'You've done your bit, so you're okay. But I'm so nervous that my upper lip keeps sticking to my teeth! It's just so dry. I'll never be able to sing looking like this.' And he bared his gums at me forlornly like Humphrey Bogart having a bad time in the swamps in *The African Queen*.

I tried to reassure him. 'I've got something that might help. It's happened to me – and I always rub some clear Vaseline under my lip and on my teeth. Here –' And I reached into a drawer and pulled out a tube of the stuff.

'Christ,' he said. 'I've never heard that one. Are you sure this isn't a gag?'

'If it was a gag,' I said, 'I'd use glue. Just try it.'

He rubbed some under his lip, strode off, and moments later I heard the strident tones of *Seven Brides* coming loud and clear from the footlights. Then Howard Keel's large frame was picking its way through the melee, and sweeping me off my feet with a huge bear-hug. 'That's one I owe you, Norman,' he said.

Actually, it's a spot of Vaseline he still owes me. I never did see that tube again. But what a smashing, unaffected bloke that man is, so I won't let a little thing like a tube of Vaseline come between us!

When the show was over we lined up backstage to meet the royal guests. I was standing between Max Bygraves and Ted Ray. The Queen, wearing a beautiful sash over a sparkling evening gown, extended her hand to me, but said nothing. I bowed low. I said nothing either – the instruction was to wait for the royal visitor to speak first, then come up with a suitable reply. It struck me as all being rather forced, but protocol is protocol and I went along with it.

We stood in a kind of frozen Madam Tussaud's tableau for a few seconds, me with my head bowed, eyes on her feet, waiting for a word. Then I realised Her Majesty was struggling to keep her expression calm. Finally a broad smile spread across her features like a shaft of sunlight, and she said in a curiously choked voice:

'It's – it's all been so happy!' before passing on with what seemed to me unnecessary haste.

Years later when I was a guest performer at a private show at Windsor Castle, one of the ladies-in-waiting revealed the truth. 'Did you know that the Queen just cannot keep a straight face when you are in the vicinity?' she confided. 'It's a standing joke in royal circles.'

'Crikey,' I said. 'I didn't know that. I'm flattered.'

I have met the Queen on a number of occasions, charity functions and premieres, and she always greets me with: 'Hullo again.' Looking at her, I must admit it does give me a curious feeling knowing that somewhere inside is a laugh waiting to happen . . .

Backstage that first time, Prince Philip fixed me with his quizzical gaze. 'How is it you don't hurt yourself?' he queried.

'Mainly 'cos I don't want to, sir,' I replied without really thinking.

'Um,' he said, raised one eyebrow, planted his hands

firmly behind his back, and moved on.

Now I signed for my second ice show, a £175,000 extravaganza called *Sinbad the Sailor* back at the Empress Hall. For this I was paid £2,000 a week, which came to an unheard-of £28,000 over the fourteen-week run. It sounds a lot, and it was. But after the tax man had his bite – top bracket 18/3d in the pound, *ouch!* – there wasn't too much left to chew on.

The ice pantomime opened on 3 December 1953. They brought in a well-built red-head from Canada named Andra McLauglin for glamour and skill – Andra, all freckles and fun, was actually her country's speed-skating champion, and when she cut off around that rink the sparks flew from the ice like a firework display.

My role was the Keeper of the Slaves. I came roaring out on the ice in an open T-Ford, a menacing machine with huge wheels and special tyres which I would drive round the ice lying on my back, not looking where I was going. The rink was oval, with its raised platform at the far end. I had come to pick up the Grand Vizier (played by Jack Harris). I was staring up at the ceiling, going hell-for-leather across the ice, and people in the front rows started to panic. You should have heard the screams! Some of the faint-hearted even got up to flee. But at the last second I'd turn the wheel and roar off at right angles, sending the next lot scattering.

What nobody realised was that there were guide lines on the rafters under the roof! All I had to do was follow the arrows. I'd spin the car like a top, execute a final twirl on the ice – and miraculously pull up right by the platform so that all the Vizier had to do was step calmly off into his seat. Jack Harris actually had his foot high in the air as I skidded under him. The timing had to be perfect, or he would have fallen flat on his face!

Then his door would fall off. I had to get hold of it, so I fixed the steering wheel, and left him sitting on the back while I actually jumped out of the car and ran alongside it as it whizzed round and round in circles. Once I'd fixed his door, I dragged myself back into the car – then my door fell off. That left me lying on the running board with my face just inches from the ice hissing past.

Finally I would clamber into the back with the Vizier – only for the whole seat to collapse and send us both hurtling out on to the ice. It was a marvellous routine, and had the whole arena yelling! It looked dangerous, and it was, but as long as you knew what you were doing, you'd survive.

A stunt that nearly put me out of *Sinbad* altogether was a trampoline act. The show had been running a week. I was rehearsing by myself on a Friday morning, bouncing up and down, working up to a dramatic one-and-a-half back somersault. I flipped up and over – but went too wide, landing on my head on the ice. I hobbled away in agony, with my head hunched unnaturally forward – and this time it wasn't for laughs. Over the next hours, I gradually began to lose the use of my left arm. By midnight it was paralysed, just hanging down.

Next morning I couldn't feel my hand or my forearm. In a panic I rang an osteopath in Harley Street. I was in his consulting rooms by noon. He said: 'I'm going to have to operate. You've got trapped nerves and a chipped bone, and I'm going to have to do some cutting.'

I said: 'When do you want to do it?'

He said: 'As soon as possible.'

'I can't miss a show,' I told him. 'Will you do it on Sunday?'

Somehow I managed to get through the Saturday shows, matinee and evening. On Sunday morning I reported to his surgery. They put me under a general anaesthetic, and when I came to in the afternoon the arm felt much better. By the next evening I was back on the ice. The only thing that had to be left out was the comedy scene where I played the harp with rubber strings, and ended up getting entangled in them. My arm just wasn't strong enough.

The climax of *Sinbad* was a gigantic song sheet lowered from the rafters. I unfurled it to get the audience singing with me: *'I'm going away, a-way, a-wa y-y-y . . .'* I would grab hold of an iron bar underneath it, and be hoisted off the ice and up into the air. The gag was that if the kids didn't sing out, up it would go – and me with it. The louder they sang – down would come the song sheet, but inevitably I would end up dangling eighty feet above the arena – with no safety net – yelling for all I was worth: 'C'mon – you've gotta help me. *Sing!'*

That was really risky, and even more when I only had one good arm. But it was a show-stopper, and we just couldn't lose it. For the next ten days after the operation I simply hung my bad arm over the bar, and let my good arm take all the strain. My record of never missing a show still stood.

By now I was beginning to feel financially secure and confident that my good fortune would continue. It was time to give up our caravan life. Freda and I started house hunting, and found a place less than two miles from the caravan site – in Arkley in Hertfordshire, on the fringe of the Green Belt. It was a smart bungalow in Galley Lane built in the hacienda style that always appealed to me. It had diamond-shaped, leaded windows that looked out on to a delightful garden, complete with a Japanese plum tree that every summer would carpet the lawn with petals of pink blossom.

There was a conservatory that grew as hot as India. A goldfish pond. And an apple tree where I once persuaded my boxer friend Freddie Mills to scrump for apples with me – we filled two sackfuls which I took back to the Empress Hall to distribute among the surprised cast.

I was now beginning to get a lot of mail from fans and

charity organisations. I was writing scripts, songs with lyrics, and, to be truthful, I couldn't cope, so I advertised for my first personal secretary – and was surprised at how many women applied for the job. I finally chose a delightful girl named Sheila Emmett. She was efficient and very helpful when I was learning scripts for my films.

I was getting around two or three hundred letters a week. Many were from youngsters, and sometimes it was hard to decipher what they said. But one was particularly delightful: it came from a small boy of eight who had seen me being chased by a bear in a Christmas pantomime. 'I pray for you every night,' he wrote. 'I say: God bless Mummy and God bless Daddy, and please don't let the bear catch Norman Wisdom'!

I also got my share of strange requests. One woman wanted Sheila to cut off a piece of my clothing when I wasn't looking. I wrote back and said: 'Madam, you can have the whole suit if you'll send the money when I'm fined for running around without it!'

Another lady said she would love to have a lock of my hair. I wrote back: 'Will you also love me when I'm bald?'

My second film was *One Good Turn*, in 1954, again directed by Paddy Carstairs with Maurice Cowan as producer and co-scriptwriter with Paddy and Ted Willis. After the huge success of *Trouble in Store* the Rank Organisation couldn't wait to get me in front of the cameras again. I could do no wrong!

I liked the outline from the word go. This time I am an odd-job man at an orphanage where I was brought up, good-hearted, optimistic, eager to please. Naturally I overlook the girl who should be the love of my life, the sweet Australian zither player, Shirley Abicair, and I'm more intent on buying a toy car I'd foolishly promised one of the young orphans, Jimmy (played by Keith Gilman), if only I can raise £12 to get it for him.

The film gave me another chance to sing one of my own

compositions. With 'Don't Laugh at Me' still in the charts, they were calling for more. I came up with a soulful little ballad called 'Please Opportunity', which I sing against a fairground closing down for the night. I have just survived a mauling from the local bruiser in a boxing booth – shades of Argentina! – and I wander through the park as the boards go up, watching the last stragglers heading for home as I sing that plaintive little song of unrequited love.

I have always tried to do my bit to keep the atmosphere light on the set, and I would make a point of pulling people's legs – especially Paddy Carstairs.

A large underground drainpipe featured in the film, like a small tunnel. In one scene I drive through it hell-for-leather at the wheel of a tiny car. I'm proud of the fact that I do all my own stunts, and being a pretty accomplished driver I had no difficulty in persuading Paddy that I could do this one myself.

What I didn't reckon was that the floor of the tunnel would be curved. I went belting in like the proverbial dose of salts, went slightly left – and whoops! Over I went. I slid along that tunnel upside down with the car on top of me, and lay there spread-eagled, eyes closed, mouth open, giving vent to loud and realistic moans.

I heard Paddy's shout down the tunnel like a hollow echo. 'For Christ's sake, call an ambulance, someone! Where's a doctor?' Then he was kneeling beside me, patting my cheeks, unbuttoning my collar, feeling for a pulse. This went on for at least a minute, when I finally couldn't control myself any more and burst out laughing.

Paddy recoiled from six inches away. His jaw dropped. I could see the relief spread over his face. Then he drew back his hand – and *wallop!* He slapped me across the face with a noise like a pistol going off. In that confined space it sounded a bit like the shot that killed Harry Lime in *The Third Man* – and it left my head reeling.

'Don't ever pull a gag like that again.' Paddy got to his feet and strode off. Out of sight, I heard him start to laugh. And rubbing my cheek, I thought to myself: No, I don't think I will.

The only other flare-up I had with Paddy Carstairs came on *The Square Peg,* made in 1958, with Hugh Stewart producing and Eddie Leslie and myself contributing to the script by Jack Davies and Henry Blyth.

The story revolved around Norman Pitkin, a road-digger whose boss is Mr Grimsdale – a role immortalised by Edward Chapman who made such a unique contribution to my films. He would step into the polished shoes vacated by Jerry Desmonde – and today kids still shout out to me: *'Mr Grimsdale! Mr Grimsdale!!'*

In the film we inadvertently get drafted into the Pioneer Corps and posted to the Front Line, where a local German general turns out to be the spitting image of Norman.

With only a couple of days to go to the start of filming, Jack Davies suddenly had a bright idea. By now I was also living in West London, in a second-floor flat at No.4, Phillimore Court, off Kensington High Street, and Jack had come round to discuss the script.

'Tell you what,' he said. 'Why don't you play the German general? It will fit the story line perfectly.'

'All right,' I said. 'I'm game. I'm okay on accents, so I think I can get away with it.,

Paddy was approached. 'Absolutely not,' he said, vehemently. 'It's out of the question. I've got to have an actor. It's an acting part, not comedy.'

Jack stuck to his guns, and even went over Paddy's head to the producer. Hugh Stewart thought for a moment, then nodded. He liked the idea. Paddy was presented with a *fait accompli,* and had to go along with it. Ominously, his hat stayed on his head. I thought he might have kicked it into the trenches.

That day I appeared in my general's uniform – Iron Cross, polished jackboots, the lot. Still Paddy didn't say a word. The first assistant called out: 'Positions, please,' and cocked an inquiring eyebrow at the director.

Paddy simply said: 'Action!', turned and walked away. He strode deliberately over to his desk near the big double doors, sat back and folded his arms, and let us get on with it. He was certainly making his point. No-one was taking any notice of him, so he wouldn't take any notice of us! It was one of the most unnerving scenes I ever had to get through.

I ploughed valiantly through my lines. 'Zer iss some problems mit ze men, iss zet so?' I laid the accent on thick, but not enough to overdo it.

Out of the corner of my eye I noticed Paddy moving towards us from the darkness. Suddenly: *'Cut!'* And he was standing there. Then he put his arms round me – and kissed me on the cheek. That was as handsome an apology as I ever had in my life! More importantly, Hugh Stewart had witnessed the entire incident. He quietly took me aside. 'Now he knows he's got an actor!' he murmured.

Sadly, I never got another chance to prove it. That was the last film I did with Paddy. He decided he wanted to return to his first love, making suspense thrillers for television. He also directed a number of plays at the Richmond Theatre, and films with Tommy Steele and Charlie Drake before his death in 1970 after a prolonged illness. We had certainly shared some of our most fruitful years together – and had more than our share of laughs along the way.

CHAPTER FIFTEEN

In 1954 I starred in the *Palladium Show* which ran for a record eighteen months. Actually the Palladium was booked for pantomime at the end of our season, but because the show was so successful, it was transferred to the Prince of Wales Theatre. Walter Wahl, the Three Monarchs and Gillian Moran were in support – and of course, the inimitable Jerry Desmonde.

Few people knew it, but the main curtains at the Palladium were worked by water pressure. Don't ask me how, because I'm no engineer. All I do know is that Jerry and I were on stage doing a sketch – when the heavy main drapes suddenly started closing on us. It turned out that a water main had burst in Regent Street, and there was no longer enough pressure to keep the curtains open.

I thought someone was messing about – until I saw the frantic face of the stage manager, and heard him hissing: 'Hurry up! Quick, get a move on – Jerry and I started speaking faster, then we were forced to babble with growing incoherence as the dark red drapes descended inexorably closer. The band were in hysterics. A shout came from the wings: 'You've got eight seconds!' By now the audience had cottoned on that the curtains couldn't be controlled, and they joined in the laughter. We finished the last line of the sketch with my head pressed against Jerry's, just two panic-stricken faces in the dwindling spotlight – wipe-out and uproar!

I was in the middle of the *Palladium Show* when my film *One Good Turn* opened in the West End. The big night was at the Odeon, Leicester Square, and I had been asked to make a brief appearance on stage. I worked out that I had half an hour between shows, and that if I had a car waiting I could make it there and back again and still have ten minutes to see the crowds – and be seen. I had a word with the stage manager, who recoiled in horror.

'No,' he stormed. 'You can't do it. You'll never get back in time.'

I protested: 'But I promised –'

'I can't help that,' he said. 'You're not going – and that's final!'

I capitulated. 'Oh, all right.' And I sloped off, looking peeved.

Inside my dressing-room I called for my car to be waiting outside. Then I wrote out a notice, and pinned it on the door: GONE TO THE PICTURES. BACK IN 10 MINUTES. And off I went in my little suit and cap, hopped in the car, and shot off down Regent Street to Leicester Square. The manager had been right: the crowd outside the Odeon caused a massive snarl-up around the square.

'Here I go again,' I thought, bounding out of the car and scurrying through the crowd. With the help of some friendly bobbies who cut a swathe through the mob, I was able to get to the foyer, mingle with the invited guests, sign a few autographs, get photographed with a group of fans, shout 'Hullo, how are you?' from the stage as I promised – then scarper back to the car.

Talk about cutting it fine! The lights for the second house at 8.45 p.m. were just dimming as I dashed in through the Stage Door – to find the manager waving my note, his face apoplectic.

'I told you I'd make it,' I said jauntily, trying to control my breathing. And the publicity next morning (NORMAN STOPS THE TRAFFIC) made it all worthwhile.

Any sane person would have known the pace was too much. But I was intoxicated by a heady cocktail of success and hard work, loving every minute, and it took hold of me like a drug.

The last show at the Palladium would end around 11.00 p.m. After changing and signing autographs, it would be 11.15 p.m. before I set off home to Arkley. I'd crawl in about 12.30 a.m. and fall into bed exhausted. Most of the time I was asleep before my head touched the pillow. Then up again at 5.30 a.m., knock back a glass of milk from the fridge, and off to the studio to be in make-up by 7.30 a.m. and on the set of my new film, *Man of the Moment*, at 8.00 a.m.

The first sign that something was wrong was when I broke out in a rash of boils and carbuncles! Don't let me spoil anyone's breakfast, but, believe me, I was not a pretty sight. I kept going on both the film and the show until they wound up which, oddly enough, happened in the same month, August 1954.

Those last weeks were murder. Falling on my backside or arms on the stage hurt me so much that I would shout out in pain, but I still kept a ghastly grin stitched to my face. The cast knew I was not well, and often in agony too. Occasionally my ears would catch the soft *Pfut!* of a boil bursting, which would give me temporary relief in that area – and then I would see one of the chorus girls slipping . . . Word got round, and my dresser said severely: 'Really, Norman, the girls are quite upset. You're turning the stage into a skating rink. Why don't you put some insulating tape on them?'

Once the film and the show were over, I had myself admitted into St Stephen's Hospital, and had the whole lot removed under a general anaesthetic. I was three days inside, just lying there with a blissful smile. Oh, the relief! The chorus girls would be happy too.

On the third day, I was honoured with a visit from the Matron. 'We can't believe it, Mr Wisdom,' she said, studying my file.

'The boils?' I inquired.

'No,' she said. 'I mean a star like you suffering from malnutrition! We just can't believe it.' Crikey, I thought, she's right. I realised I hadn't even been giving myself time to eat. From that day I have always had three square meals a day.

When I came out Freda gave me a badge. *Even a workaholic needs Christmas day off.* She gave it to me in the middle of summer, but the message was the same.

Sunday lunch – or dinner, I call it – has always been a tradition with me and even today I like to sit down at one o'clock, on the dot. My mum was always a stickler for promptness. I would visit her whenever I could at her flat in Deal for Sunday dinner with Freda and my brother Fred and his wife Christine. I'd call her on the Saturday: 'Maudie, I'll be there just before one.

And she'd say: 'Right, dinner will be on the table at 1 o'clock.'

If ever I was late, even by a couple of minutes, she would be standing just inside the door – and wallop! She would cuff me round the ear-hole – then burst out laughing.

The dish Mum would give me never varied. Roast lamb, roast potatoes, carrots and mushy peas. Maybe rhubarb and custard or prunes as a sweet. Not what you'd call exotic, is it? Then how about Shepherd's pie or tripe and onions? Or stew with dumplings? That's what I call real food.

Remember, before I went into the Army I was nearly always hungry. Anyone who has known real hunger and not been sure of where the next meal will come from will understand how I felt when I knew that in the Army I could rely on three square meals a day.

Army food is basic: stew and dumplings, Shepherd's pie, steak and kidney pudding, butter beans, chicken, maybe roast lamb if you're lucky. As far as I'm concerned it was marvellous food, and I won't hear a word said against it!

Today, if I go into the River Room at the Savoy Hotel and I'm given the best table by the window overlooking the Thames, I'll still want my Shepherd's pie. That's why I don't go to the Savoy very often.

I prefer my local fish and chip shop near Epsom, just five minutes' drive from my flat, where you get the most marvellous cod and chips. That's what I call a smashing meal. You can keep your caviar and foie gras. I've tried both – and I don't like them. What a waste of time! I know it's rare sturgeon, but caviar to me just tastes like cod's eggs!

In the same way I like gammon. But I like it with boiled onions, parsnips, pease pudding and potatoes. That's gammon for me, and I'd rather have it like that than with melon. I went in to a posh restaurant not long ago, and was offered pear and watercress soup. Strike me lucky! I'd rather have an ordinary tin of Heinz tomato or vegetable soup. Or what about cream of chicken, eh!

I have a weakness for strong curries – India again, right? I buy them at Marks and Spencer in the Isle of Man or in Epsom, and that is a gorge I really look forward to. Not quite as hot as vindaloo, but enough to stop you hanging around next day! I'm a good cook – as long as all I have to do is open a can of Mulligatawny soup and a tin of curried chicken. Then I'm a wow at the stove, and very good at stirring it with a spoon!

The best curry story I know happened in Bournemouth. It was in 1970. I was at the Winter Gardens with Tony Fayne my stage partner. Roy Castle – who was both a brilliant musician and entertainer as well as being a very good friend – was in another summer show on the pier. Roy did have one weakness: he adored Indian food. On the last Saturday we arranged to meet at an Indian restaurant near the seafront after the show, one that stayed open late. Roy liked curries, and had always boasted to me: 'The hotter the better'.

I made the reservations, and Tony and I hurried to be there ahead of him. The manager knew me, because I'd eaten there before, and showed us to our usual table by the window. I told him: 'Listen, I want you to make the hottest curry you've ever done. One that makes vindaloo look like weak tea. Okay? I'll pay you a special price for it.'

'Very well, sir!' His dark eyes gleamed at the challenge. And sure enough, they came up with a curry that would have blown the head off a bullock. Tony and I had a quick teaspoonful in the kitchen, and we both needed a glass of iced water to cool off.

In came Roy Castle, as chirpy as ever. Oozing respect, the manager said: 'We have a special dish for you tonight, sir.'

'Show me,' said Roy, waving a hand in anticipation.

Tony and I sat back as a trolley appeared, and a silver dish of something brown and liquid and frightful was placed in front of the star guest. Roy dipped in his spoon, and started wolfing it down as if he had just come off the streets of Calcutta. Tony and I exchanged a wink, waiting for the explosion and the perspiration.

Instead: nothing. It was unbelievable. Roy finished the lot, keeping up a patter of jokes and stories about his show while we sat with our mouths open in disbelief . . . mixed, I have to say, with admiration. To his dying day, Roy never knew anything about it.

On 17 December 1954 I was invited to Windsor Castle to do a private show for the Royal family's Christmas staff party. They were all there: the Queen, Prince Philip, the Queen Mum, Princess Margaret, in fact all the Royal family, plus an audience of Castle staff and their friends. The Waterloo Chamber was hung with decorations. There was a Christmas tree, and flowers were everywhere.

As every performer does, I took a judicious look at the setting. Acoustics? Not bad, a trifle echoey. Any blind spots like pillars? No. The stage? A bit small. I would have to make sure I didn't fall off the side. Three steps down at the front, fine. On either side, displays of flowers that looked lovely in priceless ceramic vases.

It was an incredible night. Sid Philips was the band leader, and the Queen danced a succession of quicksteps and tangos with her footmen and other members of her staff. When Sid played a waltz she asked him for 'something more lively', and he went into *The Darktown Strutters Ball*. 'That's much better,' said the Queen.

Wilfred Pickles was the compere, and led the royal party into a chorus of *Have a Go, Joe*. They sat in the front row of gilt-edged chairs, and the conjuror Vic Perry showed them how to pick pockets – I remember seeing Prince Philip hastily hiding his fob watch.

When my turn came I leaped out on the stage, went through a fast twenty-minute routine, and was gratified to hear the great hall resounding with laughter. That was when I made my big mistake. Instead of staying on the stage for my formal bow, I took the liberty of walking down the steps to where Her Majesty sat in the middle of the front row, and giving a deep, sycophantic bow until my head almost rested on the royal lap.

She smiled up at me with those brilliant blue eyes, nodded an acknowledgment – it was time to go – but I suddenly realised I was stuck! Protocol requires that you always keep your face turned to the royal personage. I couldn't turn my back to the Queen!

So I started walking backwards, fumbling my way up the steps with a fixed smile . . . straight into the flower

BEWARE

WORDS AND MUSIC BY
NORMAN WISDOM

Recorded by
NORMAN
WISDOM
ON COLUMBIA RECORDS

J. ARTHUR RANK ORGANISATION
presents
NORMAN WISDOM
in
"MAN OF THE MOMENT"
From an Original Story by
MAURICE COWAN
A HUGH STEWART PRODUCTION
DIRECTED BY
JOHN PADDY CARSTAIRS
J. ARTHUR RANK
Distributors LTD

THE VICTORIA MUSIC PUBLISHING CO., LTD.
52 MADDOX STREET, LONDON, W.I

2683

Collins
MUSIC HALL

1/6
NET

PROGRAMME

BEWARE

WORDS AND MUSIC BY
NORMAN WISDOM

CLAUDE LANGDON in association with HENRY HALL

PRESENTS

London Melody

at the EMPRESS HALL, London

Written & Produced by
EVE BRADFIELD

LYRICS BY
PATRICIA NASH

MUSIC BY
ROBERT FARNON

EMPRESS HALL

Featured & Recorded
NORMAN

CH

I LOVE YOU

Words & Music by NORMAN WISDOM

RECORDED BY

NORMAN WISDOM

on
TOP RANK

THE RANK ORGANISATION

presents

NORMAN WISDOM

in

FOLLOW A STAR

also starring

JUNE LAVERICK · JERRY DESMONDE

HATTIE JACQUES and RICHARD WATTIS

PRODUCED BY
HUGH STEWART

DIRECTED BY
ROBERT ASHER

2/-

FRANCIS, DAY & HUNTER LTD.

138-140, CHARING CROSS ROAD, LONDON, W.C.2.

ABOVE: With Johnny Mans

BELOW: During his touring days with Terry White at the piano,
and overlooked by 'straight man' Tony Fayne

LEFT: With Sir Harry Secombe

BELOW: With fellow actors, John Inman and Andrew Sachs

ow: With Nicholas
ons and David
am

COMIC HERITAGE

ABOVE: Norman visits the studios where he made his legendary films

RIGHT: Celebrating
the anniversary of
VE Day

ᴠᴇ: Norman tries his hand at being
gent

ʀɪɢʜᴛ: Signing autographs after
a hectic stage performance

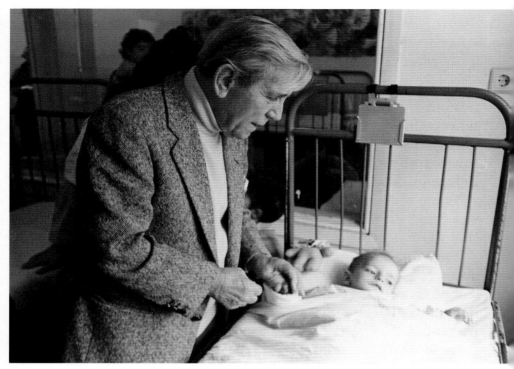

ABOVE: Visiting hospitals in Tirana, Albania

BELOW: With Albanian schoolchildren

arrangement. There was an almighty crash that I can still hear in my occasional nightmares as the vase broke, and flowers and plants spilled out on to the floor. I rolled over backwards in the debris, while the whole of the royal front row sat abruptly upright. The Queen had a hand to her mouth in concern – most likely on my behalf.

There was a deathly silence as I struggled to my feet, surveying the wreckage. Then I looked at the Queen. And said: 'Don't worry, Your Majesty – I'll pay!'

The Queen led the laughter, and I was able to scurry away, red-faced but intact.

The Queen Mother was everybody's favourite. She was a delight to perform for, and always so gracious when we were presented afterwards. On one occasion when I was asked to do a show at Hatfield House in Hertfordshire, the Queen Mum caught me out.

There was to be a huge carnival for charity, and the centre piece was a colourful marquee on the lawn. Everyone was dolled up in white tie, top hats and tails, with the ladies in elegant dresses. But nature was in a bad mood that day, and throughout the afternoon the clouds gathered overhead until the sky was a leaden grey with ominous rumblings of thunder in the distance. Finally the heavens opened, and the rain poured down on us. Eddie Leslie was with me, and we had worked out our act with the band, and checked the sound system with the engineers. But now it would be downright dangerous to go on – COMIC ELECTROCUTED IN FREAK STORM was not an epitaph I wanted.

We were hanging about in the marquee making small talk with the other guests, when glancing up I noticed a bulge in the tent overhead. A large puddle of water had gathered, getting bigger with every passing minute. I looked at Eddie. He looked at me. We nodded in unison. In one corner I found a walking stick leaning against a chair, and borrowed it.

By now the rain had eased, and several people were standing at the edge of the marquee. I shoved the stick up under the bulge – and a huge torrent of water cascaded down the canvas roof and over the top hats and dresses clustered outside. I really had not intended that to happen, honest! But it was too late to make excuses. Hurriedly I propped the stick back, listening to the outraged cries from outside, and started chatting loudly to Eddie.

A voice, familiar and female, broke in on us. 'I saw you do that,' said the Queen Mother, materialising beside us. 'You little tinker!' She chuckled quietly, and moved away.

By now I had become a proud dad. Our son Nick was born on 18 March 1953. I was topping the bill at the Coventry Hippodrome, and chalked up an impressive telephone bill with anxious calls to Barnet General Hospital where he was delivered as a bouncing 7 lb baby. He would grow into a sports fanatic – like me – and no father could be prouder than I was when he was chosen to play cricket for Sussex. Today he runs a sports shop in Haywards Heath – very successfully, I might add.

Our daughter Jackie was born the following year in the same hospital, on 21 December 1954. She would try her hand as an air stewardess for a time, and then make a career for herself working in an art dealer's in Mayfair. Neither of them wanted to go into show business, and I didn't try to force them – though I must admit that Jackie had the looks and the talent to be a very good actress. But as I told them: you must please yourselves. Needless to say, I love 'em to bits!

By this time I was making personal appearances all over the place, sometimes to publicise a new film, often for charity. I love being with kids, and the Variety Club of Great Britain and the Water Rats were two organisations I would give my time to whenever I could.

But one outing I made could have been the end of me. It

looked funny, I know – but I didn't realise how dangerous it was when I climbed into the cage with Spike the orang-outang at one of our major zoos for the photographers.

Spike was about the biggest ape I had ever set eyes on, but everyone assured me he was friendly and he didn't seem to object when I went into his cage and clowned around, swinging on the mesh and pulling faces for the cameras. The massive creature even let me cuddle up to him.

After a few minutes I heard a low voice say through the bars:

'Norman. Move very slowly, but get out of there *now!*' It was the head keeper. Very gingerly I got to my feet and casually eased over to where there was a space below the mesh just big enough for me to get through. When I was six feet away I took a fast run and literally a headlong dive – just as Spike lumbered to his feet and came after me.

'That animal is totally unpredictable,' the keeper said. 'You should never have gone in there.'

I understand that the very next day Spike turned on his own keeper – and mauled him to death. I had bad dreams for a month.

In 1957 I tried my hand at musical comedy in the classic farce *Where's Charley?* Frank Loesser, of *Guys and Dolls* fame, had written the music and lyrics, and it ran for three years with Ray Bolger in the starring role.

I liked the idea of playing Charley Wykeham, the Oxford University student who impersonates his aunt from Brazil – 'Where the nuts come from' – to chaperone a pair of young lovers, then falls in love with one of them, Amy (played by Pip Hinton). I also find myself pursued by the dapper Sir Francis Chesney, and who could be better in that role than my old sparring partner Jerry Desmonde?

I learned immediately that there is a huge gulf between farce and pantomime. With panto, you can improvise, make mistakes, even be yourself. With farce, you stick to the script. The comedy comes from situations where others are involved – and you can't play games with it. I had never learned so many lines in my life. But it was a wonderful score, and as the critic Kenneth Tynan put it so succinctly: 'The songs are airborne and the plot is secure.'

One other critic wasn't so sure. Harold Hobson of the *Sunday Times* was generally regarded as the doyen of the heavyweight critics. On the first morning of rehearsals he came round to the Palace Theatre three weeks before we opened in the West End, and came into the dressing room.

'Mr Wisdom,' he said, sternly. 'You do understand the part you are playing is that of an Oxford undergraduate, don't you?'

I launched into my most raucous Cockney accent. 'Oh yeah, wot?' He said: 'But an Oxford student would have a very refined voice, don't you see?'

I said: 'Wot? Yeah, I see wot yer talkin' abaht. But I got free weeks to practise 'ere and get it right, ain't I? So you can rest assured I'll 'ave it right on the night.' He stared at me aghast, shook his head, and walked slowly away.

Opening night, and it was a cracker! The show would run for eighteen months, and included a special royal performance in memory of Jack Buchanan following the death of the great comedian in October 1957. Backstage, I bumped into Mr Hobson heading for the champagne reception, and gave him a perky grin. He eyed me coldly. 'Very funny,' was all he said.

But he was kinder in print. Very kind, in fact. 'I was by no means alone in the madness of my delight at the meticulous timing of his jumps and falls . . . his engaging joy . . .' Madness of his delight? If only more critics were less sane!

That year I made *Just My Luck* for Paddy Carstairs – and it was exactly that for me when I found that Marilyn Monroe was filming *The Prince and the Showgirl* on the next set with Laurence Olivier. Better still, the world's most seductive sex symbol had actually asked if she could watch *me* filming. Cor, I'll say she could!

It was the film that introduced Edward Chapman into my life, though not as Mr Grimsdale. He played a character called Mr Stoneway in this story of racehorse nobbling, in which as ever I'm the gullible punter trying to raise money to buy a present for the girl of my dreams (Jill Dixon).

The girl of everyone's dreams materialised one morning, a blonde bombshell in a clinging cream satin dress, strolling on to the set with Laurence Olivier. The two of them sat quietly in canvas chairs watching me act out a scene with Edward. The atmosphere on the set was so highly charged I thought it would sizzle, and I don't know how we got any work done. At the end we had a nice little chat, and they both thanked me and left to face their own cameras next door. Marilyn gave me a very public and very seductive wink which had the studio gossiping for days, and I fell head over heels for her on the spot.

I bumped into her several times during the next few weeks. On my last day I saw her near Reception – and when I told her we were wrapping the film in a couple of hours she cried: 'Norman! Come here!' And actually lifted me off my feet to plant a smacker of a kiss full on my mouth.

It did my reputation no end of good, I can tell you. It's fair to say I was walking on air for a week.

CHAPTER SIXTEEN

I lost count of the TV sitcoms and appearances I made, from thirty-two half-hour episodes of *Nobody is Norman* to the variety bills, where I had my own *Norman Wisdom Show* to *Late Extra, Off the Record, Stars on Sunday* and the ever-popular *Sunday Night at the London Palladium*. I also recorded the 'laughing song' – *Narcissus* – with Joyce Grenfell.

The *Sunday Night* I will always treasure went out live on 3 December 1961. I still play the video over to myself at home on a quiet evening on the Isle of Man. There was an Equity strike on. Bruce Forsyth was the compere, and I had agreed to do a ten-minute spot. Equity wouldn't stop me because I had signed the contract. They were going to cancel the show. I called Billy Marsh and said: 'Look, if Bruce is willing, I'll do the whole hour with him.' An hour can be a v-e-r-y long time.

Billy called up Val Parnell, who said: 'He must be mad. He can't do an hour on television.' But the next morning he rang back. 'If Norman is prepared to risk his entire career – and rather than cancel the show – then I'll chance it.'

It was going out live. I called Bruce. 'We're going to have to rehearse for one week, solid. Is that okay with you?'

Professional from his head to his big toe, Bruce responded as I knew he would. 'Fine with me, Norm.'

The show started with Bruce chasing me through the

audience after I had the temerity to walk on wearing a large *I'm in Charge* badge in order to provoke him. He allowed me to stay around, as long as I could finish a joke without laughing.

That joke has gone down in the annals:

I was walking down the street the other day when I saw a man lying in the road with his ear to a manhole cover. I went over to him and asked: 'What are you doing down there?'
And he said: 'You have a listen.'
So I knelt down and put my head on the manhole cover, and I said: 'I can't hear anything.'
And he said: 'I know. It's been like that all bloody day . . .'

Terrible, isn't it? But you should have heard them laugh.

I was also able to include two of my favourite sketches – 'A Lesson in Rhythm' and the 'Wallpaper Sketch'. The first is a beauty, and I still use it today with Tony Fayne as my sadistic instructor teaching me the rudiments of rhythm. I first tried it out in 1954. Bernard Delfont had been doing the rounds of fringe shows off Broadway, and had spotted an American knockabout comic getting beaten up by this infernal music machine. He realised it would be ideal for me – and bought the rights on the spot for a thousand dollars! That's the way they did it in those days.

The idea was painfully simple – or simply painful. In that Palladium show, Bruce wheels out a cumbersome machine loaded with drums and a cymbal. He explains how it works. You've got 'bonker' – a rubber hammer. And 'biffer' – a boxing glove on the end of a wooden pole. And nasty-looking spikes built in to a stool shaped like a lavatory seat. I perch nervously beneath this Heath Robinson contraption, while Bruce explains how he is going to teach me to play the drums in a remarkably short space of time.

When the bonker hits me on the head it forces me to beat

the drum. When the biffer punches me in the earhole I must stop. When the spikes shoot out of the stool – Cor, ouch! – I crash the cymbals. It's a sketch designed for masochists, but it gets the loudest laughs. 'All right, Norman?' Bruce inquires. 'I haven't got all night.' And *wham!* Away we go. I get knocked all over the place, and end up senseless.

The second sketch has been called a classic: a totally silent eleven-minute routine that needs perfect timing, with Bruce as the arrogant foreman and myself as his gormless assistant attempting to paper a room. I put up a trestle table, and get trapped between two planks of wood. Then Bruce shows me how to do it – and we both get trapped. Then I get stuck up a ladder with the paper over my head. Finally Bruce ends up on my shoulders with the bucket of paste – and guess who gets it over his head?

Oddly enough, Bruce had his doubts about it when I first went over it with him. 'I don't think that sounds very funny,' he said.

'I tell you what,' I said. 'Let's rehearse it for ten minutes, and if you still don't like it we'll cut it out.'

We did. He liked it. And it became part of variety folklore. Even today I chortle when I see it on video – but no-one knows that it took literally hours of preparation to get it right, part of a dozen 13-hour rehearsal sessions for the whole show that I insisted on doing before we dared go on air. Bruce and I became great pals. But even in this book I must thank him for his incredible patience. Thank you, Bruce, my ol' mate!

I was also busy filming. In *On the Beat* (1962) I played two character parts – not just Norman Pitkin, a gormless car park attendant at Scotland Yard with ambitions to join the Force – but also one Giudo Napolitani, who sounds like an ice cream but was, in fact, a camp Italian hairdresser as a cover for being the Mr Big of a gang of jewel thieves.

This gave me the chance to mince around my Mayfair

salon like a prize teapot (one hand on hip, one limply in the air) in an outrageous black wig and moustache. David Lodge was a superintendent, Raymond Huntley the Yard chief who finally agrees for Pitkin to go undercover because of his striking resemblance to the gangster. Eric Barker, Eleanor Summerfield, Terence Alexander and Dilys Laye led a formidable acting team in support.

A Stitch in Time (1963) contained the most complex, elaborate and most daring stunt I ever pulled off. Perhaps that's why I always think of it as one of my favourite films. I was celebrating my tenth year in pictures, and my eleventh major movie. The old team of Bob Asher (director) and Hugh Stewart (producer), with Jack Davies, Eddie Leslie and myself writing the script, assembled in the familiar surroundings of Pinewood Studios to make a comedy about medical matters.

To be more precise, it was a lesson in how to create chaos in a hospital.

We roped in all the old favourites, and some fresh household names too. Once again I was Norman Pitkin, this time a butcher's assistant to Mr Grimsdale. Defending his premises from a hold-up, Mr G. manages to swallow his gold watch and chain, and has to be whipped off to hospital in a hurry.

All Norman's efforts to help his boss come unstuck. Instead he falls foul of the snooty hospital chairman Jerry Desmonde in rattling form) who is trying to wheedle funds out of Lady Brinkley (Jill Melford). Norman also manages to win over a tragic young orphan (delightfully played by child actress Lucy Appleby).

The roll-call of Britain's finest actors dwarfed anything we had ever had before. Jeanette Sterke as a nurse, Glyn Houston, Hazel Hughes as a dragon-lady matron, Peter Jones, Vera Day, Patrick Cargill, Francis Matthews (before he made his name as Paul Temple), even Johnny Briggs from *Coronation Street* as a Teddy Boy. They all wanted to be in it.

Their enthusiasm paid off. That film became my biggest-ever money-spinner, breaking records at all the twenty-six cinemas where it opened – and even toppling the James Bond saga *From Russia with Love,* one of Sean Connery's best 007 thrillers, from its number one perch. Not bad for a butcher's boy!

The stunt in question is one of those funny gags that builds and builds. I was cast – well, plaster-cast, actually – as a 'victim' in a St John's Ambulance exercise, encased from head to foot in plaster. All at once the fellows realise they're late for a football match, and rush off leaving me stranded on the stretcher-table – but I wanted to go to the football match too.

I manage to roll off it, and into a wheelchair. We're on the second floor of the ambulance station, and I manoeuvre myself to the head of the stairs – then bumpety-bumpety-bump!

The wheelchair hurtles out of control down the steps, and crashes right through the wall.

The camera angle moves outside, and you see me come smashing through the brick wall – it was plaster, but it looks like brick – and soar through the air. . . just as the ambulance with the lads at the wheel roars through the archway below.

I land on its roof, and grab at a rail and hang on for dear life as the ambulance charges off down the street. It reaches the end, swings around a bend – and sends me hurtling through a glass window into a hospital ward, sliding across the slippery floor the entire length of the ward until I smash into a wall on the opposite side.

At which point a doctor (Patrick Cargill) swings open the door, looks down at me, and says, curtly: 'Nurse, what's this man doing out of bed?'

It was a wonderful pay-off line to a scene that took us days to film. On the first morning I reported to the set, ready to climb in to my plaster 'uniform'. Bob Asher, the director, who had become a good friend, led me off into a corner.

'Norman,' he said. 'I've got news for you, and I know you're not going to like it.'

'Oh?' I said. 'What's that?'

'Well,' he hesitated. 'I've engaged a stunt man. I know you do all your own stunts, but this time I'm having a double for you.'

I was flabbergasted. 'What on earth for?' I demanded.

'Mainly because I want to finish the film,' he said drily. 'To have you crashing through that wall on to the roof of a moving ambulance is just too dangerous to contemplate.'

'Oh, please –' I began.

But Bob was adamant. 'No, it's too much. I'm sorry.'

They did the scene with me where I fall backwards off the table into the wheelchair. Then I had to sit back and watch while they photographed the stunt man from behind, as the wheelchair toppled down the stairs, through the wall and out on to the ambulance. I was still watching when the stunt man slid right across the ambulance roof, rolled off it, crashed down on to the hard tarmac and broke his arm.

'Cut! Cut!' yelled Bob Asher. The stunt man was led away, put into a car and driven off to a real hospital. A sense of gloom and doom descended on the set. At last Bob came over to me. I was still sitting encased in plaster from head to toe, because I was waiting to do some close-up shots once the stunt was over.

'All right,' he said. 'You saw that. What do you think?'

'I think it's a shame to waste a day trying to find another stunt man and explain all that to him,' I said thickly, through the small hole that had been left for my mouth. I looked up at him. 'Isn't it?'

'All right, you little swine,' said Asher. 'You win. You can do it.' Immediately I called for two chest expanders – the kind that have five springs stretching between two hand grips. I asked for them to be spread across the roof of the ambulance and hooked on to the rain sills on either side. The effect was a little like the braking lines they use on aircraft carriers to stop jets toppling into the sea when they land – except that this time the projectile was going to be me. Finally I had them painted white so that they were invisible.

It worked like a dream. Every bit of that sequence you see in the film is me, even the back of my head as I go bumping down the stairs. To get the full impact the special effects department rigged up rails so that the wheelchair would hurtle down the stairs, tilt up, and catapult me out at the right speed to meet the ambulance.

Why risk life and limb on my own stunts? Throwing myself about never bothered me. In the gym I was always doing front rolls and somersaults. I even reached the stage where I could stand on an ordinary wooden chair and fall back off it, ramrod straight, and land on the floor without hurting myself.

You break fall with your forearms – and the harder you hit the floor, the more you absorb the impact and take it away from the rest of your body. I suffered bruises over the years, of course, but I never complained. And in the end, falling over became an art.

Let's face it – everyone has an ego. And when I fell around in front of a film crew or an audience, and I could feel their genuine admiration, it was a great boost to my morale. To hear them say:

'That was smashing! Fancy taking a chance like that' – there's nothing like it.

By now I had bought a beautiful old fifteenth century farmhouse in the Sussex village of West Chiltington. Henry VIII installed his fourth wife Anne of Cleves there, and the rooms with their diamond-leaded windows and timbered ceilings simply reeked of history. It was a tranquil setting of twelve acres in a quiet country lane, complete with a stable for Jackie's horse which I had finally been persuaded to buy her. I was happy and proud that our daughter was attending the Royal Naval College for Ladies at nearby Petworth, and also that Nick was a pupil at Charterhouse. I was absolutely determined that both children would have the education that had been denied me – and at least they would never be able to copy my own entry in the *British Film and TV Year Book*, which reads: *Educated – more or less.*

The house was just a stone's throw from the village square where the stocks have survived almost five centuries, and it was an idyllic place for me to relax amid the soothing contours of the Sussex countryside after the hurly-burly of London. My flat in Kensington became my office. But this was my home.

The old house was called Laker's Farm, and dated back to 1493. I was certain the place was haunted. So was my mother. One night Mum was lying in bed when she woke up feeling terribly hot. There was a sweet apple-blossom smell in the room coming from nowhere. Mum pushed back the sheets to cool herself, and that was when she felt someone bending over her, blowing gently in her face – and laughing at the same time!

Every county has its own identity, and for me Sussex means the green of the Downs, white chalk cliffs, and meandering rivers like the Arun. But ten years later the quiet country lane had become a main road, and in 1974 for the sake of peace and quiet I had a new house built to my own specifications on the estate: a Spanish-style hacienda with white-washed walls and curved arches. I brought in most of the furniture by truck from Spain, and the only setback came when the local planners wouldn't let me put Spanish tiles on the roof. I added a heart-shaped swimming pool in the garden. Two years later in the spring of 1976 we sold Laker's Farm and moved in to our new home on the other side of the estate.

I was invited to join the board of Brighton Football Club, though in fact I was an Arsenal fan. Indeed, my happiest memory was making a personal appearance on the Highbury ground – and booting a policeman's helmet (with his permission, of course) all the way up the pitch, hotly pursued by half a dozen grinning bobbies.

I quite enjoyed the six years I was with Brighton, though I can't say I relished the board meetings. We seemed to spend all our time talking about new lavatories and tea rooms. If anyone actually mentioned soccer, the manager looked at them askance. Eventually I was travelling too much to be of any use to the club, and resigned – though like so many other show-business chums I love to watch a game. One of the reasons I ended up in the Isle of Man rather than Spain was because I could see Match of the Day in English!

My seven-year contract with The Rank Organisation was fulfilled with the six films directed by Paddy Carstairs – *Trouble in Store, One Good Turn, Man of the Moment, Up in the World, Just My Luck* and *The Square Peg* – plus *Follow a Star* for Bob Asher. After that I stayed with Rank on a film-by-film basis, with *The Bulldog Breed, On the Beat, A Stitch in Time, The Early Bird* and *Press for Time*. I also made three films for independent companies: *There Was a Crooked Man* (1960), *The Girl on the Boat* (1962) and *What's Good for the Goose* (1969).

It gave me the chance to continue with pantomimes and variety, which I loved – and also to branch out into a spot of serious stage acting. In 1964 Anthony Newley asked me if I would be interested in his new stage musical, *The Roar of the Greasepaint, the Smell of the Crowd,* which he had written with his partner Leslie Bricusse. I was keen, and so was Bernard Delfont who was planning to bring it to London after a twelve-week provincial try-out in Nottingham, Liverpool and Manchester. From the start Tony and I did not see eye-to-eye on my character, Cocky. I wanted to play him my way, more robustly here, more shyly there. But Tony was directing, too, and wouldn't give an inch. In the end I went along with it.

Bernard Delfont wasn't happy with the show, either, and kept asking for changes. Everything stayed the same. Finally, at the Palace Theatre, Manchester, just two days before we were transferring to the long-awaited West End, Bernie pulled the plug. The 'Show Closing' notice went up on the board on Friday afternoon. I thought: what have I got to lose? So that night and the next, I did it my way – and we got a tremendous reception from the audience. Even the cast gathered in the wings and applauded, among them a youngster by the name of Elaine Paige who was playing a street urchin.

Thank God I did it my way, because for me, at least, something good came out of all the trauma. On the Saturday night, when the curtain had been brought down for the last time, an American director named Cy Feuer appeared in my dressing-room – and offered me the starring role in a new stage musical he was planning based on *Hobson's Choice*. It would be performed the following year – on Broadway! I accepted on the spot. The title was *Walking Happy* – and I have to say that's how I left the theatre on that last dramatic night.

First, there was some travelling to do. In April 1965 I was invited to the Mar del Plata Film Festival in Argentina as one of the guests of honour, and flew out with Eddie Leslie to keep me company. They were screening *A Stitch in Time*, and we were accorded a marvellous VIP reception from the moment we landed, with a cavalcade of open limousines from the airport and me sitting in the back surrounded by exotic girls.

Another of the guests was James Mason. At the big opening reception in the Mar del Plata Theatre before an invited audience I was due to be introduced from the stage at the very end – the star spot.

Mason said to me: 'Don't you think I should go on last?'
I looked blank. 'Why?'
In that richly distinctive voice he said: 'Well, perhaps I am a little more *recognisable* than you when it comes to stardom. My films go back many years, you know.'

'Alright,' I said. 'I don't mind.'
Mason said: 'Well, I'll go on immediately after you.'

I had done my homework, as I always did when invited abroad, and I'd learned a few opening words in Spanish. All it needs is a brief greeting: 'Hullo, everybody. I'm glad you enjoy my films, and thank you so much for inviting me.'

That's all it takes – but the effect is astonishing. People warmed to me in Russia, in Germany, in the Far East, everywhere. They knew I had taken the trouble to learn a few basic words in their language, and it was a compliment to them. Also, it doesn't cost a lot.

Unfortunately for him, James Mason hadn't. I went out into the huge theatre, and made my little speech in Spanish. *'Hola, amigos . . .'* They went wild, and cheered me off the stage.

Then James Mason was introduced, and all he got was a ripple of light applause. It was highly embarrassing, but it reinforced my view that taking that little bit of extra trouble always pays off.

It was there that they gave me the Golden Flame Award, something of which I am enormously proud – because it was for 'The Most Popular Artist of All Nations'.

Something else happened in South America that nearly cost me my life. One night a few of us were talking in the hotel bar before turning in, when one of the local film distributors named Pablo Corenthes suddenly said: 'Would you like to go to Chile tomorrow? I can fly you there in my private plane.'

Eddie Leslie and I looked at each other. Why not? It was a chance that might not come again, and an opportunity to fly over the Andes. The plane was a two-engine Comanche, and he took us on a marvellous scenic route through those awesome mountains.

We landed at Santiago Airport, where a hire car – a pale blue American Dodge – was awaiting us. Our new-found friend took us into the city, and bought us lunch at an open-air restaurant in the old quarter, close to the hotel where we would be staying for one night. It was a Sunday. The place was teeming, and it was fascinating just to sit back and watch the faces of the people strolling by on the traditional *paseo* dressed in all their finery. I felt I was on holiday.

After lunch Pablo said: 'My friends, I have some business to conduct. Please make use of the car. The driver will take you sightseeing, and I will see you back here in two hours.'

We climbed in the back of the car, and threaded our way through the crowds and out into the main boulevard. Suddenly I saw the car in front of us swerve across the road. I said to Eddie: 'Look at that bloke. He must be drunk!' Then I saw another car doing the same. I said: 'Hullo, he must have got a puncture.' They were all over the place, mounting the pavements, desperately trying to avoid pedestrians who had started to run in all directions.

Now people were screaming, and cars were crashing into each other. Women in shawls scooped up their children and ran for doorways as slates came showering off rooftops. Our Dodge rocked from side to side, and was suddenly rammed by a taxi.

'My God,' I said. 'It's an earthquake!'

Our driver screeched to a halt in one of the city squares. Through the window I saw an old church start to bulge – and then its front wall exploded outward in a cascade of bricks and stone. Its spire shook, then toppled like a falling tree. Worshippers came fleeing out of the doors and down the steps. Other buildings began to sway.

The driver turned a panic-stricken face to us. 'Better to get out, *señors*,' he cried. Without hesitation we jumped clear, just as a telegraph pole crashed on to the next car in a welter of wood and flailing wires.

Eddie and I ducked and ran across to the centre of the square. Common-sense told me we were probably better off in the open than near a building – even though paving stones were erupting around us as if some giant hand was pushing them from underneath.

People were on their knees, praying. But curiously, I was more elated than frightened. 'My camera!' I shouted above the din. 'I've got to get it.'

'Where is it?' Eddie was pale, but in control.

'In the back of the car –' And I dashed back through the milling throng to the Dodge, and made to open the door.

I was stopped by a yell from the driver. *'No! Get away!'* And I saw that an electricity cable had snaked over the bonnet, and was flashing sparks everywhere. If I'd touched the car I would have gone up in smoke too!

The earth had been shaking under my feet – and then it stopped just as suddenly, and an unearthly stillness settled on the city. Slowly Eddie and I made our way back to the hotel. The place was standing, but there was dust everywhere. Predictably, the service was nonexistent. The electricity had gone, so we simply raided the kitchen to make ourselves sandwiches out of bread and cheese.

'What about the after-shocks?' Eddie inquired, tentatively. 'There could be more to come.'

'The sooner we get out of here the better,' I agreed.

We had to wait until next morning to get permission to drive to the airport and take off. I spent a sleepless night on a mattress which I rigged up under the bed in a doorway between the bedroom and the bathroom. I remembered reading instructions in a hotel in California about what you do in an earthquake – get under a vertical wall, such as a doorway, and stay there. It's the centre of the ceilings which collapse first, and apparently you have more of a chance to survive if you avoid the middle of a room.

Outside, a pall of black smoke hung over the city. The shattered streets were a bedlam of wailing sirens and hooting car horns. The earthquake had been 7.2 on the Richter Scale, and countless old buildings had suffered. More than four hundred people had been killed, and many more injured.

The old Dodge looked even more battered as it rolled up to take us to the airport – with my camera still intact, if unused. The departure hall was full of rubble, and a staircase had buckled. Pablo looked at the mess, and said: 'Well, gentlemen, a little more excitement than we anticipated – but welcome to Chile, anyway!'

'At least I'm one up on you,' I said to Eddie.

'How's that?'

'I was in another earthquake in India,' I said. 'But all I did there was fall off my bike.' We looked out at the devastation on the airport road. The shanty town on the fringe of the city had been virtually flattened. 'It's quite humbling, the power of nature,' I mused. 'When I think what I've experienced – the heat of India, earthquakes, violent storms that lash a sea into sixty-foot waves . . .' I had their undivided attention. 'And I've been out in the rain,' I couldn't help adding, winking slyly at Eddie, 'without an umbrella!'

Pablo nodded, impressed. Eddie pulled a face at me, and turned away to hide a grin.

When our Comanche took off I sent up a quiet prayer of thanks. We flew over the mining village of El Cobre, eighty miles north of Santiago, and as the plane banked above it we saw how badly it had been hit by an avalanche that had followed the 'quake. The mud slide was over a mile wide, and had wiped out the flimsy houses in seconds. It was a scene of terrible devastation, and we flew back to Mar del Plata in silence.

Before we left the film festival I was able to show Eddie the waterfront of Buenos Aires that I had last seen as a cabin boy. We even found the field where I had my innocent young brains scrambled in a boxing booth. The port area hadn't changed a lot, even if *I* had, and it brought the memories flooding back.

Film festivals are hectic, noisy, chaotic – but fun. In Berlin, Bob Hope came out on to the stage – doing my walk! In Russia, where I was part of a British delegation to the Moscow Film Festival in July that same year, they played a season of my films in several cinemas. It was an international event that attracted names like Bob Hope and Peter Ustinov, so I was in good company.

The Russians never did anything by halves. Other actors saw their films screened at cinemas with up to 2,000 seats – but I was flattered beyond measure the night they screened *Trouble in Store* . . . at an indoor stadium that held 18,000 people – and it was packed! When I went on the stage to make my little speech, I must have looked like an ant to the people at the back – but what a wonderful welcome they gave me.

Russians have an earthy sense of humour, and they seemed to identify with Norman Pitkin and all the terrible scrapes he got into – even when dubbed into Russian.

At the end they surged from their seats to surround me on the stage when I said in my most fluent Russian: 'Hullo, everyone, you're lovely – and thank you!'

CHAPTER SEVENTEEN

The summer of 1966 brought another milestone in my
career: the stage musical *Walking Happy* on Broadway. Cy
Feuer had been true to his word. The classic British play
Hobson's Choice set in Salford, Lancashire, which first
opened way back in 1915, had been turned into a lavish feast
of song-and-dance with music by Jimmy van Heusen and
lyrics by the legendary Sammy Cahn. Up to then most
people only remembered the 1954 film with Charles
Laughton, Brenda de Banzie and John Mills.

Cy thought I was just right for the starring role of
bootmaker Will Mossop, toiling away in the shop run by
Henry Hobson (who was played by George Rose) and
falling for the charms of the boss's daughter Maggie (Louise
Troy). I was thrilled to bits.

But on the first morning when I was introduced to the
cast I felt as if I had inadvertently stepped into a cold
shower. They were pleasant enough. But no-one had told
me that Americans rehearse in a different manner from the
way we do it here. In Britain we learn our lines slowly, and
at the same time work out where we are going to stand and
move. In America they walk about reading the script, which
they hold in their hands, working flat out before they know
their lines or where to move. I found this latter method off-
putting, so I did it my way.

Unfortunately they didn't like it and it showed. They

began by calling me Mr Wisdom. Then it became Norman. After two weeks, someone actually said: 'Hey you!' It dawned on me that they had no confidence in their star, and therefore none in the show. The lowest point came the day we moved from the rehearsal rooms to the Lunt-Fontanne Theatre on Broadway for one week of final preparation.

We broke for refreshment during the morning as the coffee trolley entered. In the wings I saw a chorus boy beckon me with an imperious finger. 'Hey, Limey, get me some coffee, will you?' The other dancers lounging around laughed as if it was the joke of the week. I got him his coffee, and he thanked me as if I was the tea boy.

Cy Feuer called us for the run-through, a complete rehearsal. By now I knew my lines inside out and upside down and backwards. I knew every movement, every note of music. They put just the working lights on the stage, enough to get by, and we went through it from A-Z. And I didn't put a foot wrong – even if some of the others did.

After it was over the same lad who had called me Limey walked slowly over to me. 'Mr Wisdom,' he said. 'I want to apologise for my behaviour. When you're on that stage, you don't need any lights, because you are a shining star.'

Honest, I still get a lump in my throat when I think about it.

As befits the title it was a happy show, one of the happiest I ever worked in. And it was a hit. My reviews were great, even though there was no slapstick – apart from one moment where I was tugging an overloaded barrow through the streets and it suddenly tilted up to send me sky high, clinging to it for dear life like a nervous acrobat without a safety net. The appeal was in the warmth of the story line, and the affection that flowed over the footlights to captivate the audience.

In the influential *Daily News,* their critic John Chapman said: 'They hardly make entertainers like Norman Wisdom any more. Now that we have found him, we should adopt him and never let him go . . .

That show received a cluster of awards. Two for me, including the prestigious New York Critics Award. Plus a shoal of nominations in the sought-after Tony Awards – no fewer than six in all. I was nominated for Best Actor in a Musical, but lost out to Robert Preston for *I Do! I Do!* That year, 1967, was dominated by *Cabaret*.

But the public flocked in, and kept us there for 161 performances before we set out on the road for a nation-wide tour that took us across the States to the West Coast and the climax in Los Angeles.

That was a wonderful month, so different from the last time I had tried to conquer tinsel town. Almost every night there would be a knock on my dressing-room door at the Dorothy Chandler Pavilion – and I would find myself staring into the face of a world-famous celebrity. That great clown Jerry Lewis looked in one night, and his first words were: 'We've gotta do a movie together.' I was all for it. It turned into a hilarious meeting where we both pulled faces at one another to see who had the most rubbery features. After five minutes we called it an honourable draw.

The idea that Jerry mooted was that we would team up with the French comic Fernandel, whose face was even more pliable than ours, and the Mexican clown Cantinflas, and get some crazy scheme going together. It died on the drawing-board, as so many things do in show-business.

Mary Tyler Moore, Edward G. Robinson, even John Wayne, they all came to say hullo. Wayne – 'Call me Duke, everyone does' – towered so tall I thought his head would scrape the ceiling, but what an interesting man he turned out to be, far removed from his 'Yupnope' image.

Richard Burton and Elizabeth Taylor, too. Burton had that marvellous pitted face, a lived-in map, and he shook my hand and said:

'Norman, I'd never heard you sing. That's quite a voice you've got.' This was a bit rich coming from an actor who to my mind had the greatest speaking voice in the world.

He gave a bellow of laughter when I replied: 'Come to think of it, I've never heard you sing, either.'

I also found myself at a Hollywood charity lunch at the Beverly Hills Hotel sitting next to Joan Crawford, who had been widowed from her fourth husband Alfred Steele, board chairman of Pepsi-Cola, and was busy promoting the drink. I reminded her that our last, and first, meeting had been at the Marble Arch Pavilion – ahem, how many years ago? Enough to make her pause for thought. She remembered the premiere, but one lift boy looks like another.

'You ruffled my hair and gave me a kiss,' I told her.

'I did?' she said. 'Then how about this for an encore –, And she reached below the table and gave my thigh a squeeze. I reached for the nearest glass of Pepsi double quick.

During our month's run there, I received the accolade of putting my hand-prints in the cement outside Grauman's Chinese Theatre, thus joining the ranks of the Hollywood immortals, from Judy Garland to Gene Kelly to Chaplin – his feet, of course – to Douglas Fairbanks to. .. well, you name it. In actual fact I had to put my right hand and right foot in the fresh concrete, which took a bit of balancing. But at least I could say: I've arrived!

My size six foot was actually bigger than both Chaplin's and Fred Astaire's, who had very small feet. As for Judy Garland, her prints were tiny.

Sometimes uninvited guests do barge into your dressing-room, and if you're taking off your make-up and preparing to have a shower it isn't always easy to be as courteous as one might wish. But I always did my best. In Los Angeles my mind was still filled with one such incident that had happened towards the end of the Broadway run. There had been a knock at my dressing-room door. In came a middle-aged gentleman with a kindly face who looked like everyone's favourite uncle.

He complimented me on my performance, and I thanked him. There was a pause. Then he said: 'Actually I'd like you to do a show for me.' I thought, Hello, I've got one here!

'How nice,' I said. 'What's it about?' I was only half-listening as I was desperate to get back to my hotel, put my feet up and have a bite to eat.

'It's called *Androcles and the Lion,*' he said. I almost laughed out loud.

'Oh,' I said. 'What's my role?' I knew that no-one certainly in England would ever cast me in a George Bernard Shaw play.

'Androcles, of course,' said my visitor.

By now I was starting to get irritated. 'Have you cast it yet?' I queried with a touch of sarcasm.

'Oh yes. I have Noël Coward as the Emperor Caesar – It was getting more farcical by the minute. I turned on him.

'Please, I'm very tired. I've had about enough –'

The avuncular figure held up his hands. 'Forgive me. I forgot to introduce myself. My name is Richard Rodgers,' he said.

Realising I was staring a legend in the face, I almost wanted to go on my knees, but invited him to sit down instead. The composer who had given us so much pleasure with great musicals like *South Pacific, The King and I* and *The Sound of Music* actually wanted *me* to play the title role in a TV musical of Shaw's play? Isn't showbiz amazing?

Mr Rodgers explained. It was a satire set in the days of ancient Rome, about a slave who removes a thorn from a lion's paw. Years later he is thrown to the beasts in the arena, only to find the maneater he is facing is the very same one he helped – who recognises him and saves his life.

It was to be a TV special for NBC, due to go out on 15 November 1967. We taped over five days at their studios in Brooklyn, with a cast that included Ed Ames (as Ferronius), Brian Bedford (Lentulus) and Patricia Routledge (as my wife Megaera). Geoffrey Holder was in the lion skin, and I didn't envy him sweltering under the studio arc lamps.

As the first day of rehearsals approached, I found myself getting a trifle nervous. Alright, I had worked with some big names – but Noël Coward was a daunting figure to face. Anyone who answers happily to the label 'The Master' has to be approached warily. I needn't have lost a minute's sleep. He was urbane, ultra-polite, the living epitome of the man we knew from stage, screen and TV. And he put us all at ease with his humour.

Admittedly there was one moment where I thought I had overstepped the mark. Coward had a long stretch of dialogue with me, but he kept moving away from the spot they had marked for him with a cross of white tape on the floor. Each time the director Joe Layton shouted: 'Cut!' And they would start all over again.

'Noël, could you please try to stay on your mark,' he pleaded after the third effort.

Coward responded with a raised eyebrow, but said nothing. I could sense storm clouds gathering. As it was we were up against the clock, because we had to be finished by midnight on the fifth day, when a technicians' strike loomed.

The camera rolled for the fourth time – and I saw Noël instinctively start to back away. Covertly I reached out a hand and grabbed hold of his toga – out of sight of the camera.

Coward finished his dialogue, straining against my hand. The director called: 'Cut! That was lovely' – then the Master turned on me.

'What on earth do you think you are doing?' he demanded, brushing my hand off like an irritating fly.

'Well, you didn't move off your mark, did you?' I retorted.

'Oh, that,' he said. 'Of course.' And smiled wryly. 'Thank you dear boy, thank you.'

One of the more elaborate scenes called for Noël to address the crowd from a balcony of the Senate in an impassioned speech. It began: 'Lo and behold –' There must have been at least 300 extras gathered below in full costume. He came out and began: 'Lo and behold – ' then paused. The cameras went on rolling. Coward's mouth opened again: 'Lo and behold – ' and closed. The silence was agonising.

Finally it opened again. And he announced loudly: 'The Master has forgotten his f-ing lines!'

The Senate steps had never heard a speech quite like that one, and nor I suspect had GBS when he wrote it. The studio erupted in laughter, and Coward got it word-perfect next take.

It was an unusual role for me. No-one in Britain in a million years would have cast me as Androcles, but unexpected things happen in America. I enjoyed it – and I sang several numbers, including 'Velvet Paws' which was a nice catchy little piece. The show went out as planned, with an excellent critical reaction. 'Coward played Caesar with the blithest spirit possible,' said the influential *Variety*. 'And Norman Wisdom was a perfect choice for Androcles.'

At the end of the run Noël Coward gave me a book of his poems and lyrics, and wrote in the fly-leaf: *To Norman. Thanks for all the wonderful times we've had together – Noël*

Unfortunately I lent the book to someone and never got it back – but that always happens, doesn't it? I just hope nobody gets the wrong idea if they come across it. Noël and I were just good friends.

That year I was invited back on the Ed Sullivan Show,

and found myself rubbing shoulders with a star-spangled banner of celebrities. While I was in the make-up room I glanced along the mirror. In the next chair sat Kirk Douglas, and beyond him was Johnny Mathis. Also on the bill were Count Basie and Woody Herman, and Johnny Weissmuller – complete with Tarzan yell. All in one night. Unbelievable.

Equally unbelievable was that at this point my marriage broke up.

Chapter Eighteen

I thought I had the perfect marriage. Freda was proud of me, and she had proved to be a smashing mother, bringing up the kids with the aid of a nanny. Everything seemed fine until I went to America to do *Walking Happy*. It kept me there eighteen months, then a further three months, and it was in that time that Freda found someone else.

Looking back I can't say that I blame her. I was away from home a lot, and I was making my work my priority. I never knew anything about it until I got home from America to find she had found someone tall and good-looking – that's how I always summed up the new man in her life if ever I was asked.

My main concern was for the children. We both wanted custody. When the divorce judge awarded me a decree nisi at Kingston, Surrey, on 15 February 1969, he decided that the kids had reached an age when they could choose for themselves. Nick and Jackie were interviewed by social workers – and I can only say it was an incredibly proud and exciting moment for me when I learned that both children had chosen to stay with their Dad.

I was lucky to find Madge Perodeau, a widow who was the mother of a former secretary of mine, who came to live with us in Sussex as the new nanny after my marriage ended. We called her Magic – and she was wonderful with the kids.

She fussed over them, and called them 'My boy and girl', and we would all go out together like any other family. She agreed to try a 'probationary period' of four weeks – and stayed six years! She was also a fabulous cook, and prepared all my favourite dishes – with gravy her speciality.

Freda and I stayed good friends, and the children were able to see her regularly. On occasions we still get together for a 'family curry' at Epsom, or a fish-and-chip lunch, and now I'm a granddad – Nick and his wife Kim have a lusty little lad called Laurence, who was born in 1989 – I love him!

The unhappy truth is that show business has been responsible for so many divorces, and mine was just another sad statistic in a long list of casualties. My absence made her heart grow fonder – of somebody else.

As for me, sadder, a little wiser, but accepting the inevitable, I plunged myself back into my work.

If my personal life was at a low ebb, my American career was going full blast. *Androcles and the Lion* had received excellent reviews, and I had been singled out for praise. I signed for a leading role in *The Night They Raided Minsky's*, a major film for one of Hollywood's biggest companies, United Artists.

The story covered the last day in a notorious New York burlesque show before it was closed down by the vice squad. My character was Chick Williams, known as the 'top banana' in a comedy act with my straight man, Raymond Paine, played by Jason Robards. The cast was exciting. It was the first film for Elliott Gould, then married to Barbra Streisand, who played Minsky. Veteran star Forrest Tucker, as leathery as the saddles he adorned in countless Westerns, played a racketeer. Our own Denholm Elliott and Harry Andrews were there, while Minsky's dad was played by Joseph Wiseman, who was the unforgettable Dr No in the first James Bond thriller. Britt Ekland provided the glamour as a would-be dancer who unintentionally turns burlesque into striptease when her dress gets torn.

Add to all this the director William Friedkin – later to make *The French Connection* and *The Exorcist* – and you will see the kind of company I was keeping.

In those days Jason Robards had a reputation as a man who liked a drink. I never saw it interfere with his performance, but if there was an excuse to celebrate – Jason would be there. On one notable occasion he had been on a binge for three days, and an important scene was coming up.

'Where is Jason?' I enquired of an assistant, as the minutes ticked by, and the time got ominously nearer. We were on location in the Lower East Side, one of the less salubrious areas of the city.

'Over there –' He jerked a thumb across the street at a seedy bar.

I went in, and found Jason crouched on a stool studying a glass of whisky with rapt attention. I slid on to the stool next to him.

'They'll want us in half an hour,' I said. 'Are you ready?'

'Sure I am,' Jason said to the glass. 'But I'm not moving from here unless you join me in one for the road.'

He knew I didn't drink. I thought for a moment. 'Er – lemonade?' I said hopefully.

'Scotch!' Robards said loudly to the barman. 'A large one for my friend.'

I shut my eyes, thought of England, and downed it in one. 'Good boy,' said Jason, approvingly. He took my arm, and walked ramrod straight out into the street to the make-up caravan. Thirty minutes later we were in front of the cameras, Jason was word perfect, and I was struggling to clear my head. Since they all knew I didn't drink, I'm not sure what they made of me that day – but I got through it somehow.

'You're a terrible man,' I told him at the end of the scene.

He gave me a broad wink. 'Yeah,' he grinned. 'Ain't it fun?' Jason was a smashing fellow, and was one of the guests when I was the subject of *This is Your Life* for the second time in 1987 – the first being in 1957.

Harry Andrews played Britt Ekland's father, a religious bigot named Jacob Schpitendavel, which is not a moniker I would wish on too many people. In one scene I had to throw a glass of water in his face in a row in the theatre bar. That morning Friedkin beckoned me over.

'You know you're going to throw that water in his face?' I nodded. 'Well,' said the director. 'Don't tell him.'

I said: 'I've got to. Besides, it's in the script.'

'I know,' said Friedkin. 'But he thinks we're finishing this part of the scene before he gets it. I want to capture his expression.'

Now Harry is a big bloke, and to my mind the best sergeant-major we've ever had in all those war films. I was a little bit nervous about this one. What if he thought it was a gag?

'Don't worry,' said Friedkin, with a grin. 'We'll hold him off you!' In the bar the cameras rolled. Harry put on his thickest Schpitendavel accent. And *whoosh!* I let him have it, right in that lantern-jawed face.

'Cut!' shouted Friedkin. 'That was great!'

Harry blew his top. His bellows of indignation filled the theatre. 'What the hell did you do that for – why didn't you warn me?' he stormed.

'Don't blame me,' I said, edging away. 'He told me to.'

'Don't you listen to him,' shouted Harry. 'He's only the f-ing director!' And off he went to get dried. Thankfully he saw the funny side later – and we didn't have to do that scene again.

In another scene I had to tumble down a whole flight of stairs into the theatre. Now this is something I had done many times in my career and as usual I worked out the whole fall to the last inch. Step by step, I knew which way I would be facing, where the camera would be to capture my expression, and where I would end up.

I was meticulous when it came to the physical stunts as the following incident shows.

The photographer from the film told me he wanted to shoot off a few prints of my prolonged pratfall down the stairs.

'Where is the best place to get your face?' he asked.

I led the way to the curving staircase that loomed above us. 'There –' I pointed to a step half-way up. I would be approaching it from the top, curled in like a ball on the curves, flattening out on the straight bits. 'Put yourself over there so you're not in the shot, and when I pass you on that step I'll be facing you with my eyes wide open. It's the only chance you'll get. If you miss it, you've lost me 'cos I'm rolling in the other direction.'

He said: 'Are you sure?'

I gave him a mock glare. 'Sure I'm sure.'

We shot it in one, and afterwards he came rushing up waving the Polaroid print. 'It's dead on,' he whooped. 'But you went by me so fast it was unbelievable.'

There was a sad postscript to that film which left us all feeling low. In the story the principal comedian – the 'top banana' – was originally an elderly comic known as Professor Spats, played by a famous star of vaudeville, Bert Lahr. The 'Prof' gets superseded by the brash young Chick, and we had some wonderfully poignant scenes where the old man was trying to educate me in the traditions of burlesque. Bert was seventy-two, and his claim to screen immortality was that he played the Cowardly Lion in the 1939 film of *The Wizard of Oz*.

But two weeks before the end of shooting, the producer Norman Lear called us all together in the studio and announced: 'I've got some terrible news. Bert Lahr died last night.' The news cast a gloom over the remaining days.

In Billy Friedkin's words it also, professionally speaking, cost me a 'certain' Oscar for supporting actor, as all our scenes together were cut. Bert only appeared as a sad figure shuffling across the stage at the end.

But the reviews were marvellous for all of us, and *Time* magazine compared me to Buster Keaton.

A year later I returned to New York to star in the farce *Not Now, Darling,* a typically British lose-your-trousers romp that had run and run in London with Leslie Phillips in the lead. We opened on 29 October 1970 to a critical panning as the Butchers of Broadway leaped joyously upon us with sharpened knives – it's amazing how they can kill a show stone dead without giving other audiences a chance to see it for themselves.

My own reviews were good, and I received the Roseland Theatre Owners Award for best comedy actor. I liked the United Press line:

'A masterful little comic. If you are breathing you will laugh.'

Too many people obviously held their breath. The show closed twenty-one nights later.

It was time to go back to Britain, and into summer shows, pantomime and cabaret – clubs were opening all over the country, and they were the new goldmine for comic prospectors. Colour TV had arrived and reigned supreme, cinemas were more than half empty, and the entire film industry was feeling the draught.

My main concern was to find myself a new sparring partner. There was only one serious contender, and I was delighted when in 1968 Tony Fayne agreed to join me. With his tall, schoolmasterly manner and commanding presence, he was the ideal foil. Tony is also particularly good at looking annoyed!

He hails from Bristol, and had begun his career doing

impressions at the Bristol Empire in 1940. He then teamed up with David Evans to specialise in satirical songs at the piano and a wide range of sporting impersonations.

I remembered hearing him on the radio in *Starlight Hour,* and I first shook his hand in *1954* when he and David were brought in as a speciality act when the London Palladium Show transferred to the Prince of Wales.

Tony always had a tremendous talent, and when, sadly, David fell ill and he was forced to go solo his success story continued. That was in 1959, when he made some very amusing records, partnered the old Cockney comic Arthur Haynes, and carved his own niche as an entertainer. Billy Marsh was his agent too, and it was his suggestion that we teamed up.

We met up over a coffee in Soho, and I said: 'Okay, Tony, how do you feel about it? If you agree, we can both be on the move again.'

He extended a large hand over the table. 'I'm with you,' he said. 'I think we're going to go places.'

I don't know which crystal ball he had been studying, but the places we went to included Canada, Iran (when the Shah was in charge), Australia, Tasmania, New Zealand, Hong Kong, Malaysia and Africa. Clubs were coining in the loot, and I remember Ernie Wise once told me, 'Whenever we get hired in a club, I tell Eric: it's like a bank raid!' And it was.

We got a good act going, Tony and I. One sketch that I particularly enjoyed was when the curtains part to reveal a large sign that announces: *The Tony Fayne Show.* Tony strolls languidly on, immaculate in dinner jacket, and starts to warble and soft-shoe-shuffle his way through *Singin' in the Rain* in a style that would not have shamed Gene Kelly. That's when I break in from the stalls, ten rows back, in my Gump suit, joining in enthusiastically and exhorting the audience to do likewise.

Tony tries to keep going, but finally grinds his teeth in frustration and challenges me to come up on stage and do better. Everything turns topsy-turvy as I take over his show, and he has to get me off the stage. The sketch ends with us both perched on stools that go up and down like elevators as we sing *Tie a Yellow Ribbon*. It finishes up with Tony crooning away oblivious of me hanging on like a drunken parrot high above him! That was one of the funniest sketches, and wherever we went it brought the house down.

It was that act which the BBC later chose in December 1976 for their entry to the Knokke-le-Zoute festival in Holland – and it won the top Golden Seal award. Not bad for a first-time double act!

But on our initial tour of Britain, when we were still getting to know each other, a problem arose – or rather, a drunk arose, and headed towards the stage with a fixed, glassy-eyed intent.

It was a club in Sunderland. I was in the middle of my opening number, and Tony had strolled out to interrupt it. Before he even had a chance to open his mouth there was a flurry from the side, and on staggered this drunk.

He started swinging punches at Tony, who dodged about adroitly ducking the blows. I tried to make light of it by going into my shadow boxing routine – but seconds later I was brushed aside by a large gentleman in a tight-fitting dinner jacket who walked up to the intruder, said: 'You don't want to do that' – and knocked him clean out with one punch. The Club bouncer, earning his pay for the night. The drunk was dragged off, and we went on with the show.

Over the next twenty years Tony and I became great pals. We both like golf – my handicap is around 18, his are his clubs (actually, he plays to a respectable 12). Our first venue as a stage team was Bournemouth, a season at the Winter Gardens. I chose it deliberately, because Tony lives nearby in the New Forest. We broke all house records.

On that first tour together a very funny comic named Freddie Starr was on the supporting bill, a shock-haired young man who even then had a wild and way-out line in laughter.

He would stand in the wings every night watching me – and I suspect that is why out of all my imitators, in my book he is the best. I know they say that imitation is the sincerest form of flattery – but you should see some of them attempting to do my walk. Freddie has a reputation for being an absolute terror, but with us he was a lamb. It was a couple of years later that he became a star in his own right – and deservedly so.

It was in the seventies that I really spread my wings to all corners of the globe. After all, my films had already done so, the invitations came in thick and fast, and Tony and I agreed it was a good time to see the world. I would usually make it a maximum of ten weeks – then back for a variety tour in the UK and a pantomime.

On these tours we had our tight-knit foursome: Cohn Norman, then our musical director, Tony, a secretary and myself. We would travel with a load of instruments which I would always supervise personally into the cargo area at Heathrow. I never travel first-class – I go economy with the others. On long trips, especially around the world, I want to be with my mates.

One secret I learned was to get on to local time immediately I set foot on foreign soil. If I arrived at four o'clock in the afternoon I would prop my eyelids open with matchsticks if necessary until 9.00 p.m., then hit the sack and sleep the clock round.

Down Under I found, I was very popular. Just as well, because I know that if the Aussies don't like you, they eat you for dinner. But they had enjoyed my films, they found me funny, and on all the seven trips I have made to that vast continent I have had a marvellous time.

Mainly I played the clubs. My first ever date on my opening tour in 1973 was in the South Sydney Junior League Club, a colonial-type building with propeller blades lazily swishing the ceiling, a noisy bar, and a jovial atmosphere. Everyone was rooting for me, and I won them over in the first minute.

Oh, there were some great times in Australia. Once I found myself in a bar with a ship's captain who told me an incredible yarn. He had come off his ship in Darwin, and celebrated his home leave with a few pints of Four-X, or some equally strong brew. Driving to his home in the outback, he suddenly saw a kangaroo jump into his lights. He braked hard – but hit the poor beast, which flopped down dead in the road.

The skipper had a rare sense of humour, and thought he'd play a joke on his mates he was due to see in the next town. So he dragged the kangaroo into the back of his Jeep, took off his blazer and put it on the animal, then drove off. Ten minutes later the kangaroo made a remarkable recovery, and started slugging the captain with its paws.

He screeched to a stop – and the kangaroo leaped out of the Jeep and hopped off into the night, resplendent in the captain's double-breasted blazer. 'It hasn't been heard of since, sport, and neither has my jacket,' my new-found friend bemoaned.

But we both cherish the thought that somewhere in the Australian bush a kangaroo is hopping around, even as you read this, clad in a smart blue blazer against the desert chill. Hopping mad too, no doubt.

The worst thing that Tony Fayne ever experienced in all our years together happened on our 1973 Australian tour. We found ourselves in a remote area of the Gold Coast up towards the Great Barrier Reef in a small town called Goolamgatta. Tony woke up one morning to find he had gone partially deaf! He hastened to the only doctor in town.

'Tony,' shouted the doc in broad Aussie tones. 'Yer've got wax in yer ears.' He handed my partner a small phial. 'Here, put these drops in yer ears every two hours, okay?'

'Okay,' said Tony. 'Thanks a lot.'

He dutifully poured the drops every couple of hours, as instructed – but as he stepped out on to the stage that night he went stone deaf! 'It was like a shutter coming down,' he told me afterwards. He couldn't hear anything I said. He was conducting the band, but couldn't hear what they were playing. He didn't know if he was shouting or speaking normally. He couldn't even hear if the audience was applauding.

Of course I had no idea my straight man was living in a nightmare world of numbing silence, and went happily on with the act. And somehow we got away with it. He read my lips, he knew the act by heart – and it proves how good his timing was that none of us ever suspected he was mutton-and-Jeff.

In 1974 I had my first sight of Teheran, in the days when the Shah ruled from his peacock throne. Tony and I found ourselves appearing in a club called the Sheka Fah Nous in the heart of the red light district. Our dressing-rooms were about the size of a lavatory – and smelled like it. The lighting was a ghastly blue, which played weird tricks with our eyes. It was thirty-five quid a head to set foot inside, and that was just the food. The drink you had to order by the bottle – and everything was a hundred pounds a bottle, Scotch, Vodka, even Martini. In other words, a rip-off joint.

The customers, mostly men in dark suits, hardly understood a word either Tony or I said. But it didn't seem to matter. They roared with laughter at the slightest gesture, threw carnations on the stage, and generally it was a riot. The women at their tables were showgirls from the club, exotic Indians and Philippines, who would sidle up between acts to get as much drink out of the clientele as possible.

Tony took one look at them, and muttered: 'Call girls, every one.'

In the month we were there we were treated like royalty, with a luxury hotel suite each and a chauffeur-driven car constantly at our disposal. I could have had caviar and vodka coming out of my ears – unfortunately I don't like either. I just missed my Shepherd's pie like mad.

Whenever we set foot in the streets or the markets I was recognised. College students and little kids alike would point and shout:

'Meestair Norman! Ah, Meestair Norman!' and follow me around trying to touch me. My films were always being shown at the local cinemas, dubbed into Farsi, the local lingo.

We gave a private show for the Shah at his palace on the outskirts of the city, just Tony and myself with our pianist, with not even an orchestra to back us. Luckily there was a grand piano, so I was able to give them some of my favourite routines. The only hiccup was during rehearsals when the Shah's sister refused to move the piano to where we wanted it. Tony insisted. In the end he put on all his considerable charm, and said: 'Come on, darlin'. It'll make all the difference.' I flinched at Tony's cheek, but she enjoyed being called 'darling' and melted visibly. Finally the piano was trundled over to where we wanted it.

The show took place in a huge banqueting hall, all marble pillars and fountains. Three hundred guests stood around in kaftans and robes and all the Iranian clobber, with the Shah himself in a dinner jacket with velvet sleeves sitting on a gold throne at one end. We were presented afterwards, and I nearly got a crick in my neck chatting to the Shah's wife Empress Farah Dibah, who was over six feet tall and towered over me. They had both seen my films, and liked them enough to beckon the royal finger in the direction of the palace.

One curious anomaly Tony and I noticed was that the

thick Persian carpets left our shoes covered up to the ankles with very common-or-garden dust. At least the bo had solid gold taps.

The travel bug was taking me everywhere. The Pink Giraffe Club in Hong-Kong . . . rubbing shoulders with Prime Minister Ian Smith in Rhodesia . . . perspiring away pounds in the cloying humidity of Malaysia . . .

The high spot of 1972 was an extensive winter tour of South Africa. Our winter, their summer. Tony is a great cricket fan (so am I), a member of Lords Taverners (me, too) and used to bowl a useful googly for North Middlesex. So we were both delighted to find the Australian cricket team in the same plane when we took off from Heathrow for Johannesburg. Not only that, but also on the plane was that legendary hell-raiser Trevor Howard. He was on his way to film scenes in *Ryan's Daughter* on the marvellous sand beaches of Durban that the director David Lean had decided would double nicely for Ireland.

It was in Durban that Trevor and his delightful wife Helen Cherry came to my flat for lunch. They arrived at 10.00 a.m. and Trevor got stuck into the bar, kicking off with large gin-and-tonics. By the time the cold lobster salad was served up Trevor was so pie-eyed he couldn't tell a claw from a carrot. But he had a fund of stories that kept us in stitches until we poured him out at sunset.

Our touring company included singer Julie Rogers and comedian Joe Church, with dear old Eddie Calvert playing the trumpet in the band. Sad to say, his career had taken a tumble – but what a player that man was!

We played Capetown, Port Elizabeth and Durban, as well as Johannesburg – where, because of the altitude, they had oxygen cylinders stored in the wings. The dancers needed it – Tony and I didn't. In those days TV was still in its infancy, people flocked to the cinema and theatres for their entertainment, and we sold out at every performance.

On the way back Tony and I dropped in on Zimbabwe, or Rhodesia as it was known then, to give a show in Salisbury. The Prime Minister, Ian Smith, was in the audience, and came backstage afterwards. He invited me to coffee in Government House next day, and I took a book along that he had written. Would he sign it for me? 'Certainly,' he said. 'What would you like me to write?'

'Oh, just sign it Smudger!' I said, lightly, reminding him that in the Army all Smiths were known as Smudger.

I still have it on my shelf in my study: 'To Norman, from Smudger Smith.'

Apart from world-wide tours, variety and panto, the seventies and eighties kept me busy with television. I appeared on shows like ATV's *Music Hall, It's Norman* and my own weekly sitcom series *A Little Bit of Wisdom,* in which I'd get into all sorts of scrapes, from tangling with spies to getting tangled up in supermarket trollies. Another series in similar vein was *Nobody is Norman Wisdom.*

I also tried my hand at the popular panel game *Celebrity Squares,* which was an excuse for general mayhem and mirth in the studio. Spike Milligan had the reputation of being the most uncontrollable leg-puller, and anyone prepared to sit below him was warned to take an umbrella, as he had a habit of pouring water from his carafe down their neck. He would also tear his note pad into tiny shreds and sprinkle it like confetti over the poor wretch's head, muttering:

'Sorry, my dandruff's getting worse!'

I would look on the set as a gymnasium, and used the staircase as a frame, swinging on the steel squares, and scampering up and down it to ask other contestants the answers.

Arthur Mullard came up with the most outlandish ripostes. Once he was asked: 'Is it true that a polar bear disguises itself as a pile of snow?' Arthur replied: 'If that's true, how does a brown bear disguise itself?'

One broadcast that will not soon be forgotten by anyone who saw it, and certainly not by me, was the live Pebble Mill show from the BBC studios in Birmingham in February 1975. Bob Langley introduced me, and Donny McLeod was to interview me. I bounced out in front of the studio audience, and went happily into overdrive – and thousands of viewers at home saw me in what is known as a state of undress. Out of camera range Bob Langley kept hissing at me: 'Trousers . . . undone!' and rolling his eyes significantly downwards, but I thought he was joking. Somebody was holding up a big card with the same message, and it was panic stations in the control box.

I went blithely on with my chat, totally unaware. Suddenly the vital part of the show, so to speak, became to get Norman to do his trousers up! Finally the irrepressible Kenny Ball, who was there with his Jazzmen to provide the music, came out with it: 'Well, Norman, I've gotta tell you – your flies are undone!'

I must have got caught up with one of my props before coming out – and at least I was able to point out that I'd been a flyweight champion. A number of viewers rang up, but most of them were on my side. As I said afterwards when it made headlines: Although my office door was open, you couldn't see the office boy!

CHAPTER NINETEEN

Money and I have always been uneasy bedfellows. I've earned a lot, and spent a lot. While it is true that I did become Britain's highest-earning comedian, the figures that were bandied around made even me blink. On 6 April 1956, for instance, the *News Chronicle* revealed I had jumped into the £200,000-a-year class, which catapulted me into the world strata of high rollers, with a movie contract with Warwick Films, backed by Columbia Pictures.

The truth was somewhat less heady: it was to be a five-year contract at £45,000 a year – still no small potatoes – for one film a year. They were to be on the lines of the old *Road* films with Hope and Crosby, starring me in all sorts of comedy capers. The first picture was to be *An Englishman in Las Vegas,* a madcap adventure with Edward G. Robinson and the statuesque Anita Ekberg for love interest – and who would argue with *that*?

The project came about in the oddest way. I was in my Kensington flat one morning when the phone rang. The voice sounded familiar. 'This is Cary Grant.'

'Oh yes?' I said. 'Pull the other one.'

He said: 'No, honestly it is. And I want to come and meet you. I can be round in half an hour.'

Blow me down, thirty minutes later the doorbell sounded – and there stood the tall, suave figure of the screen's most popular leading man, resplendent in blazer and slacks with a knife-edge crease that could have cut through a steak.

I gave him a cup of coffee and we chatted for a few minutes. Then, in that uniquely mannered voice of his, he said: 'I'll come to the point. Would you be interested in making films in America?'

I could scarcely believe my ears. 'Of course I would,' I managed to say.

'Warwick Films are very interested in you,' he said. 'Let me have your agent's name.' And after a few more pleasantries he got up and left.

That afternoon Billy Marsh rang me. 'We've got an appointment with Warwick Films in Mayfair tomorrow morning, ten o'clock sharp,' he said. 'Some joker on the phone gave his name as Cary Grant to my secretary and left a message. But I've checked it out, and they want us round.'

'Funny you should say that,' I said. 'I had a bloke in my flat today who looked just like Cary Grant, too.,

Billy said: 'What are you talking about?'

I said: 'But it *was* him.'

Next morning I was there with Billy at ten o'clock sharp. Cary Grant was conspicuously absent, but in a plush fourth-floor office two smooth-talking executives spelled out the good news. They had projects 'in the pipeline', and wanted to make me a Hollywood star.

Sadly, it didn't work out. Negotiations went on and on for eight long months. But unbeknown to me I had fallen among the money-men whose idea of a laugh is when the balance sheet is in the black, and the deal fell through.

Why Cary Grant to make the overtures? I never did find out. The formidable boss of Warwick Films, one Irving Allen who was built like a Sherman tank and had a voice to match, issued a statement about a 'script disagreement', adding: 'Mr Wisdom did not think it was funny enough. We agreed with him.' In fact that little episode cost me £2000 in solicitors' fees and a headache at the end of it.

It was no fault of my agent. Billy worked tirelessly to try and get the small print sorted out, but to no avail. Personally, I admit to being extremely naive when it comes to money. I simply say: As long as I can suffer in comfort, then I'm all right. I'll never know what happened.

I have been lucky to have some marvellous people watching my interests – when, sadly, Billy Marsh had a stroke in 1990, his place was taken by Johnny Mans, a great character who used to be a stand-up comic before moving to the other side of the drapes and who had been working with me for some years planning my tours. He is my business manager, agent, confidante and friend and that's what I like – friend! You can really enjoy yourself if you are working with someone you like. On top of that he has a lovely wife, Becky, and two smashing kids, Elliot his sports crazy son and Lucy his beautiful little daughter. I cannot help cuddling them when I see them, although I feel that Elliot is beginning to prefer shaking hands, with a smile of course. Yes – he's growing up. And Johnny's daily phone calls ensure I keep on my toes with one project or another in the pipeline. The rest of my small but trusted team are my adviser Ken Bowers, a financial wizard who lives less than half an hour from my flat in Epsom, and Mrs Clare Faulds, my advocate in the Isle of Man.

I always liked messing about in boats. But in 1960 I was well and truly messed about when I decided I would like to build my own yacht – or at least design it from scratch. I settled down in my study and got to work. Finally I had prepared the plans for a 94-foot cruiser, which I showed to a boatbuilder I knew in Shoreham, Sussex. 'How much do you reckon that would cost me?' I asked. I didn't know anything about the engine size or technical details, but I had designed the hull, the interior decor, the cabins, all the way down to the slanting windows that would give her a streamlined look. I named her *Conquest*. He pored over the plans, and came up with what seemed a very fair figure: £14,000. So I gave him the green light, and building started immediately.

After a few weeks the price had gone up to £17,000. The builder decided to take her to Gibraltar to fit the engine and complete the finishing. Over the next eighteen months the cost jumped to £30,000, then spiralled up to £70,000 – and by the time *Conquest* was ready to be launched she had cost me over £200,000! Gor blimey – I was in trouble. I knew I'd have to work flat out to pay those sort of bills. That was one of the reasons I pushed myself so hard; filming by day and doing two shows a night.

But what a beauty that boat was. Sleek lines, oak panelling, polished mahogany and teak fittings, luxury cabins, a spacious main lounge, and a Cordon Bleu chef looking after the galley. The upper sun deck had two swivel chairs that Sean Connery gave me from his first James Bond film, *Dr No*. Ironically, I was forced to turn it into a business to keep her going, and put her out for charter in the Mediterranean. It meant that in the fourteen years that I was the proud owner I hardly set foot on her. Tragic! But I've often said there are two happy days in the life of a yachtsman – the day he buys it and the day he sells it.

My second happy day came in 1976 when I sold it to a German industrialist – but at a loss.

Another financial headache I could have done without was the Silver Bullion Saga that made headlines in 1968. In fact I achieved the dubious distinction of being immortalised in the pages of the Income Tax textbooks which are the Bible for aspiring Inland Revenue inspectors. You'll find me buried away amid the dusty shelves in a case that made headlines, and established a precedent, in the High Gourt on 8 November 1968.

The background was cloaked in the kind of mystery that only Treasury Department bureaucrats can fathom. Ever since World War II the United States Treasury had supported the price of silver, so that the world could rely on at least one stable commodity. In five years its value had not varied by more than three per cent, Fort Knox was bulging at the seams, and Goldfinger hadn't raided it yet.

Six years previously, in 1962, my financial adviser Cecil Halpern, who was both a friend and a mathematical genius, and his partner Ken Bowers, came up with a wheeze that would make me a few bob on a safe bet – and, more important, create a hedge against the alarming possibility of the pound being devalued.

At this time I was earning around £40,000 a year, and paying 18/3d on every pound that I earned in the 'higher bracket', a crippling charge which embraced a ten-shilling surtax as well as the exhorbitant rate.

I felt a certain sympathy with George Bernard Shaw, who was paying 19/6d in the pound when he had three plays running in the West End and came up with the memorable comment: 'I am merely an agent for the Inland Revenue, earning sixpence in the pound commission!' I knew how he felt!

Cecil did a deal with Johnson Matthey, the international precious metal company based in Hatton Garden, whereby I bought £200,000-worth of silver bullion from them with a guaranteed buy-back price in a year. Within that time I would make some money on the silver market, and be paying interest on the £200,000 loan which would be tax deductible.

It was a straightforward deal, Cecil explained, neat and uncomplicated. He sat me down in his city office and explained patiently and at great length exactly how it would work. After an hour, it was as clear to my addled financial brain as the mud on the bottom of the Thames. But that's what Cecil and Ken were for – to look after my loot. 'Go ahead,' I told him. 'Whatever you say is fine by me.

'If all goes as planned,' Cecil assured me, 'you should get about £20,000 clear profit. And no tax. And if anything happens to the pound, you've got a cast-iron shield – made of silver.'

That sounded okay to me. But . . . in the middle of the transaction, out of the blue the US Treasury suddenly removed their support for silver that had kept it stable – and the price went through the roof.

Ken came bounding round to my house in West Chiltington, and waved a piece of paper in my face. 'You won't believe it,' he shouted. 'But that twenty grand has suddenly become £50,000!'

The second piece of paper came through some months later, and was rather less attractive. A demand from the Inland Revenue to pay 18/3d in the pound on my windfall. They couched it in terms like 'under the provisions of an Adventure in the Nature of the Trade . . .' but in any language the message was the same: *Pay up – or else!*

On 12 March 1968 we faced each other in the Chancery Court. *Wisdom* v *Chamberlain* (*Inspector of Taxes*), and this was one place where my trembling lower lip wasn't going to cut any ice at all! The lengthy arguments boiled down to the income tax boys agreeing I was not actually trading, as it was a one-off effort, but claiming that I intended to make a profit under any guise. I pleaded that I bought the silver to protect the value of my capital in case of devaluation, and how could I have seen that the price would jump sky-high?

Mr Justice Goff, bless him, went along with me all the way, and gave me costs as well. Perhaps he had seen one of my films, though I didn't actually get round to asking. Cecil, Ken and I left the court in high spirits, with a big grin on my face for the photographers and then off to a celebratory lunch in the Strand.

The grin lasted precisely eight months. The legal eagles at the Inland Revenue, considerably peeved by the verdict, weren't going to let me off the hook that easily. Their bloodhounds had their teeth sunk in good and proper, and were about to start shaking me.

They took the case to the Court of Appeal, where three eminent judges led by Mr Justice Salmon obviously found it fishy. They agreed I had bought the silver as 'an adventure in trade', and that I should pay tax on it. They also refused me leave to take it to the House of Lords.

The end result was: Inland Revenue one, Wisdom nil. I put on a brave face, if not a happy smile, for the cameras and the reporters in the Strand as I left. But inside I was feeling pretty sick that the tax man had stung me for so much money. The case ended up as an important legal precedent, written into heavy tomes in any library where red tape abounds.

Fortunately for me, my friend Ken Bowers has a long memory. He was seething quietly over the affair, and his chance for revenge came a whole decade later after Cecil had retired. Around the end of the seventies inflation was running high, small businesses were faced with acute cash flow problems, and the Chancellor introduced some elaborate allowances for off-setting the cost of increased stock against tax.

'Norman,' said Ken one morning when he dropped by my house for a coffee and a chat, 'I'm going to establish you as a metal trader.'

'What? Why? How?' I inquired, in that order.

Ken explained, keeping it simple. The London Metal Exchange fixes the price of metals twice a day. Traders have the choice of buying or selling that day – known as 'Spot' – or in one, two or three months' time – 'Futures'.

It was all way over my head, but then being short I thought to myself: so far, so good. 'The Inland Revenue have established that you were an adventurer in a metal trade. Now's the time to cash in on it,' declared Ken. 'I'll buy spot for you, and sell in the future. You're entitled to stock relief, and you can't lose.'

And I didn't. I became a trader in copper wire bars, of all things, and it took ten years. But at the end of that time I had recouped all the money I had been lumbered for in the silver tax. 'Honours even,' said Ken in triumph. I celebrated with an extra glass of ginger beer.

I'm not really a gambler, just a professional berk. But in 1981 I stuck my neck out again. Acting a part totally out of character has never worried me, and on the evening of June 5 I proved it with *Going Gently*, a total departure that took everyone by surprise.

The producer Innes Lloyd approached Billy Marsh and asked him if I would be interested in a serious role. I read the script and thought: 'Hullo, I can do some real acting here.' I was invited to the BBC TV Centre to have lunch with Innes and Stephen Frears, who was one of the most prolific directors in television, and would later make a name for himself with films like *My Beautiful Laundrette* (1985) and *Dangerous Liaisons* (1989).

I found myself sitting opposite a rather serious young man with a thoughtful expression that did not change throughout a somewhat strained meal. I let the pair of them do most of the talking. They explained the approach and the mood behind what was basically a two-hander play set in a terminal cancer ward where Fulton Mackay in the next bed to me taunts me about our mutual condition. Judi Dench was to play the no-nonsense ward sister who could not let her pity shine through. It wasn't a barrel of laughs, that's for sure. It was heart-rending stuff, and called for me to find depths in myself I had never had a real chance to plumb.

After lunch Frears invited me along the corridor to his office to 'discuss it further'. I sat opposite him, and he said: 'You realise, Norman, that my main concern in having you in the play is that there is no place in it whatsoever for laughs.'

I said: 'Oh, I don't know. If I'm wearing a hospital night-gown I can get out of bed and walk off, only to have the gown catch on a bed-spring. The spring could expand, and then *boing-g-g!* It jerks me back to the bed, and if I put my foot in a chamber-pot at the same time, it'll have everyone in fits –'

He sat there looking thunder-struck. Finally he managed to stutter:

'This – this is unbelievable –'

I looked at him straight, and demanded abruptly: 'Why the bloody hell did you send for me? Wasting my time. I don't have to be messed about by the likes of you – it's a downright liberty!'

He said: 'Oh please Norman, calm down. Calm down!'

I said: 'I am calm. But how's that for acting!'

Frears sat back and took a deep breath. Then he smiled and said: 'Norman, you've got the part.'

The very first scene we shot gave me an idea of what I'd let myself in for. It was a harrowing scene where I'm lying between the sheets in our small ward, with Fulton Mackay in the next bed. A name-tag has been tied around my wrist, and obviously the end isn't far off. Fulton is talking about how long we've got to go, and I'm up to my neck in self-pity.

The camera was on me in full close-up. 'Why me?' I keep asking. 'What have I done? I don't smoke, I don't drink. I've led a clean life. As far as I know I've done the right things . . . I haven't disappointed God . . . I've done my best.'

It was a tremendously difficult scene to get through, and I am sure the director had deliberately chosen it to see if I was up to it. All I can say is that when he said: 'Cut!' there was a silence that seemed to go on for ever. Looking around I saw tears in the cameraman's eyes. Frears just walked over, and without a word ruffled my hair. And I thought: I can do it. And I did.

To assist us in the film Frears brought in a nurse as

adviser to explain to us how cancer patients behaved. We called her Celia. She gave us fascinating, if sombre details about the irrational moments, the tantrums, the self-pitying, everything she saw and had to live through every day. When Frears introduced her, he said: 'Now you listen carefully, Norman. This lady knows what she's talking about.' I listened.

It was because of Celia that we included the scene just before the end where I petulantly call for a bowl of soup – 'The thickest pea soup you've got, thick enough to eat with a fork' – and I refuse to have anything else! I was too ill to touch it. .. but what a scene that was.

I used to smoke Senior Service cigarettes and I liked the odd slim cigar, usually a Panatella – which I would inhale. All I can add as a postscript is that since that play I have never touched either.

I would hate to think it was an identity crisis – but I found I was really enjoying roles completely at odds with the character everyone has known and – I hope – loved over the years. So when in 1991 the chance came to play a gangster in a film called *Double-X*, I jumped at it. As a villain who double-crosses the Mafia I get blown up by a bomb, I'm betrayed by my mistress (played by lovely Gemma Craven) and finally get it in the neck (literally) in a gangland execution. All good, dirty stuff.

The hit-man was played by William Katt, best known for his role as a young Robert Redford in the Western, *Butch Cassidy and the Sundance Kid – The Early Years*. As usual I insisted on doing all my own stunts, one of which was to be blown into the air on a quayside at Stranraer in Scotland, and land heavily on the pavement. After it was over young Mr Katt approached me, his mouth still slack with disbelief. 'How did you do that, and get up and walk away?' He shook his head. 'I thought you'd have broken every bone in your body.'

'Easy,' I said, clapping him on the shoulder. 'Just put it down to experience.' I only wish Edward G. could have seen me as a gangster. The film came out in June 1992.

I must have written thirty songs, from 'Beware', 'Please Opportunity' and 'Follow a Star' to 'Don't Laugh at Me'. There is one recurring theme, love and loneliness – perhaps a reflection of the character I created. And I suppose there must be a little bit of me in there, too.

It was in 1977 that I had my first taste of the Isle of Man while appearing in a three month summer season show. I had never been there before – and what a surprise it was. I fell in love with the place on sight, and grew to appreciate its beauty, its charms and its tranquillity even more during the time I was appearing at the Gaiety Theatre in Douglas. Up to then I had only thought of the island as a place where fast motor bikes went scorching round the country roads once a year in the TT races, and where the cats looked a bit different at one end.

But it came alive for me with the friendliness of the local people (just 66,000 of them) and the pace of life. The local phrase is *Traady-Liooar,* which means 'Time enough', and as for crime – a story in the local *Isle of Man Examiner* recently had the stark headline, 'Ski jacket stolen'. Big news!

I moved over in 1980. That is how long it took me to find my ideal spot for a second home, and build my dream house from scratch. I had been touring the island, and in a remote area called Kirk Andreas on the beautiful north-west coast I came upon a rundown old cottage – with an incredible view of rolling fields stretching away to a hazy mountain range in the distance. And I knew. This is it!

I designed the house myself out of local Manx stone. A touch of Mediterranean hacienda coupled with a 'random stone' effect of a period house built a long time ago. In fact it was completed in 1984. I rented a place two miles away in Bride while I went about obtaining local planning permission, which isn't too easy on the island. The house was built in eighteen months.

I took my treasured Bentley Continental with me. Later I sold it – I told you I'm a berk! I bought a black Rolls Royce Silver Shadow, and in 1986 sold it for my present luxury, a two-tone Rolls Royce Silver Spirit (licence no. NMN 17) that I keep for special occasions.

As a tax haven the Isle of Man ranks much the same as the Channel Islands. Income tax is twenty per cent, and there are no further surcharges of any kind. But just in case you're wondering – with a home in Surrey I pay UK taxes in full. I also suspect I found a kinship with the island's motto above the famous Three Legs symbol: *Quocunque Jeceris Stabit,* which means 'Whichever way you throw me I shall stand'.

Whichever way, I decided I couldn't find a better place for a second home for the rest of my life, and I put all my energies into making it my own hideaway. The interior was particularly exciting to design. I wanted my favourite Spanish feel to the place, with lots of Spanish and Italian furniture. The patio has green and brown tiles to match the garden, with wrought iron railings around the balconies. My study leads on to the summer house, with oak panels and genuine oak beams. It is a small, cosy room lined with photographs and theatrical posters – pride of place going to the framed telegram from Sid Field's family.

In the lounge is my grand piano, a beautiful polished French Erard, where I play and compose my music. In one corner stands a display cabinet with my trophies: British Academy Award, the Golden Flame from the Argentine, Top Comedian seven times, seven engraved silver spoons from John Paddy Carstairs, one for each of the films he directed – plus many trophies including the Lifetime Achievement Award from my fellow comics. What a swankpot! But why not? I did get 'em, didn't I?

One wall is dominated by a dramatic 3ft 6ins by 2ft 6 ins

oil painting of me as Aladdin, kneeling on the stage of the London Palladium with a spotlight searing through the dimness, holding the magic lamp in both hands. It was painted by Francis Russell Flint, who specialised in landscapes. But during the 1956 run of the pantomime he spent three weeks crouched over an easel in the wings to produce a magnificent work of art. And that lamp is in my cabinet too, presented to me by Bernard Delfont after the record-breaking panto. On close inspection you find that parts of the lamp are actually an ashtray and a door-handle, but you would never know it. Aladdin must have rubbed the props department, and the result was sheer magic!

The lounge is my favourite room, bright and cosy with its light cream walls, beige carpet, and bay windows. It's a room where the sun always seems to shine. At 7.00 p.m. on the dot I'll open up the carved wooden double-doors that conceal a monster TV set, plant myself down in my favourite armchair, and settle back for an evening's viewing. With any luck there'll be a big fight on, or a good soccer match.

I sit back to watch the box and munch a toasted ham sandwich made by my secretary-cum-minder Barbara, bless her, and sometimes I'll gaze out through the window at a view that never fails to move me. Past the clipped lawn is a gentle valley that stretches for miles before soaring up into the hills in the distance.

The price for the view is a keening wind that can sweep through the valley from the south-west without warning and gives 'Mr Green Fingers', otherwise my cheery gardener Rodney, an extra headache. But his weekly visits keep the garden in trim, and I am specially proud of the spiky cordyline palm trees that come from Australia and add to the semi-tropical feel of the place. In the summer the garden is a riot of colour, the beds filled with a variety of flowers,

from delphiniums to the mass of red and yellow lupins in all
their glory.

Yes, it's lovely to come home, and what I still find hard to
believe is it's all mine, and not a dream.

CHAPTER TWENTY

I am sitting up front in the coach with George the driver, watching the grey vista of the North Sea slip away into hazy infinity. We are saying goodbye to Lowestoft, after another sell-out show. Boarding houses slide past the window, with names like Adair, Sunningdale, Esplanade. Oh look, there's even a *Mon Repos*! Another town, another theatre, another programme for the scrapbook. The Wolverhampton Grand seems an age away. Last night was the Marina Theatre. Tonight, the Embassy, Skegness. Tomorrow, the Fairfield Halls, Croydon.

Tonight? Ah, Skegness. It was at the Pier Theatre in nineteen something-or-other that a schoolgirl of thirteen named Tonia Clark laughed so much when I was fooling around conducting the orchestra that she actually dislocated her jaw. Her parents had to take the poor girl to hospital to have it reset. I sent her a note of sympathy, while the theatre manager Mr Jack Bradley was quoted as saying:

'In a case like this we would normally give the family complimentary tickets to see the show again. In Tonia's case, we just daren't!'

Memories are made of this, as the song said.

The band behind me on the coach all have their own stories, and spin away the hours and the miles with yarns that will keep us entertained far into the night.

The forty-seater coach has a crown emblazoned on the

270

side. Royalty! Inside is a life-size cardboard cut-out of Norman Wisdom sitting in splendid isolation on a rear seat, ready to be taken out and propped against the door of the next theatre. The interior is cheerful grey. Video, fridge, coffee-maker. A loo downstairs. We've got the lot.

I call it 'The Lorry', because it carts all our vital belongings around. Instruments, clothes, cardboard boxes full of sheet music are packed into the back. Our driver George has been with us five years. Every morning he tops up the hundred-gallon tank, and off we go. We are self-sufficient down to the sleeping compartment below stairs with its twin bunks, though often the boys will kip down on lilos spread on the floor between the seats if they want to save on digs.

The coach becomes our travelling home, and over the next six weeks we will become very attached to it. I look back at the others, and give them a wave. Tony Fayne, occupying his usual seat three rows back, once said: 'There isn't a bad egg amongst 'em.' All of them are freelance musicians. Terry White, pianist and musical director, Cliff Longhurst, drummer, Harry Bence on alto-sax, Gary Branch on clarinet when he's not playing tenor-sax, Paul Higgs, keyboard, and Dale Gibson on trumpet. And our company manager, John Ditchfield, who looks after the cash when he's not looking after his bass guitar. They're a great bunch, a team from start to finish.

I sit back and close my eyes, listening to the soporific *thrum-thrum* of the wheels as we speed north. How many miles have I travelled, criss-crossing the country from theatre to club to TV studio over the years? Fleeting images rise like ghosts in my memory, shine briefly, and fade back into darkness.

Voices, too. My mother: 'My, Norman, how you've grown . . . The Lipton's manager: 'All right, shove off!' . . . The dockyard foreman: 'Show me your shoes . . .' My father: 'Get out!' . . . Shipmates: 'Don't let us down' . . . Marshal Foch, and the coffee stall owner: 'Bullshit them' . . . The bandmaster: 'What's a sharp?' .

The sergeant: 'Bury that!' . . . And the Regimental Call: 'We are the Tenth, the shiny, shiny Tenth' . . .

Oh, those were the days!

And the rise from the obscurity of a bare changing-room in a draughty provincial variety hall to the star dressing-room at the London Palladium with my name on the door . . . my lucky No. 8 at Pinewood Studios . . . the tours to the far corners of the globe.

But most of all the friends I made.

The coach slows, turns in to a car park, and comes to a halt by the Stage Door of the Embassy Theatre. The future beckons, and right now the future is the next show.

I wonder briefly if the ten-year-old lookalike will be there tonight, a small boy dressed in a Gump suit and cap, with his parents in tow who follow me round the country.

Or the group of six of my fans who dress up in my outfit and sit together in the front row, cheering me on even though they must have seen me a score of times and know every line of my act backwards.

Tony Fayne's voice in my ear. 'Norman! We're here!'

We are, too.

'Let's go,' I say.

. . . And the show begins.

Chapter Twenty-One

The show went on until 1998, when dear old Tony Fayne felt it was time to call it a day. I like to think he'd had enough of seeing my pained expression as he tortured me with that infernal 'Biff Bang' machine, and couldn't stand my discomfort any more. But I suspect less altruistic reasons were the cause of his deciding to chuck it in and tend the roses in his garden in Hampshire. He just wanted a quiet life – and we had been friends for thirty years enjoying ourselves to the full and touring the world.

Had we really been together thirty years?

'I'm going to miss you, young Norman,' he said, shaking hands after the final curtain call as our last tour came to a close in Tunbridge Wells.

'Me, too, Tony,' I said.

'I mean,,' he said, 'who am I going to be able to vent my rage on if I'm feeling a bit out of sorts? I always looked forward to thumping you around!'

Oh . . . well . . . Thanks, Tony, anyway. We gave each other an affectionate bear hug, and went our separate ways. I would see him from time to time, dropping in to his home on the edge of the New Forest for a cuppa and seeing if he was up to a game on the golf course with his handicap of 16 against my 362.

'Golf? There's no contest.' Who said that? Well, he did.

If the *Tony Fayne Show* was over, and my sparring partner

would slide into graceful and well-earned retirement, I still had loads to do.

Like those trips to Albania.

Why Albania? The short answer is: *Because they kept asking me!* In fact they had been asking me for years, and I had no idea why because nobody told me. All I do know is that in January 1995 I had first embarked on one of the strangest and unlikeliest trips of my life, to a country that up to then had only been a vague blob on the map somewhere near Greece.

The invitations kept coming in, and finally I found out why. All my films back in the Fifties and Sixties had proved enormously popular with the locals, possibly because they had very little else to laugh at. Due to the repressive regime, the iron hand in an iron glove of a gent named Enver Hoxha (who died in 1985 after forty years of ruthless dictatorship) Albania's intake from the decadent Western world was, to put it mildly, sparse. But no-one, not even the most zealous commissar could find any threat to destabilise the country from little Norman Pitkin, the name they gave me in many of my films – or 'Pitkini', as the Albanians called me. Subversive? I wouldn't know how to spell the word, or want to. Apparently the dictator decreed that Norman Pitkin was a 'proletarian hero' to Mr Grimsdale's capitalist ogre.

Albania is shaped like a duffel bag. Geographically speaking, you'll find it nestling against the Adriatic Sea opposite Italy, blocked from the rest of the Balkan peninsula by rugged peaks, among them the 'Prokletije' or 'Accursed Mountains'. Roughly the size of Wales, it is surrounded by Yugoslavia (north), Macedonia (east) and Greece (south).

I know, because when I heard I was going there I did my homework out of courtesy to my hosts. And the more I learned about the place the less reassuring it became. Like so many countries in that part of the world it had survived a chequered history through a succession of empires –

Roman, Byzantine, Ottoman, and a bloke called Ahmed Zogu who crowned himself King Zog I in 1928 and hung in there until 1939 when war was declared and he legged it into exile. After 1945 the downtrodden populace found themselves in the grip of communism, which lasted until Hoxha's death.

Today, outsiders like to make jokes about the country, which I think is unkind. The people I met were warm, friendly, generous and stoic. But I must admit the general image doesn't have a lot going for it. Like the survey they did in 2002, where some bright spark found our railway system in Britain was the third worst in Europe – beaten only by Macedonia and (you've guessed it) poor old Albania.

Well, I never did take a train there. But when you're shivering on the platform at Clapham Junction waiting for the 8.15 a.m. to Victoria, remember the folk standing on Drashi or Gotitza waiting for the 5.15 a.m. to Tirana. They tend to get up earlier there.

Rather more ominous were the reports that dubbed the place 'Europe's outcast', pointing out that ninety-five per cent of the 3.5 million population owned guns, and that the cities were plagued by a daily round of murders and power cuts.

This was yet another audience I was looking forward to playing to. I flew in to Tirana airport, along with my agent and business manager Johnny Mans, my old Army pal Pat Dickinson, another friend Bill Hamilton, and pianist Jimmy Noon as accompaniment, so to speak. 'You never know – I might have to burst into a rendering of *Don't Laugh at Me,*' I told him. 'Keep those fingers flexed!'

Standing in the wings for future trips was my personal assistant Sylvia Murray, a lovely lass from Northampton who was a housing manager before taking on the task of caring for my every whim. She is the proverbial treasure, with all the attributes I ask for: a nice, friendly, sensible person who can cook, type, look after me and laugh at my jokes. Actually, I don't keep falling over all the time. Just some of it.

The first hint of what we were all in for came when we landed. I thought it might be the right thing to wear my Gump suit, and had changed into it a few minutes before the 'Fasten seat belts' sign flashed on.

As we emerged from the plane, we saw a bunch of armed guards at the foot of the steps, all looking my way. 'I thought they liked my films,' I said to Johnny. 'Don't tell me I'm going to be hauled off to the slammer!' But I pretended to trip on the steps, and people were laughing before I touched the tarmac.

The soldiers in fact were a guard of honour, and the whole place was in uproar. The arrival terminal was bedlam, with cameras flashing and literally hundreds of people cheering and waving, straining to get a glimpse of me. There were shouts of welcome from all sides.

'Mr Pitkini! *Mr Pitkini!*' I waved back as best I could in the melee, and I have to admit there were tears misting my eyes. This was as good as any reception I'd ever had in Blighty. The last time I had seen anything like it was in newsreels of the Beatles arriving at London airport back in the Sixties. I went through some of my routine, tripping over my feet and pretending to run away, and they loved it. I even fell down three stairs into the reception area, and they fell about too. Finally someone dragged me off into a side room, where a camera and a tripod had been set up and a television presenter was waiting to interview me. He was a smooth, middle-aged man who did his best in two languages – broken English and what I took to be Albanian – when in the middle of our chat, he suddenly held up his hand, stopped the camera, and asked for my autograph! I presume it wasn't going out live, but that was another first.

They put us all up in the splendour of the former dictator's palace, though I'd have happily settled for something less grand. This was the right royal treatment. Norman Zog the First – how does that sound? Okay, forget it! Just an idea. The communist regime had collapsed in 1990, opening the way for all sorts of schemes and scams to come on the market with the 'new freedom' – including rival gangs, a 'Balkan Mafia', and an unhealthy line in drugs and arms dealing. You could say the place was somewhat volatile.

The trip had been put together by several charities, including ADRA (Adventist Development and Relief Agency), Task Force Albania and MenCap on the Isle of Man, of which I'm president. We would be there four days. Over dinner at a local restaurant on my first evening in this strangely fascinating place I learned some intriguing facts that you won't find in any guide book. The menu, for a start, was interesting. I ducked the *kukerc*, even though it was a traditional delicacy of lamb's intestines stuffed and fried and served with yoghurt and olives, and went for plain scrambled eggs on toast. The local firewater of *raki* brought tears to my eyes, so I settled for orange juice and let the rest of the party get on with the toasts.

My informant, a cheerful young interpreter organised by the welcoming committee, finally got down to basics. 'Mr Pitkini, you can buy a Mercedes here for just $5,000. Except that you cannot take it out. It will have been stolen from some other country and brought in here illegally.

'You will be arrested at the border. Or you want a fully automatic Kalashnikov assault rifle? Just three dollars on the streets of Tirana.'

'Blimey,' I said. 'Thanks, but no thanks.'

The streets of Tirana are something else. The spot where at least a dozen of them converge is the huge Skenderberg Square, which seems about the size of your average golf course as I discovered on our first stroll through the city. The cars come at you from everywhere, souped-up old bangers roaring by in a cacophony of screeching brakes and honking horns. Look out, *Pitkini*, here comes another one!

The fun part of the trip was to be a public appearance at a cinema which they'd named after me. By now I'd found out that the despotic Mr Hoxha had been paranoid about Western influences on his country, and made it a prison offence for anyone caught with their TV aerials turned across the Adriatic towards Italy. Amazing! People could only watch what he allowed them to watch. Even more astonishing was that apparently he had taken a shine to my films, which were run and rerun at cinemas and on TV. No wonder I had become a household name.

The new boy on the presidential block was a former heart surgeon named Sali Berisha, who had been elected in 1992. I met him when he was at the height of his powers – just in time, because he was toppled by a popular uprising a couple of years later.

But at least I achieved another high spot on that first trip: an official reception at Government House in my honour, with lots of dark-suited dignitaries standing around and stiffening to attention when a band played the National Anthem.

I should mention here that the Albanian National Anthem was once described thus: 'It is as long as a Wagner opera and sounds like the Marine Corps band performing the whole *Ring* cycle while falling down all the stairs at the Washington Monument'. So you'll get an idea of the noise.

But there was President Berisha himself waiting at the end of the room to shake my hand. 'Welcome to our country,' he said, in excellent English. 'You are so funny!' And he burst out laughing.

I hadn't even opened my mouth, or given the smallest hint of a trip, but it seemed a promising start. *I can do with audiences like you!* 'Thank you very much,' I responded.

'I have something for you,' he said, gesturing to an aide.

Next thing I knew, a medal on a ribbon was being draped around my neck – and that's how I was given the Freedom of the City of Tirana.

How about that? It goes with two Freedoms I've already got, London and Douglas in the Isle of Man, and today it's hanging up in a glass frame in my study. And right proud I am of it, too. Do you know anyone else who's got one? (Don't all rush!) Actually, they did confide that the last person to get it was Mother Theresa. So I was in good company. That night the *raki* flowed, though I steered clear of it, a lot of back-slapping went on, and generally it was an evening I will never forget. I messed about a bit, though I didn't actually roll around on the floor, but it was enough to keep them laughing.

Prior to the reception had come the serious business, and the real reason that I was in Albania at all. Apart from the cinema, there's the Pitkini Centre, would you believe – a welfare centre for kids which was my first port of call. I would also visit hospitals and children's homes and other welfare projects. In one orphanage I spotted a slide in the playground. Guess who was shouldering the kids aside to get up the ladder and whizz down?

The 'No 1 Hospital Tirana', to use its bleak official name, was an eye-opener. Not to mince words, it was close to a culture shock to see that grey slab of a building on a huge run-down estate, and witness what passes for medical facilities in this poverty-stricken little country. Doctors virtually chain-smoke when they do their rounds, the equipment looks as if it's inherited from Florence Nightingale, and all in all it makes our National Health Service seem like *Shangri-la*.

But the kids are marvellous, and so brave it makes you want to weep. I pulled faces at them, and made funny unintelligible noises which (forgive the pun) had them in stitches. Alright, I couldn't speak more than a few words of their language, and nor could they speak English. But somehow I got through to them because laughter is a universal language, isn't it?

During those four moving days, and other days that would follow when I went back to Albania, I just felt proud to be accepted, as someone kindly said, as 'an ambassador of laughter'. I'll go along with that.

Their Minister of Culture Mr Teodor Loco put it another way at a dinner held in my honour at the Palace. 'Mr Pitkini's art is above all politics. Totalitarianism is very dark. But the humour that comes from him is like a light, a joy for us all. It is well known that people need humour in their times of difficulty, and for twenty-five years he has been giving us that humour.' Wasn't that nice?

My last night was memorable. Actually, unforgettable. When did I ever sing *Don't Laugh at Me* with bats swooping around in the ceiling like swirling leaves in a squall. But it happened at the Academy of Fine Art where the students put on a special performance for me, everything from opera to comedy.

The building itself, with its peeling wallpaper and cracked plaster pillars, had seen better days. But the show had a youthful zing about it that was totally captivating, and judging by what I saw I couldn't help thinking there was hope for this small country with its resilience, optimism and creative talent.

My turn. I had nothing rehearsed, but they were shouting so insistently that I had to go up on stage to say a few words and thank them. I climbed the steps hesitantly, faced the back curtain in apparent bewilderment, then turned to face the audience and recoiled with mock stage fright.

Finally I managed a small speech of appreciation, interrupted when I appeared to slip and bang my head on the mike (yes, they did laugh), made sure Jimmy Noon had found the piano in the corner . . . and launched into *Don't Laugh at Me*.

That was a scene I won't forget in a hurry. The students cheered Mr Pitkini to the echo, the bats buzzed me one last time, and I reckon I found myself a new fan club that night. I might even make a film there one day.

CHAPTER TWENTY-TWO

It wouldn't be the last trip I'd make to that corner of the Balkan Peninsula. Fast forward to the new Millennium and the summer of the year 2000. A little matter of the World Cup had come up to tax people's minds, and believe it or not England had been drawn against – yes, Albania, in one of the qualifying rounds. Playing away in the first leg, which meant a return trip to the place where I was a Freeman of the capital city.

What on earth was I to do? I went out there, of course. It was my duty, wasn't it – and I love soccer like a second religion. But as an avid England supporter, how could I avoid offending my new-found friends? Besides which, Albania were the underdogs, the no-hopers, and I didn't want to rub it in.

Johnny Mans came up with the answer, and presented me with it an hour before kick-off. The trip had been arranged by John van Weenen, head of Task Force Albania. We knew there was a good contingent of England fans who had obtained their visas, paid their travel and hotel expenses, transferred their money into *Leks* (120 to the pound, and get rid of it all in Albania!) and would be cheering themselves hoarse in their allotted corner of Qemel Stafa stadium. Johnny had already arranged that I should be in soccer strip, and when I asked, 'But what shirt am I going to wear?' he just winked and said, 'Wait and see.'

Johnny had arranged a room at the ground, and when we got there he escorted me through, fished into a bag, and waved a shirt at me in triumph. 'There! What do you think of that?'

I had to take my hat off to him. The shirt had been specially made, half and half with a stitch down the middle – one side England's white, the other Albanian red-and-blue. 'I think it's the polite thing to do,' said Johnny with a grin. Plus one white sock and one red-and-blue. Clever, or what?

Both factions certainly thought so when I suddenly appeared from the tunnel before the kick-off, trotting down the side line in my double-coloured shirt and white shorts to where the English supporters were massed in one corner of the stadium. The place went mad! I had to jog past the massed Albanian areas to get there, and they cheered me first when they recognised the mascot in their midst – it didn't matter whose, though of course I wanted England to win. 'Norman-o! *Norman-o!*' they screamed, drowned only by our lads yelling 'Norman Number One! *Norman Number One!*' when I reached them.

That was one game I won't forget in a hurry and, for the record, England won 3-1.

The second leg was equally dramatic. Because England had walloped Germany 5-0 in Munich, our tails were up, and everyone thought it would be a slaughter when Albania took us on again on our home territory. The arena was Newcastle United's ground, with a sell-out 52,000 crowd roaring on David Beckham's boys and just twenty Albanian fans allowed into the country to spur on their team.

The Home Office put the block on scores of other visa applications 'to prevent supporters claiming asylum'. Sad, really, but what can you say? England coach Sven Goran Eriksson told reporters: 'I feel sorry for the Albanian fans being unable to see their team play football on such a momentous occasion. I also feel sorry for the team not having the support they need at such a big game.' Sporting words – but not much help to little Albania, whose valiant lads succumbed by a plucky 2-0. The choice of ground couldn't have been better for me, though. At Newcastle I'm lucky enough to be invited into the directors' box for home games, thanks to my mate Pat Dickinson who lives close by and lets them know when I'm around. I'm not swanking, but it's a wonderful way to see a soccer match!

It's funny how life seems to throw up coincidences. The same year I first found myself in Albania saw me bouncing around in a truck bound for Chernobyl, of all places. Call it weird if you like, but there is actually a Norman Wisdom Centre in that place which has the unhappy distinction of being known for one of the worst nuclear disasters of the century. Since that terrible day in 1986, the area has been a virtual wasteland, though people still live there, clinging to some kind of life and refusing to leave their homeland.

My charity work includes being patron of International Aid Services, which is based on the Isle of Man. This supports the Norman Wisdom Children's Hospice in the town of Mayak, near Odessa, and with its two hundred beds is said to be the largest children's hospice in the world.

For a long time I had been mightily impressed with the work they do, with volunteers giving up their annual holidays in the UK to go out and help with construction and repairs.

Finally I had the chance to take a look at the sharp end of the operation. A friend named Robert Kelly, who is closely associated with the charity, set the wheels in motion. In May 1995 I found myself in a car park near Chorley in Lancashire with eighty other people, all of us eyeing three large trucks and two coaches that would be our homes for the next three days and nights. I knew it would be a tough journey, but I've lived rough before and this didn't give me any worries. Besides, it was all in a good cause.

The trucks were loaded to the roof with blankets, food, medical supplies and other necessary provisions. I could have taken a coach, but I opted to sit up front in one of the lorries with the driver and, as we set out for Felixstowe to catch the ferry, a sudden thought hit me. *I've done this before!* And my thoughts went back to the miles of English highway I'd put under me on my tours of the country over the years.

There was no crown emblazoned on the side of the vehicle on this trip, and no videos, fridges or loos. But who cared? Not me! There were plenty of places to stop off for a sandwich or a call of nature on the long journey through France, Germany and Poland, and I was so excited by the whole incredible experience that I wouldn't have felt any discomfort if I had been sitting on bare springs prodding me through the upholstery.

We slept in the trucks and on the coaches. No five-star hotels on this trip. All the money on these 'missions of mercy' goes straight to where it belongs – to the poor and needy kids, and the care they must have to keep them alive. I can sleep in most places, so I dozed happily as the truck ploughed on through the nights, with a change of driver every so often to give me a new buddy to talk to when I felt like it.

There was a genuine sense of purpose about the whole adventure, with committed volunteers from every walk of life coming together for these few days, knowing that the IAS had been credited with saving the lives of up to three hundred people in the area, providing support for three hospitals as well as the kids' hospice with my name above the door.

Finally we rumbled into Chernobyl – and that was a sight I'll never forget, however long I live and however hard I try. It was like the aftermath of a war zone, a once-beautiful place of old buildings mixed with new, but now reeking with an air of utter desolation that seemed to creep through the bricks of every building like a virus through the pores of your skin. An occasional old car or tractor bumped out of a side turning into the empty, barren streets. A few stunted trees and withered plants sprouted stubbornly from the hard earth. It was shivery and spooky, and the extraordinary thing was to find old people still clinging to their lives even in that Godforsaken spot.

Through an interpreter, I managed to ask one old peasant woman in a headscarf why she stayed there.

'Where else can I go?' She shrugged her thin, bony shoulders. 'I've never been out of this place in my whole life, and I am too old now to start looking for somewhere else. I will stay here and keep myself alive until it is no longer necessary.' I'll never forget that reply.

But I was there to bring some cheer into the lives of the new generation, and that meant the children's hospital. I had been into several such institutions in my trips, where the kids don't speak my language and I don't speak theirs, but somehow we always communicate and understand one another. I pull faces and make rude noises and generally mess about, and their little faces light up and they laugh themselves silly. Marvellous!

But I remember Chernobyl in particular. In this hospital I toured the wards and saw that some of the children looked really ill. I had taken bags of sweets along, but many of the kids were too ill to know about it. They were aged between five and fifteen, and a number of them were actually unconscious, breathing through tubes and lying in long rows, their beds side by side like a huge school dormitory. The nurses told me that many of them had radiation sickness, mainly leukaemia, and wouldn't live long. It was heart-breaking, they looked so helpless. Staring down at them lying there, I found a huge lump in my throat. It was terribly upsetting.

But one unexpected ray of sunshine came in the form of

young Lucus, a kid who must have been about seven, lying on his back with a tube in his nose but a bright gleam of determination sparkling in his eyes as he watched me approach through the ward. I caught his gaze, pulled a face, pretended to fall over the bed, and watched him dissolve into laughter even if he could hardly move under the sheets. I had a chat, most of it one-way, left a packet of sweets by the bed, patted his shoulder and went on my way.

Eighteen months later I was back, doing the rounds as you might say. Same hospital, same ward – and same kid in the same bed. Only this time Lucus was sitting up, a huge smile spread across his face – and his arms were outstretched towards me! I practically ran into them. We sat and hugged each other, and the months just dropped away.

He is still there, like so many of them whose names I never knew. But they've got TV there, and apparently they show my films every now and then. How do I know? Because I get a card from him each Christmas, that's how, along with simply-written letters and cards from other kids. That alone makes the whole thing worthwhile.

Some of the other volunteers stayed on to help out until the next convoy. What can you say about such people? 'Angels of mercy' seems too facile a description. But to these youngsters and the hard-pressed staff who care for them – angels themselves – that's what each new arrival must seem like.

Me, I went home on the same truck that had brought me. Sleeping where I sat, blinking out bleary-eyed through rain-swept windows at the border posts, thinking about one of the most unusual and unexpected chapters of my life.

People still ask me if I was frightened of the effects of radiation myself – and if not, why not.

You never know what stays in the ground, or for how long, and those trees and shrubs didn't look particularly happy. The boffins are always telling you one thing or another, so that in the end you don't know who to believe. Personally, I think you have to go by your instincts, after weighing up all the professional advice available. I was assured that it was all clear, and I had to take their word for it. I didn't even bother with a jab for anything. And so far – no ill effects!

Life is full of surprises, isn't it? I wouldn't have missed the experience for anything.

And I like to think I left a little bit of myself behind there.

Chapter Twenty-Three

Did you know I died three years ago? Well, a lot of people *thought* I had, including MPs at the House of Commons where I was being taken around on an official visit. I had to rush off early to catch a plane from Heathrow back to the Isle of Man, and apparently someone went up to a policeman and asked, 'Where's Norman Wisdom?'

The copper answered, 'He's gone.'

The other bloke thought I'd passed away, and the rumour went round Parliament, and all the way to Fleet Street the way rumours do. In the newspaper offices they were starting to prepare my obituary when someone managed to get hold of Johnny Mans. 'Is it true Norman Wisdom's dead?' he asked.

'Christ!' Johnny ejaculated. 'First I've heard of it.'

He knew where I should be, and rang Heathrow. They put out an announcement for me, and when I finally picked up the phone Johnny's voice was on the other end shouting, 'Are you still here? Are you all right?'

'Yes, I'm still here. Why shouldn't I be?' I asked.

'There's a rumour you're dead,' he said, without preamble. 'You had me really worried.'

'Well I'm not,' I said. 'This is the Departure Lounge, not the Dearly Departed Lounge!'

To prove my health and fitness, if nothing else, I've popped up in several TV shows as well as numerous charity events. Oh, and the cruises. Mustn't forget my annual seasonal flotation around the Caribbean. I'm so used to spending Christmas in a swimming costume under a hot sun that I'd feel quite out of place if it was snowing. I give my lectures and meet and greet the folks on deck. It's a lot of fun, and I get a nice tan as well.

As for TV, a studio is like a second home to me, and I always feel a lift in my stride when I walk on to a set and see the cameras waiting. One of my favourite programmes is *Last of the Summer Wine,* and when I was invited to appear in the Christmas episode in 1994 I jumped at the chance. We actually filmed it in September, and I had a wonderful week in the heart of the Yorkshire countryside swapping stories with the likes of Bill Owen, Brian Wilde and Peter Sallis. Thora Hird and Jean Ferguson were in the cast, and it was like one big family.

My character was a nutcase named Billy Ingleton, who had always wanted to be a professional concert pianist. I remember a scene in a pub where I had to get up on a high stool and make heavy weather of it, turning it into a personal struggle: my personal 'mission impossible'. Well, that scene could have come straight out of my live stage act, so I couldn't miss.

Talking of pubs, I've never played a drunk. I've always wanted to, because for someone who doesn't drink – now that really would be acting! I'm told the secret of playing a drunk is to behave like a man who is desperately trying to appear sober. Think about it! He may keep falling over, but he's doing his best to stay upright. That makes a kind of sense to me and I'd love to give it a shot.

My well-known love of practical jokes got me into the headlines again when I appeared in an episode of the hit BBC TV hospital series *Casualty.* I played a pensioner who is devastated when his wife is struck down by a fatal heart attack. It was described by the producers as 'a very poignant role, with Wisdom playing a sweet old man bewildered by what happens to his wife.'

Bewildered or not, I certainly livened up the rehearsals. My wife, played by the actress May Boak, was lying on a slab, and I sat beside her giving it all the emotion I could. 'Life will mean nothing to me now . . . nothing. I don't know how I'm ever going to live without you . . . Please come back . . .' Real tear-jerking stuff, and I could see that even some of the hardened crew were moved. Then, still talking, I surreptitiously tickled her feet – and that did it. May squealed and burst out laughing, and the whole thing came to a grinding halt.

It took us a bit of time to get going again, but it all worked out nicely in the end. The critics who gave us a thumbs-up never knew how we had struggled to keep a straight face in the actual recording, which went out on 17 October 1998.

I had more fun at Pinewood Studios, my old stamping ground, when we had a photocall to talk about a film idea called *Adam and Evil,* which remains my long-standing ambition.

The place hasn't changed since my own glory days, though they've built a few new sound stages, including the massive 007 set at the back of the lot. But the mansion is as fabulous as ever, with a unique atmosphere unlike any other film studio in the world.

Adam and Evil is very close to my heart. It has been a project that has been in my mind for some years, ever since I acquired the rights to an unusual J.B.Priestley story called *Tober and the Tulpa.* It's a black comedy about a lonely musician who falls in love with the cardboard cut-out of a beautiful blonde in a travel shop window. Then she suddenly comes alive, takes over his whole life, and makes it a misery. Weird, eh? And what a great title! I've turned it into a script that would make a smashing film. I even persuaded Bo Derek that she'd be the ideal actress for the lead part. I'm still hoping, and my fingers remain crossed!

Then I have a short 45-minute film up my sleeve that I wrote called *He Who Laughs Last*. There isn't a word of dialogue in it, just pure mime. The theme is centred around a day in the life of an old tramp – guess who? – just wandering around and getting into all sorts of hot water. It starts when I wake up on a park bench under a 'blanket' of newspapers, and follows me through the day as I live off my wits and manage to have a marvellous time into the bargain. My body language does the talking, and it's right up my street. There's one other project on the cards: a series about a burglar who robs the rich to pay the poor and needy. All in a good cause, you might say, and I rather like the title of this one, too: *Robbing Hood*.

What else? TV has kept me happily ticking over. You may have seen my house featured in *Through the Keyhole*, and the squire of the manor with it. Most actors and celebrities protect their privacy like the gold in Fort Knox, and particularly their homes. But I'm proud of my house, and I don't mind the public having a peek inside via the TV cameras. After all, I designed it, didn't I? They opened the programme by showing a suit on a hanger, plus a cloth cap with the peak turned up, as clues to who lives there. You didn't need to be Sherlock Holmes to realise who might stick his head round the door and welcome you inside.

Still up there in the Isle of Man, I was mine host in the holiday TV series *Wish You Were Here* when I was asked to take viewers on a conducted tour over the island. I gave them the full works about the peace and tranquility of the place, the beautiful views – which they could see for themselves – and the lovely countryside. I meant every word of it.

Halfway into the shoot, I couldn't resist showing them a statue of a little chap sitting on a wooden bench outside the town hall at Douglas. Carved out of bronze, he's at one end of the seat, with a certain Gump suit and cloth cap as the giveaway. Yes, me again. Tourists tend to have their photos taken sitting on the bench beside him, and one of the gags I like to play if I happen to be passing by is to walk up quietly behind them and just stand there, staring into the distance, or pulling a face. You should hear the screams when they notice me.

A local sculptress named Amanda Barton did the deed. I posed for her for three days, and somehow managed to stay still enough for her to get an amazing likeness. A statue of me – blimey, what an honour! There's one of Lord Nelson not far off, so I'm in good company. Cabin boy and Admiral!

I do the odd voice-over for commercials, and sometimes appear too. One I did for Woolworth's on TV was quite funny. They were advertising a range of nutcrackers around Christmas time, and the idea was that I would walk out of a Woollies store and bump head-on into a tree. Cracking my nut, geddit?

Then I'd rub my bonce and say: 'Ah, that reminds me. Nutcrackers!'

During the first rehearsal, I couldn't help fooling about. I noticed a bollard on the pavement, but pretended not to see it, walking slap into it. 'Ouch!' Then writhing around holding myself in a certain place, staggering about the street and shouting, 'Aagh! Nutcrackers! Nutcrackers!'

The director held up a hand, and stalked over.

'Norman,' he said. 'Shall we try again!'

Chapter Twenty-Four

Tuesday, 6 June 2000. I woke up early with butterflies playing skittles in my stomach. The first thing I did was look out of the bedroom window of my flat in Epsom. Force of habit, really, dating all the way back to the film days when I wondered what the weather was doing and if we'd be able to shoot outside that day. Now, three floors up in the modern block, I glanced out at the morning sun slanting through the trees and above it, a bright blue sky.

Frankly, I wouldn't have minded if it had been raining the proverbial cats and dogs. I had a date with the Queen.

I was off to the Palace to meet Her Majesty and receive the knighthood that others (not me) had said privately and publicly was 'long overdue'. I never gave it much thought, I promise you, because I'd already got a gong – the OBE ('Old Boys' Emblem') in 1995 for comic services rendered – and that was more than I'd ever anticipated anyway. Some people pointed out that Charlie Chaplin had to wait several decades for his knighthood. But if anyone actually said to me, 'Norman, it's about time . . .' I'd give them a one-word reply: '*Cobblers!*'

I first heard about it in a phone call from Johnny Mans just before Christmas. I thought he was kidding. I've fallen down a lot in my life, and usually got paid for it. This time if there'd been a feather floating about and I'd bumped into it – crash! Pick him up someone, he's just keeled over.

A few days later came a letter confirming that I was to be dubbed a Knight Bachelor for Services to Entertainment, and that if I accepted the honour I wasn't to breathe a word about it until the official announcement to go with the New Year's Honours List. How long can you hold your breath? But somehow I managed it, and only Johnny, my son Nick and daughter Jaqui knew.

Was I nervous? 'Course I was nervous. Blimey, who wouldn't be? You show me anyone who's going to meet the Queen and says they aren't, and I'll say they're telling porkies. Even yours truly, a seasoned campaigner who had met Her Majesty a number of times, had a case of the flutters that morning. But the day reflected my mood; I was buoyant, optimistic, excited, and determined to enjoy myself. I'd woken up plain Mister, and I'd be going to bed as a Sir!

But I want to put something on record, here and now: I never, ever, let it go to my head. I've never got used to myself as 'Sir Norman'. People still call me Norman or Norm – or '*Hey, you!*'

If it ever got to me, all I'd have to do is think back to the days when I was an errand boy at Lipton's riding around on my bike, and that would put me straight. I know what a lucky little devil I've been.

Back to the big day.

I'd brought my morning suit all the way down from the Isle of Man, hired once again from Peter Luis in Douglas. They know my measurements by now – they ought to – and the suit always fits just right. I haven't changed the size of my measurements in years, not even the topper! I got myself dressed without fumbling with the studs or cuff links, had a gulp of tea and a quick bowl of cereal, then it was down to a waiting Mercedes, and off to Buck House.

You're allowed two guests, and they all sit in the grand

ballroom on red plush chairs, with a military band like the Coldstream Guards or the Grenadiers playing cheery music on an upstairs balcony. Nick and Jaqui were there to see their dad ennobled – as distinct from benighted – and I don't know who was more proud, me or them.

The Queen stands in the centre of a semi-circular stage in front of a throne, with a courtier just behind her with the list of recipients. He bends forward to murmur in her ear as each person walks out from the wings to bow – or, in my case, bow the knee.

My turn. I knelt on a purple stool, and sure enough Her Majesty was there in front of me in a lovely blue dress, but suddenly holding a sword and tapping me on each shoulder. I didn't see anyone hand it to her, but they do these things so discreetly and efficiently that the whole thing went as smooth as silk. Until I tripped up, that is.

Well, I couldn't resist it. 'Many congratulations,' she said to my kneeling figure, which was better than *Get up, tich!* 'It's so nice to see you again. Well done!' And behind the spectacles those brilliant blue eyes twinkled and smiled.

'Thank you, ma'am!' (remembering to pronounce it as in 'ram', not 'arm'). Then I was backing away, as instructed, praying there were no potted plants I might have overlooked behind me. I made it, and headed for the wings like a performer leaving the stage.

It must have been instinct that made me do it – the instinct of an old music-hall ham who can't resist milking it for just one more laugh. Or maybe the fact that the audience sitting out there on their gilt chairs don't applaud, but sit in silent pride as their loved one shakes the royal mitt, takes his gong and makes off. I'm not used to silence when I leave a stage, so perhaps that was why I got it into my head to trip over my own feet and stumble into the sidelines.

Well, that broke the silence all right. The place echoed with guffaws. Turning with an apologetic shrug, I caught the Queen beaming a big smile coupled with a slight shake of the head as if to say: *Behave yourself, Norman!* She's lovely, she is.

Anything for a laugh, I say.

Afterwards, bursting with pride, I posed in the Palace forecourt for photos, then took the family to the Grosvenor Thistle Hotel nearby where we'd got the Gallery Suite reserved for the celebration party. My mates Andrew Sachs and John Inman were there to raise a glass, along with Jacqui, plus two grandsons – eleven-year-old Lawrence, and Gregory, five, sons of Nick and his lovely wife Kim. Those kids are great. They've both got a wicked sense of humour, so maybe they'll follow me into comedy. 'Well done, granddad,' they chorused, as I showed off the ribbon in its velvet case.

Now that's the kind of day I'd like to live over and over again.

EPILOGUE

Saturday, 21 July 2001. The Grosvenor House Ballroom, Park Lane, London. Comic Heritage have laid on a celebrity luncheon to honour their most senior patron and former president. That's me, in case you haven't tumbled to it. A piano plays cheery numbers from hit musical shows in the reception area as 250 invited guests mingle to sip aperitifs and swap show-business gossip before heading for their tables.

I like Comic Heritage. They're a good bunch. They're the organisation which puts up blue plaques outside homes where famous comedians once lived or worked. Charlie Chaplin, Peter Sellers, Tony Hancock, Kenneth Williams, Frankie Howerd, Eric Morecambe and Dick Emery are but a few of the legendary names, now sadly no longer with us, who have been honoured. And they hold functions which raise thousands of pounds for charity.

This occasion is one of them. All right, I'm not yet ready for my final curtain call, and I've yet to have a plaque erected either on the wall of my beautiful house in the Isle of Man or the building in Paddington where I grew up. But today's event is a milestone for me.

A 'lifetime tribute luncheon to Sir Norman Wisdom' has proved enough to bring the household faces flocking to pay their own respects – some people used the word 'homage', but that's a bit much for me – and it's all very flattering, and to be honest rather overwhelming.

A toastmaster summons us into the opulent ballroom where a dozen round tables are waiting under glittering chandeliers, chinaware shining, silverware gleaming. We're going to tuck into a sumptuous spread of strawberry salad, chicken breasts, and blackcurrant ice-cream in a chocolate honeycomb. The white wine is *Domaine de Richard 2000*. Well, I'd settle for sausage and mash and a lemonade shandy, but you can't be rude.

But the role call of guests might have baffled anyone who'd just dropped in to see the fun. At the top table with me is my mate the Albanian Ambassador, Mr Agim Fagu (I have to be careful how I say his surname) while down on table No. 9 I see Neil Hamilton and his wife Christine.

David Graham, founder of Comic Heritage and organiser of the event, takes the microphone. 'Mr Ambassador, ladies and gentlemen, please be upstanding and give a huge ovation to our special guest . . . Sir Norman Wisdom!'

Pause for effect as the applause swells and engulfs the stage.

This is the bit I like. Small, bewildered, I appear from nowhere, stumble up the steps to the small stage and wander around like a lost sheep, blinking and shaking my head as if to say: *What am I doing here?* Once again, the body language saying it all.

But then it always did. I like to think I can speak volumes with a slump of my shoulders, a wistful look in the eye, a turn of my head. Now I'm the Gump, completely out of my depth but doing my best to get myself out of a fix.

The first knight of comedy (who called me that?) is in his element!

Finally I make it to the microphone, and when the applause dies away I launch into the act I've updated to fit into my new role as a 'senior citizen of the boards'.

'Making a speech has never been my favourite way of performing. It means there's a lot to think about and a lot to remember. As you get older three things happen to you. First your memory goes. Then . . .' I stop, and finally they catch on and the laughter rolls around me like a wave. '. . . I can't remember the other two!'

More gags roll off the conveyor belt, and I'm sure some of the audience are wondering how many I've told over the years. Truth is, I must have forgotten more than I've had hot dinners.

Like the one where I go into a barber's and ask for a haircut 'to match Sylvester Stallone's.' I frown. 'After a few minutes I looked in the mirror and saw he'd made a terrible job of it – short back and sides here, almost bald there, some of my hair hanging over one side of my head and nothing on the other. It was a total mess.

'I yelled: 'Strewth! What have you done? I wanted it to look like Sylvester Stallone. He doesn't have his hair cut like this!'

'The barber replied: *'He would if he came in here!'*'

What was that about the old ones being the best?

I end by singing *Don't Laugh at Me* (what else?), before taking my place at the top table, between the unlikeliest foreign ambassador on the social circuit and the producer of some of my most successful comedies, Hugh Stewart, now a stalwart of ninety.

Harry Fowler takes over the microphone, and begins an auction that will raise £2000 for charity. A signed picture of myself with Frankie Howerd and Bill Fraser fetches £220. Framed black and white photographs from 1950 signed by me reach £340. A poster goes for £250. People are digging deep into their pockets, and all for charity. What a great, generous bunch they are.

More speeches.

Jack Douglas: 'To make people laugh is one of the

greatest things in the world.' No-one's arguing with that. Hugh Stewart adds his weight: 'I never found anyone like Norman in my life. Some people tried to change him, but he has an instinct for knowing what's right and it never let him down.' Amen to that, too.

And finally, the Albanian Ambassador himself. As I've told you, I'm big in Albania. I would even make a trip there in March 2002 with a joke record I'd made with Tony Hawks and Sir Tim Rice called *Norman Wisdom is Big in Albania* to try to get it top of the hit parade. Tony, a true funny man down to his funny bone, had laid a mad bet with a TV series for the Discovery Channel that he could get a song to the top of the charts anywhere in the world – and they chose Albania. I was all for it, and the three of us went out there to promote this lively ditty with a crew from Wall-to-Wall TV. As Harry Fowler, introducing the diplomat guest, put it: 'Norman is the biggest thing since sliced bread in Albania!' There's an accolade for you . . . I think.

The whole thing takes on a surreal air as Mr Ambassador Fagu, in grey suit and pink tie, gets to his feet and proclaims that 'Mr Wisdom is one of the greatest artists that Albania has received in recent years.' (Strewth! Who were the others?) 'I myself was dismissed from school for seeing Mr Pitkin and lying to the headmaster that I had been to the dentist. The enjoyment that Mr Wisdom gave me not just that day but all my life was bigger than the punishment from my school. This lunch will be one of the most remarkable days of my life.' Praise indeed.

My turn again.

There's a song I wrote a few years ago and, since the words are all mine, I can reproduce it here to see what you think of it. Along with *Don't Laugh at Me*, it has become a favourite for me to end my act on when I go on cruises or stand up to do my bit at charity functions like this. I call it *Falling in Love*, and I watch their faces as I go all moist-eyed when I'm singing.

My Turn

It goes like this:

Falling in love is a youthful delight,
It starts just before you leave school.
It would even start sooner if it weren't for the fact
That you're frightened of looking a fool.
Then hey presto, there's a change! You begin to feel proud
'Cos you've chosen a partner and you're out of the crowd
Holding hands gently to show that you care,
And with a shy little kiss you start an affair.
Now the first time I fell in love
Could only be classed as superb,
The second affair was also quite nice,
But the one I liked best was the third.
Although four I was sure would be top of the list,
It was beaten by five, six and seven.
And when eight was perfection with all that I wished,
Number nine must have dropped in from heaven.
As the list grew bigger, it became just a habit
Any chance of a date it wouldn't wait – I'd just grab it!
Now I've made up my mind to be much more fastidious
And try to avoid all the ones that were hideous . . .
Then later my age was reaching the stage
Where the choice had to be more elastic
They were wrinkled and aging, their faces needed caging
But to get one at all was fantastic!
Then common sense showed me the way,
Said: I mustn't be greedy no more.
Settle down with one only, then never be lonely
With a wife and some kids I'd adore.
So I started to court an old hag,
I knew it was time to get wed.
But then when I asked it, she said I was past it –
And that made me wish I was dead!
But I'm still trying hard, and nobody's barred

So I thought that I ought just to mention:
That with no luck so far, whoever you are . . .
I've got a small house and a pension!

Is that the story of life, or is that the story of life!

Oh, and in case you're wondering, I've still got my own hair. And my own teeth.

Honest!

The remarkable day ends in the late afternoon. I sign more autographs, and head for Park Lane where my car is waiting. On the way out, someone mentions a forbidden word. I stop dead in my tracks, and scowl at the impudent fellow.

'Retire? I don't know the meaning of the word. As long as I can make people laugh, I'll never retire. And I'll still keep falling down. The only thing is that as I grow older I may take longer to get up again!'

And I laugh and shake his hand and walk out into the sunshine of Park Lane in high summer.